EVIDENCE OF EDITING

Society of Biblical Literature

Resources for Biblical Study

Susan Ackerman, Old Testament/Hebrew Bible editor

EVIDENCE OF EDITING

Growth and Change of Texts in the Hebrew Bible

By
Reinhard Müller, Juha Pakkala, and Bas ter Haar Romeny

Society of Biblical Literature
Atlanta

Copyright © 2014 by the Society of Biblical Literature

All rights reserved. No part of this work may be reproduced or transmitted in any form or by any means, electronic or mechanical, including photocopying and recording, or by means of any information storage or retrieval system, except as may be expressly permitted by the 1976 Copyright Act or in writing from the publisher. Requests for permission should be addressed in writing to the Rights and Permissions Office, Society of Biblical Literature, 825 Houston Mill Road, Atlanta, GA 30329 USA.

Library of Congress Cataloging-in-Publication Data

Müller, Reinhard, 1972–.
 Evidence of editing : growth and change of texts in the Hebrew Bible / by Reinhard Müller, Juha Pakkala, and Bas ter Haar Romeny.
   p. cm. — (Society of biblical literature resources for biblical study ; no. 75)
 Includes bibliographical references and index.
 ISBN 978-1-58983-747-8 (paper binding : alk. paper) — ISBN 978-1-58983-748-5 (electronic format) — ISBN 978-1-58983-883-3 (hardcover binding : alk. paper)
 1. Bible. Old Testament—Criticism, Redaction. I. Pakkala, Juha. II. Haar Romeny, R. B. ter. III. Title.
 BS1171.3.M85 2013
 221.6'6—dc23   2013029558

Printed on acid-free, recycled paper conforming to
ANSI/NISO Z39.48-1992 (R1997) and ISO 9706:1994
standards for paper permanence.

Contents

Abbreviations vii

Introduction 1

1. Added Detail in the Samaritan Version of Leviticus 17:4 concerning the Sacrifices 19

2. An Expansion to the Passover Law: Leviticus 23:5–8 and Numbers 28:16–25 Compared 27

3. From Glosses to Larger Expansions: The Masoretic Text of Numbers 13–14 Compared with the Septuagint and the Samaritan Pentateuch 35

4. Late Additions or Editorial Shortening? Joshua 20 in the Masoretic Text and the Septuagint 45

5. A Qumran Manuscript as Evidence of an Addition in the Masoretic Text: Judges 6:7–10 59

6. A Secondary Omission in the Masoretic Text of 1 Samuel 10:1 69

7. An Addition in a Qumran Manuscript as Evidence for the Continuous Growth of the Text: 1 Samuel 10:27–11:1 79

8. The Septuagint Provides Evidence of a Late Addition in the Masoretic Text: 1 Kings 6:11–14 101

9. From Small Additions to Rewriting in the Story about the Burning of Jerusalem 109

10. Evidence for the Literary Growth of Gedaliah's Murder in
    2 Kings 25:25, Jeremiah 41:1–3 MT, and Jeremiah 48:1–3 LXX 127

11. Techniques of Rewriting Prophecy: Jeremiah 48 Compared
    with Isaiah 15–16 143

12. Evidence of Psalm Composition: Psalm 108 as a Secondary
    Compilation of Other Psalm Texts 159

13. Revision of Ezra-Nehemiah in 1 Esdras: Expansions,
    Omissions, and Rewritings 179

14. Evidence for Large Additions in the Book of Esther 193

15. Evidence for Expansions, Relocations, Omissions, and
    Rewriting: Joash the King and Jehoiada the Priest in
    2 Kings 11–12 and 2 Chronicles 22–24 205

Conclusions: Empirical Evidence of Editorial Processes 219

Bibliography 229

Index of Sources 243

Index of Authors 253

Abbreviations

≈	ideas, verses, or passages that roughly correspond with each other.
AASF	Annales Academiae scientiarum fennicae
AB	Anchor Bible
Ant.	Josephus, *Jewish Antiquities*
ASV	American Standard Version
ATANT	Abhandlungen zur Theologie des Alten and Neuen Testaments
ATD	Das Alte Testament Deutsch
ATD Erg.	Das Alte Testament Deutsch Ergänzungsreihe
BBB	Bonner biblische Beiträge
BETL	Bibliotheca ephemeridum theologicarum lovaniensium
BHK	*Biblia Hebraica*. Edited by Rudolf Kittel. Leipzig: Hinrichs, 1905–1906. 1925^2, 1937^3, 1951^4, 1973^{16}.
BHQ	*Biblia Hebraica Quinta*. Edited by Adrian Schenker et al. Stuttgart: Deutsche Bibelgesellschaft, 2004–.
BHS	*Biblia Hebraica Stuttgartensia*. Edited by K. Elliger and W. Rudolph. Stuttgart: Deutsche Bibelgesellschaft, 1983.
BKAT	Biblischer Kommentar, Altes Testament
BWANT	Beiträge zur Wissenschaft vom Alten und Neuen Testament
BZ	*Biblische Zeitschrift*
BZAW	Beihefte zur Zeitschrift für die alttestamentliche Wissenschaft
CBC	Cambridge Bible Commentary
CBQ	*Catholic Biblical Quarterly*
DJD	Discoveries in the Judaean Desert
ETL	*Ephemerides theologicae lovanienses*
FAT	Forschungen zum Alten Testament
FOTL	Forms of the Old Testament Literature

FRLANT	Forschungen zur Religion und Literatur des Alten und Neuen Testaments
GKC	*Gesenius' Hebrew Grammar*. Edited by E. Kautzsch. Translated by A. E. Cowley. 2nd ed. Oxford: Clarendon, 1910.
HAT	Handbuch zum Alten Testament
HKAT	Handkommentar zum Alten Testament
HOTTP	The Hebrew Old Testament Text Project
HSM	Harvard Semitic Monographs
HTKAT	Herders theologischer Kommentar zum Altes Testament
HTR	*Harvard Theological Review*
ICC	International Critical Commentary
IEJ	*Israel Exploration Journal*
IOSCS	International Organization for Septuagint and Cognate Studies
JSJSup	Journal for the Study of Judaism Supplement Series
JSOTSup	Journal for the Study of the Old Testament Supplement Series
JSPSup	Journal for the Study of Pseudepigrapha Supplement Series
J.W.	Josephus, *Jewish War*
KAT	Kommentar zum Alten Testament
KeHAT	Kurzgefasstes exegetisches Handbuch zum Alten Testament
KHC	Kurzer Hand-Commentar zum Alten Testament
KJV	King James Version
LCL	Loeb Classical Library
LXX	Septuagint
MT	Masoretic Text
NCBC	New Century Bible Commentary
NEB	New English Bible
NRSV	New Revised Standard Version
OBO	Orbis biblicus et orientalis
OTL	Old Testament Library
POut	De Prediking van het Oude Testament
RB	*Revue biblique*
RevQ	*Revue de Qumran*
RSV	Revised Standard Version
SBLDS	Society of Biblical Literature Dissertation Series

SBLMS	Society of Biblical Literature Monograph Series
SBLSCS	Society of Biblical Literature Septuagint and Cognate Studies
SBLSymS	Society of Biblical Literature Symposium Series
SP	Samaritan Pentateuch
SSN	Studia semitica neerlandica
ST	*Studia theologica*
STDJ	Studies on the Texts of the Desert of Judah
SubBi	Subsidia Biblica
TECC	Textos y Estudios «Cardenal Cisneros»
UBS	United Bible Societies
UTB	Uni-Taschenbücher
VT	*Vetus Testamentum*
VTSup	Vetus Testamentum Supplement Series
WBC	Word Biblical Commentary
WMANT	Wissenschaftliche Monographien zum Alten und Neuen Testament
ZAW	*Zeitschrift für die alttestamentliche Wissenschaft*
ZBK	Zürcher Bibelkommentare

Introduction

1. The Purpose of This Volume

This book seeks to demonstrate that substantial editing took place in the history of the Hebrew Bible. It presents empirical evidence[1] that gives exemplary insight into the editorial processes. The examples show how successive scribes updated the texts to accord with changed historical and social circumstances and with new religious concepts. On the basis of evidence that is collected here it can reasonably be assumed that editorial reworking of the Hebrew Bible continued unabated for centuries before the texts gradually became unchangeable. Their growing religious authority does not seem to have precluded scribes from changing the form, meaning, and content of the texts. On the contrary, for some scribes the religious authority attributed to the texts was reason to update or otherwise improve their wording in order to make sure that no blemish could be found in them. The empirical or documented evidence indicates that editorial modification was the rule rather than the exception, and accordingly signs of editing can be found in all parts of the Hebrew Bible.

Already in the nineteenth century several scholars acknowledged that the texts of the Hebrew Bible are the result of editing, but since then there have always been different perceptions as to how much the biblical texts were edited and to what extent one should take such processes into consideration. There have also been scholars who rejected the idea of editing completely[2] or assumed that editing was only a marginal phe-

---

[1]. The term "empirical" in connection with textual evidence was initially used by Jeffrey Tigay (*Empirical Models for Biblical Criticism* [Philadelphia: University of Pennsylvania Press, 1985]).

[2]. E.g., John Van Seters, *The Edited Bible: The Curious History of the "Editor" in Biblical Criticism* (Winona Lake, Ind.: Eisenbrauns, 2006), 297, 391, 398–401, and passim.

nomenon that did not affect the meaning of the texts substantially.³ In this book we seek to demonstrate that editing has been so substantial and frequent that biblical scholars may not neglect or bypass editorial processes as irrelevant. Instead, one should determine the existence, extent, and impact of editorial changes on the texts of the Hebrew Bible if they are used as sources for historical purposes. This is suggested by empirical evidence that can be found in many parts of the Hebrew Bible itself and in its ancient witnesses.

With the term "empirical evidence" we refer to such cases where the same passage or text is preserved and documented in parallel versions (e.g., the Passover laws in Lev 23 and Num 28, the description of the destruction of Jerusalem in 2 Kgs 25 and Jer 52, or the prophecies concerning Moab in Isa 15–16 and Jer 48). Factual changes that took place in the transmission of the text can be observed by comparing these versions. Another kind of empirical evidence can be found among the manifold variations that occur in the textual traditions. Here we are referring to the differences between the Masoretic Text (MT), the Samaritan Pentateuch (SP), biblical manuscripts from Qumran, and the ancient translations, the Septuagint (LXX) in particular.

The evidence that is collected in this volume shows that the distinction between textual criticism and literary or redaction criticism (*Literarkritik*)⁴ cannot be drawn very sharply. If one compares the ancient witnesses of a certain biblical text, one will find not only errors of copyists and different translation techniques but also many deliberate changes of the transmitted texts. The documented evidence of the textual history indicates that editorial processes went on at rather late stages (here one should mention, for instance, the expansion of Judg 6:7–10 that is not yet contained in a manuscript from Qumran, or 1 Kgs 6:11–14, which is not found in several LXX manuscripts). Literary or redaction criticism assumes that similar changes took place at earlier stages, although there is, in most cases, no empirical evidence of such changes. Indeed, literary criticism investigates primarily cases where documented evidence is missing, while textual criti-

---

3. This is often implied in studies that use the "final" (mainly) MT as the sole object of investigation.

4. In this volume we will use the terms "literary criticism" and "redaction criticism" instead of "source" or "composition criticism." The term "literary criticism" used in this volume should be clearly distinguished from the literary criticism used in the interpretation and reading of modern literature.

cism investigates cases where the evidence is preserved. Apart from this difference, the two methodologies deal, at least in part, with the same kind of editorial changes.⁵ One of the goals of this book is to bridge the gap between text-critical evidence of late editorial processes, on the one hand, and the literary- or redaction-critical methodology that assumes such processes for earlier stages of the literary history, on the other.

2. The MT and Other Textual Traditions

The evidence provided in this book underscores that the MT cannot be the single starting point when investigating the Hebrew Bible.⁶ The option of assuming *a priori* that *one* textual tradition is in some way superior to the other preserved textual traditions is untenable from a scholarly point of view. Yet, one still recurrently finds the underlying or implicit assumption that the MT is in some way superior to the other traditions or even sacrosanct.⁷ To be sure, the MT is a witness of high quality, and in many cases there are good reasons to assume that it represents a relatively old textual tradition. Yet, the Hebrew Bible also contains many passages where the primacy of the MT has been challenged for good reasons. There is empirical evidence in various parts of the Hebrew Bible that the MT contains substantial editorial additions of a very late origin (e.g., in Num 13:33; Judg 6:7-10; 1 Kgs 6:11-14; and throughout the book of Jeremiah). Thus,

---

5. See the material presented by Emanuel Tov, *Textual Criticism of the Hebrew Bible* (3d ed.; Minneapolis: Fortress, 2012), 283–326.

6. In effect, this is done in many volumes of the series Forms of Old Testament Literature published by Eerdmans; see, e.g., Ehud Ben Zvi, *Hosea* (FOTL 21A.1; Grand Rapids: Eerdmans, 2005), 6.

7. See, e.g., Jan P. Fokkelman, *King David (II Sam. 9–20 and I Kings 1–2)* (vol. 1 of *Narrative Art and Poetry in the Books of Samuel: A Full Interpretation Based on Stylistic and Structural Analyses*; Assen: Van Gorcum, 1981), 448, who writes on the text of Samuel: "the reliability of the Hebrew renders a consultation of the old versions as a source of inspiration or change almost superfluous." This statement implies that he uses the LXX only in exceptional cases to reconstruct an earlier text. In earlier editions of his *Textual Criticism of the Hebrew Bible*, Emanuel Tov also attached high importance to the canonical status of the MT. Thus the first edition (1992) presented, for instance, the shorter text of Jeremiah as a layer of growth preceding the final composition that was not to be taken into consideration in the reconstruction of the original text, whereas the second edition (2001; see pp. 177, 317) still excluded literary developments later than the MT.

the starting point of investigations should be not the MT alone but the variety of texts. In each case, the textual basis has to be established from all the textual witnesses.[8] To take the MT as the sole source of historical investigation, as is done in many studies, would seem to be highly questionable or even arbitrary from a scientific point of view. Some of the material in this volume shows that in many cases a more original version of a passage is documented in witnesses other than the MT, while the MT is substantially edited and contains secondary readings.[9]

A clear example of this can be found in 1 Kgs 11:38–39. Compared to the oldest manuscripts of the LXX,[10] the MT of this passage has a considerable plus. The additional text gives a certain theological interpretation of the division of Israel's unified monarchy. However, the version that is represented by the LXX does not refer to this interpretation and can be understood without knowledge of the plus. There is good reason to assume that the shorter text of the LXX goes back to a Hebrew *Vorlage*[11] that is more original than the MT reading.[12] It would be difficult to explain why the additional passage should have been secondarily omitted in the LXX.[13]

---

8. Anneli Aejmelaeus ("What Can We Know about the Hebrew *Vorlage* of the Septuagint," in *On the Trail of the Septuagint Translators: Collected Essays* [Leuven: Peeters, 2007], 106) has noted that different readings have to be weighed "against one another" when the oldest reading is reconstructed.

9. "Secondary" here refers only to the chronological age of the readings in comparison with more original readings. The content of the readings is by no means secondary, since they may also contain significant historical information and are witness to the further development of the text.

10. Some Greek manuscripts, such as the Lucianic text, follow the MT, but this is probably a later harmonization after the MT.

11. "*Vorlage*" refers to the source text from which the Greek version was translated.

12. Thus, e.g., Immanuel Benzinger, *Die Bücher der Könige* (KHC 9; Freiburg i. B.: Mohr Siebeck, 1899), 84; C. F. Burney, *Notes on the Hebrew Text of the Books of Kings: With an Introduction and Appendix* (Oxford: Clarendon, 1903), 171; Simon J. DeVries, *1 Kings* (WBC 12; Waco, Tex.: Word, 1985), 149; Martin J. Mulder, *1 Kings 1–11* (vol. 1 of *1 Kings*; Historical Commentary on the Old Testament; Leuven: Peeters, 1998), 597.

13. According to Mordechai Cogan, *1 Kings: A New Translation with Introduction and Commentary* (AB 10; New York: Doubleday, 2001), 342, "the ideas expressed here need not be altogether secondary," but he does not explain why the passage should have been omitted in the LXX. Marvin A. Sweeney, *I and II Kings: A Commentary*

INTRODUCTION 5

1 Kgs 11:38–39 MT[14]

והיה אם תשמע את כל אשר אצוך והלכת בדרכי ועשית הישר בעיני
לשמור חקותי ומצותי כאשר עשה דוד עבדי והייתי עמך ובניתי לך בית
נאמן כאשר בניתי לדוד ונתתי לך את ישראל ואענה את זרע דוד למען
זאת אך לא כל הימים

³⁸ And if you will listen to all that I command you, and walk in my ways, and do what is right in my eyes by keeping my statutes and my commandments, as David my servant did, I will be with you, and will build you a sure house, as I built for David. <u>And I will give Israel to you,</u>³⁹ <u>and I will afflict the seed of David, but not forever.</u>

1 Kgs 11:38(–39) LXX

καὶ ἔσται ἐὰν φυλάξῃς πάντα, ὅσα ἂν ἐντείλωμαί σοι, καὶ πορευθῇς ἐν ταῖς ὁδοῖς μου καὶ ποιήσῃς τὸ εὐθὲς ἐνώπιον ἐμοῦ τοῦ φυλάξασθαι τὰς ἐντολάς μου καὶ τὰ προστάγματά μου, καθὼς ἐποίησεν Δαυιδ ὁ δοῦλός μου, καὶ ἔσομαι μετὰ σοῦ καὶ οἰκοδομήσω σοι οἶκον πιστόν, καθὼς ᾠκοδόμησα τῷ Δαυιδ.

³⁸ And if you keep all that I command you, and walk in my ways, and do what is right before me by keeping my statutes and my commandments, as David my servant did, I will be with you and will build you a sure house, as I built for David.

It can be assumed that similar additions were made in many texts of the Hebrew Bible, although in most cases no empirical evidence has been preserved.

(OTL; Louisville: Westminster John Knox, 2007), 158, presupposes the MT without discussion.

14. The following markings are used in this volume: expansions and plusses are <u>underlined</u>, rewritten or slightly modified texts are displayed in <u>dashed underline</u>, parallels between passages are displayed in <u>dotted underline</u>, and relocated texts are displayed in gray. Omitted sections are maked with strikethrough. When three texts are compared (for example, ch. 10), the first stage of expansions is underlined, and the second stage is double underlined.

3. Evidence of Substantial Rewriting

Editing did not mean just making additions to given texts, as it is conventionally assumed in literary-critical and other methodologies.[15] The empirical evidence preserved in the textual witnesses also shows that editors could replace parts of the transmitted texts with new passages. Such a process of editorial reworking is documented, for instance, in Deut 34. In this passage the MT and the SP contain different descriptions of the boundaries of the land that Yhwh shows to Moses. Although the Samaritan version is shorter than the MT, it is probably secondary, since in this version the boundaries of the promised land are considerably expanded and Moses is able to see the entire territory between the Nile and the Euphrates. This is probably a harmonization with the description of the land in Gen 15:18, which mentions exactly the same boundaries of the promised land (cf. Deut 11:24; Josh 1:4). As a result, the SP contains a substantially different version of this passage from the MT.

Deut 34:1–3 MT

ויעל משה מערבת מואב אל הר נבו ראש הפסגה אשר על פני ירחו ויראהו
יהוה את כל הארץ את הגלעד עד דן ואת כל נפתלי ואת ארץ אפרים
ומנשה ואת כל ארץ יהודה עד הים האחרון ואת הנגב ואת הככר בקעת
ירחו עיר התמרים עד צער

[1] And Moses went up from the plains of Moab to Mount Nebo, to the top of Pisgah, which is opposite Jericho, and Yhwh showed him the whole land: <u>Gilead as far as Dan,</u> [2] <u>all Naphtali, the land of Ephraim and Manasseh, all the land of Judah</u> as far as the Western Sea, [3] <u>the Negeb, and the Plain—the valley of Jericho, the city of palm trees—as far as Zoar.</u>

Deut 34:1 SP

ויעל משה מערבת מואב אל הר נבא ראש הפסגה אשר על פני יריחו
ויראהו יהוה את כל הארץ מנהר מצרים עד הנהר הגדול נהר פרת ועד
הים האחרון

---

15. Thus, among many others, Christoph Levin, *The Old Testament: A Brief Introduction* (Princeton: Princeton University Press, 2005), 27–28; Uwe Becker, *Exegese des Alten Testaments* (3rd ed.; UTB 2664; Mohr Siebeck, 2011), 84.

And Moses went up from the plains of Moab to Mount Nebo, to the top of Pisgah, which is opposite Jericho, and Yhwh showed him the whole land: <u>from the river of Egypt to the great river, the river Euphrates, and</u> as far as the Western Sea.

In this case, the MT very probably preserves a more original version of the passage than the SP.[16] This would seem to accord with the common scholarly tendency to assume that the SP contains many secondary readings in relation to the MT.[17] Yet, the example shows that ancient editors—even those behind the transmission of the Pentateuch—were able to replace one passage with another. There is no reason to assume that this technique would not have been used in the earlier literary history of the biblical texts, that is, prior to the editorial changes that were made in the textual tradition represented by the SP[18] after it diverged from the textual tradition of the proto-MT.

4. Evidence from Parallel Texts in the Hebrew Bible

A different type of evidence that is nonetheless highly relevant with regard to literary- or redaction-critical methodology is provided by Chronicles in relation to its sources. The evidence of Chronicles is distinguished from the text-critical evidence where the same passage or text is preserved in two variant editions. Chronicles shows how a text developed when an editor used an older literary work as a source text in order to create a new composition. In this regard, scholarship has largely ignored Chronicles and

---

16. This is assumed by virtually all commentators; see, for instance, S. R. Driver, *Deuteronomy* (ICC; Edinburgh: T&T Clark, 1902), 421–23; and Richard D. Nelson, *Deuteronomy* (OTL; Louisville: Westminster John Knox, 2002), 393–96, who both do not discuss the reading of the SP. An exception is Carmel McCarthy, ed., *Deuteronomy* (vol. 5 of *Biblia Hebraica: Quinta editione*; Stuttgart: Deutsche Bibelgesellschaft, 2007), 168*; according to her, "it is difficult to decide which one [i.e., MT or SP] gives access to the 'original.'"

17. Thus, many scholars; see, e.g., Michael Fishbane, *Biblical Interpretation in Ancient Israel* (Oxford: Clarendon, 1985), 71. As an *a priori* assumption the secondary nature of the SP should be rejected, however, and the SP should be considered a significant witness when establishing the textual basis of any passage in the Pentateuch.

18. Many of these changes might be of a pre-Samaritan origin, as the investigation of the so-called Reworked Pentateuch manuscripts from Qumran shows; see Magnar Kartveit, *The Origin of the Samaritans* (VTSup 128; Leiden: Brill, 2009), 259–312, with literature, and ch. 1 in this volume.

other works of similar or related genre in relation to their sources (e.g., Jubilees and the Temple Scroll) because they represent entirely new compositions.[19] Nevertheless, these works still show how texts could develop. When we investigate the texts of the Hebrew Bible, the history of which we do not know, it is quite possible that some of them relate to their preceding literary stage in a similar way as Chronicles does to the book of Kings. Concretely speaking, when we reconstruct the literary history of a passage in the book of Kings, we cannot exclude the possibility that its authors related to their sources as the Chronicler did. In fact, much speaks in favor of similarities. Consequently, Chronicles in relation to its sources provides primary evidence for a possible course of editing in the Hebrew Bible. The editorial changes in Chronicles range from small additions, such as the ones conventionally assumed in literary criticism, to substantial changes, rewritings, and replacements. One example suffices to demonstrate the relevance of the material.[20]

Second Kings 11 describes the rebellion (or *coup d'état*) of Jehoiada to replace Queen Athaliah with Joash as the monarch. Extensive literary connections throughout 2 Chr 23 imply that the Chronicler followed the parallel account in 2 Kings; he has adopted several passages word for word. However, clear ideological or theological tendencies are evident when we look at the differences between the parallel verses. The Chronicler has increased the role of priests and Levites throughout the passage. Moreover, there is a notable interest in the temple. Second Chronicles 23:1–2 in relation to 2 Kgs 11:4 illustrates these motifs.

2 Kgs 11:4 MT

ובשנה השביעית שלח יהוידע ויקח את־שרי המא(י)ות לכרי ולרצים ויבא אתם אליו בית יהוה

In the seventh year Jehoiada ~~summoned~~ and took the commanders of the hundreds ~~and of the guards~~ and ~~had them~~ come ~~to him in Yhwh's temple~~.

---

19. Julius Wellhausen (*Prolegomena to the History of Israel* [Edinburgh: Black, 1885], 228) and many other scholars after him assumed that Chronicles would not be a typical representative of editorial processes. Instead, it would be a midrash or commentary on the texts that were used as sources.

20. See also chs. 9 and 15 for more extensive examples in Chronicles.

2 Chr 23:1–2

ובשנה השביעית התחזק יהוידע ויקח את־שרי המאות לעזריהו בן־ירחם
ולישמעאל בן־יהוחנן ולעזריהו בן־עובד ואת־מעשיהו בן־עדיהו ואת־
אלישפט בן־זכרי עמו בברית ויסבו ביהודה ויקבצו את־הלוים מכל־ערי
יהודה וראשי האבות לישראל ויבאו אל־ירושלם

¹ In the seventh year Jehoiada <u>took courage</u> and took the commanders of the hundreds, <u>Azariah son of Jeroham, Ishmael son of Jehohanan, Azariah son of Obed, Maaseiah son of Adaiah, and Elishaphat son of Zichri.</u>
² <u>They went around through Judah and gathered the Levites from all the towns of Judah, and the heads of families of Israel,</u> and <u>they</u> came <u>to Jerusalem.</u>

Whereas in 2 Kgs 11:4 the (mercenary?) Carian soldiers and the guard play a central role in the coup, they are replaced in 2 Chr 23:1–2 with priests and Levites. The Chronicler was evidently offended by the lack of priests in the events, especially since the coup was against the evil Athaliah to instate a more pious ruler in Judah. One should also note that in the source text the soldiers enter Yhwh's temple, but this would have been an incomprehensible idea in the Second Temple context of the Chronicler. The soldiers entering the temple were thus replaced by the people coming to Jerusalem. The following story contains similar modifications, which form a consistent pattern and show an ideological tendency. Ideological and/or theological concepts have been a central motive for the editorial changes. The editorial changes we can observe in Chronicles should be included in the discussion about how other texts, where similar evidence is not preserved, may have been changed.

5. Processes of Editing Should Not Be Neglected in Studies of the Hebrew Bible

In contrast to these examples, we do not possess empirical evidence for most of the texts in the Hebrew Bible. It is only in some cases that we have parallels or differing manuscripts that give insights into the editorial processes, but we can assume that these documented cases attest to merely a fraction of the actual changes that have taken place in the transmission of the Hebrew Bible. Although much of the evidence comes from relatively late periods in the development of the texts, there are good reasons to assume that similar editorial processes took place during the earlier periods of the textual transmission that are largely undocumented by variant editions.[21]

As a consequence, the investigation of the development of the texts of the Hebrew Bible and its possible prehistory cannot be ignored as merely an optional method that can be used but that can also be neglected or entirely skipped.[22] The historical investigation of the texts should not be seen as the task of some scholarly traditions only. In other words, the present volume seeks to underline that the quest for editorial processes is a necessary methodological step in *any* use of the Hebrew Bible for historical and scholarly research. Without understanding the history and nature of the source, we cannot reliably use this source at all.

The importance of textual and literary or redaction criticism was already understood in critical research of the nineteenth century. Scholars in this period came to the conclusion that both are necessary methodological steps. The most prominent scholar in this respect is Julius Wellhausen, who started with investigations into the documented textual history. On the basis of his observations from the textual witnesses, especially in the book of Samuel, he also sought to reconstruct the earlier stages of literary growth.[23] He thus recognized the close connection between textual and literary criticism.

However, this kind of historical- and literary-critical approach has not been accepted by all scholars. In some scholarly traditions the use of the so-called final or end text has become popular, particularly since the last decades of the twentieth century. This is seen, for example, in rhetorical and structural analyses that pay little or no heed to questions of textual history and literary growth.[24] In many cases these approaches ignore the variety of textual evidence and choose the MT as the starting point without explaining or justifying this decision. By the same token, questions

---

21. This is especially the case with those texts that received an authoritative status relatively early—the Pentateuch, for instance. On the other hand, for those texts of the Hebrew Bible that were originally created rather late—for example, Daniel, Ezra-Nehemiah, and Esther—a much earlier stage of their transmission history is preserved. This is reflected in more variety in the textual evidence, which is hardly a coincidence.

22. Many investigations that take no heed of literary criticism use the Hebrew Bible as it was preserved (primarily) in the MT. See below for examples.

23. Julius Wellhausen, *Der Text der Bücher Samuelis* (Göttingen: Vandenhoeck & Ruprecht, 1871).

24. Here one could mention, e.g., Tamara Eskenazi, *In an Age of Prose: A Literary Approach to Ezra-Nehemiah* (SBLMS 36; Atlanta: Scholars Press, 1988).

about the prehistory of the final texts and the editorial processes that the empirical evidence attests to are ignored.

Structural analyses might be able to highlight certain structures in the latest version of the texts, but these versions are often merely random stages of the textual development.[25] Observations reached on the basis of one textual stage cannot be extended to include other textual stages that were not investigated in such analyses. Although the methodologies of structural analysis may have their justification in investigating one version, it would be hazardous to ignore the variation of textual evidence, which implies a complicated history of the texts. If one decides to use the MT only, this should be reflected in the conclusions that one draws from the observations. An approach that investigates merely the final text would significantly limit the information that one can deduce from the text. In other words, if the history of the text remains obscure to the scholar, the limits of scientific possibilities have to be acknowledged. To give an example, if one investigates the final text of Ezra-Nehemiah without understanding its complicated prehistory, one can hardly make any historical conclusions or statements by using this text as a historical source. Without a theory about the historical context of a particular section in this composition, one cannot use that section for a historical reconstruction.[26] By presenting examples of evidence for constant and substantial changes, we seek to show what the problems inherent in such approaches are.

6. Why We Should Try to Reconstruct the Literary History of the Hebrew Bible

Because literary- and redaction-critical reconstructions vary considerably and no consensus has been reached on many texts, some scholars have given up trying to understand the history of the texts.[27] This kind

---

25. Here one should additionally ask whether the scholar investigating a final text such as the MT is able to determine which period in the development of the text he or she is investigating.

26. An example of such an end-text reading of Ezra-Nehemiah is Eskenazi, *In an Age of Prose*. Although she largely ignores the complicated literary history of the text, she makes historical conclusions by using Ezra-Nehemiah as a source. One has to be skeptical about the viability of such an approach.

27. Interestingly, structural analyses have not led to consensus either; thus Marjo Korpel, *The Structure of the Book of Ruth* (Pericope 2; Assen: Van Gorcum, 2001), 5–30, presents a survey of twenty structural analyses of Ruth and concludes that they

of methodological skepticism has been advocated by some scholars in recent decades. A prominent voice is Ehud Ben Zvi, who, one the one hand, admits that the texts may have been heavily edited but, on the other, refrains from trying to reconstruct the earlier stages of their literary development. According to him, "scholarly reconstructed texts cannot but be hypothetical and unverifiable, and rarely command any consensus." He stresses that "redactional and authorial processes may not only bring new material into a source text but may also exclude and completely reshape material as the way in which the Chronicler worked with the books of Samuel and Kings clearly shows." Therefore he asks, "how can a scholar reconstruct an omitted text?"[28] While Ben Zvi is right in stressing the fact that editorial processes comprised not only expanding texts but also substantial rewriting—even omissions, as we have shown above—we cannot agree with the overall methodological skepticism Ben Zvi deduces from that. When he, on the basis of his methodological doubts, treats the prophetic books exclusively in the context of a postmonarchic setting and does not use them as a source for earlier periods,[29] we have to ask if this one-sided approach can be justified. The reconstruction of older textual material that is contained in the prophetic books is admittedly difficult, and we have to be aware of the limits of such reconstructions (see also below). However, the attempt to detect the literary history of these books should nevertheless be made, and there are many texts where editorial processes left clearly discernible traces. In many cases the texts provide clues as to how at least parts of the literary prehistory should be reconstructed.[30] In addition, the prophetic books contain several concepts that cannot have originated in the postmonarchic period but must predate this period. Thus, we need to explain how these concepts were transmitted from earlier times to the postmonarchic era and how they were transformed during the

---

present a "bewildering variety of opinion." In comparison, nineteenth-century source criticism of the Pentateuch was a model of unanimity.

28. Ben Zvi, *Hosea*, 6.

29. Ehud Ben Zvi, "The Concept of Prophetic Books and Its Historical Setting," in *The Production of Prophecy: Constructing Prophecy and Prophets in Yehud* (ed. Diana V. Edelman and Ehud Ben Zvi; London: Equinox, 2009), 73–95.

30. For example, there are good reasons to assume that the oldest material in the first part of Jeremiah comprises in particular a series of lamentations about the enemy from the north that cannot have originated in the postmonarchic period. The attempt to distinguish this material from later editorial layers is not futile altogether, although we may not be able to reconstruct these relatively old lamentations in every detail.

transmission by editorial activity. If we read the prophetic books against the backdrop of only the postmonarchic periods, we would fail to discern these transformations.

One could also mention the recently presented position of David M. Carr. Appealing to the lack of consensus, he notes that "more complicated reconstructions of textual prehistory have not stood and will not stand the test of time."[31] The texts would not preserve enough evidence "to reconstruct each and every stage of that [textual] growth."[32] The authors of this volume agree with Carr's criticism of those reconstructions that suggest a 100 percent reliability of their results. However, the underlying skepticism about the general possibilities of literary-critical reconstructions, evident in Carr's approach, should be rejected. Carr's text examples are mainly from texts where the most radical editorial processes have been at work. On the basis of the observation on these texts, he implies that the editorial history cannot be reconstructed when the documented evidence is missing. Regarding this implicit assumption, it is surprising to note that Carr—in stark contrast to Ben Zvi—is nevertheless able to reconstruct much of the history and religion of Israel during the monarchic period. This reconstruction, which results in rather conservative conceptions,[33] seems to derive from Carr's implicit assumption that the final texts of many biblical books are fairly reliable historical sources. From a methodological perspective, this is not very consistent. The current volume seeks to demonstrate that radical editorial processes represent only part of the evidence and that many examples of the documented evidence in fact accord with the conceptions and methodology of literary and redaction criticism.

Although the frustration over the lack of consensus on several historically central texts (such as 2 Kgs 23) is understandable, and the means to reconstruct the history of the Hebrew Bible are limited because of the variety of the editorial processes, it is doubtful that an overall methodological skepticism as advocated by both Ben Zvi and Carr provides any improved access to understanding the Hebrew Bible. As in Carr's case, and in contrast to Ben Zvi, the skepticism can result in rather conservative conceptions about the history and religion of Israel. In such cases one receives the impression that since the textual growth is assumed to be so compli-

---

31. David M. Carr, *The Formation of the Hebrew Bible: A New Reconstruction* (Oxford: Oxford University Press, 2011), 4.
32. Ibid.
33. See esp. ibid., 304–490 (chs. 10–17).

cated, the arduous process of trying to analyze each text in detail may be skipped. If we take the texts as they are and lean simply on conventional conceptions about the history and religion of Israel, we fail to recognize that edited or "final" texts can be rather misleading if we use them uncritically as historical sources. To be consistent, one should then abandon the entire Hebrew Bible as a historical source, but this is not what Carr and many others who share his approach are willing to do.

In this respect, the approach of Niels Peter Lemche may be more consistent. On the basis of observations on the textual or literary growth of the Hebrew Bible similar to those made by Ben Zvi and Carr, Lemche has contended that the Hebrew Bible witnesses to mainly the Hellenistic or even Roman period, the period of the oldest manuscripts.[34] The earlier development cannot be recovered anymore. In practice, Lemche denies the value of the Hebrew Bible as a witness to earlier periods, because any reconstruction of the prehistory of the text would be too speculative. However, this radical view fails to convince us either. Although most literary- and redaction-critical reconstructions can never be fully proven but remain hypotheses, it is difficult to see how the texts of the Hebrew Bible would bear witness to only the latest periods. In many cases it is unequivocally clear that conceptions predating the freezing of the texts to changes are preserved in the Hebrew Bible. They should be used as evidence for the period when they were originally written and not for the period when the oldest manuscript was copied.

For example, it has to be asked whether it is justified to regard many of the psalms, commonly assumed to preserve religious conceptions of the monarchic time, as primarily Hellenistic or Roman. Many of these conceptions would be incomprehensible in a Hellenistic or Roman setting, and reading them as witnesses to such a late context would hardly do justice to the evidence. We can observe that many texts that were later edited are still closely related to religious concepts of Northwest Semitic or Levantine origin of much earlier periods, and they should be seen against this background. Even if the texts were finished or their literary development ceased in the Hellenistic or Roman period, we can still see that they contain conceptions that are much older. It is the contention of the

---

34. Niels Peter Lemche, *The Old Testament between Theology and History* (Louisville: Westminster John Knox, 2008), 379–92, esp. 385. In part, Lemche's approach is more consequent than that of Ben Zvi, because it is fairly certain that most texts of the Hebrew Bible were finished in the Hellenistic or Roman periods.

authors of this volume that one should always make the attempt to understand the earlier history of the texts as well—despite the difficulties and time-consuming analysis—because it may be the only evidence we have of many stages in the history of ancient Israel, Judah, and Yehud. The evidence should not be rejected altogether on the grounds that it is preserved in complicated and heavily edited sources.

7. The Limitations of Literary- and Redaction-Critical Reconstructions

The classic methods of literary and redaction criticism also have to be criticized when they suggest that all stages of textual growth can be reconstructed with complete certainty, and here one may agree with Lemche, Ben Zvi and Carr.[35] The possibility that some of the processes may be untraceable by critical scholarship has to be taken into account. Some of the examples in this book illustrate that editorial changes may not always have left traces in the resulting text. Moreover, it is gradually becoming more probable that the texts may not have developed exclusively by additions. Some examples in this volume suggest that relocations, rewritings, and omissions may also have taken place. From this it follows that literary and redaction criticisms should not be used as infallible methods. Their results are often hypotheses or abstractions of a development, and they should also be understood as such. It would be a mistake to assume that literary-critical reconstructions are evidence of the same caliber as preserved textual witnesses, for example. However, it has to be stressed that despite their limitations many scholarly reconstructions have often greatly advanced our understanding of the history, culture, and religion of ancient Israel.

It is possible that the development of some texts will never be unlocked by the available methods, but this does not mean that we should abandon the Hebrew Bible altogether as a historical source. More caution is needed than some overly optimistic forms of literary and redaction criticism would imply.

---

35. E.g., Carr, *Formation*, 4.

8. Toward a Refined Methodology for the Reconstruction of the Textual Prehistory

In this book we will present examples of passages that are preserved in more than one version or edition. These examples provide insight into how texts have been factually changed during the process of their transmission. We have taken examples from different parts of the Hebrew Bible and also sought to include various kinds of examples. It is evident that there were different techniques of editing and rewriting by the scribes. This volume therefore also shows that the editors or scribes did not all relate to the older texts in the same way. Different kinds of editing may have been connected to different genres, and the issue of genre has to be taken into consideration when thinking about editorial changes. However, it seems difficult to establish a precise relationship between editorial techniques or the range of editorial freedom on the one hand, and the genre of the edited text on the other.

This volume does not pursue a conclusive explanation for the development of the texts of the Hebrew Bible. Instead, it seeks to contribute to the methodological discussion by taking various kinds of examples that address some of the problems in the use of the Hebrew Bible as a historical source. It seeks to advocate awareness of the substantial changes that took place in the development of the texts. It obviously cannot and does not presume to dictate what should be done, but it provides some suggestions and guidelines that emerge from the empirical evidence. As such, it can function as a practical guide for scholars and students who are grappling with the complexities of the literary history. It furnishes possible models that could provide insight into how other texts were edited and changed.

Besides demonstrating the importance of understanding the history and development of the texts, one of the main goals of this volume is to contribute to the refining of the exegetical methodology of literary and redaction criticism. On the one hand, the examples show that methodological nihilism, as advocated in particular by Ben Zvi and Lemche, is not justified. An attempt should always be made to reconstruct the development of the texts. Some examples indicate that one could come to reliable results even without the extant empirical evidence. In several cases one would be able to detect the main tendencies and developments in the literary history. On the other hand, the examples also show that overextended optimism about the possibilities of reconstructing every detail of the literary growth is unwarranted. In some cases, the processes of editing have been so substantial that the resulting texts were very different from the older versions. In such cases it would be difficult, if not impossible, to reconstruct the literary history accurately.

The empirical evidence that is collected here advocates a middle position between the extremes of abandoning literary analysis altogether and trying to reconstruct every little detail. Because it is impossible to ignore the development of the texts, a reconstruction of the texts' prehistory should always be pursued, but it cannot be pushed to the extreme as to the precision of the results. In some cases, one has to acknowledge that the prehistory of a text cannot be recovered. Accordingly, in the following chapters, in connection with each passage, we will also discuss the question of to what extent reliable reconstructions would be possible without the empirical evidence. We feel that when reconstructions become hypothetical, this should be admitted more frankly than has been done in the past. This is in no way problematic. On the contrary, once the edited nature of the texts is recognized, it becomes the duty of scholars to offer hypotheses, just as it will be the duty of the coming generations to improve on them.

1

Added Detail in the Samaritan Version of Leviticus 17:4 concerning the Sacrifices

1.1. The Variant Readings

Leviticus 17:4 is part of the first law of the so-called Holiness Code in Lev 17–26. After the short preamble to the code in Lev 17:1–2, the following two verses, 3–4, contain Yhwh's instruction to Moses concerning those Israelites who slaughter an ox, lamb, or goat and do not bring it to the entrance of the tent of meeting for cultic sacrifice. The MT uses the expression להקריב קרבן, which commonly refers to bringing offerings but which does not specify what types of offerings are meant.[1] Because the text discusses primarily punishments for neglecting the offering altogether, no further details or specifications are required, and the reader would hardly expect such. The main message is that those who do not follow the commandment should be killed (or literally, "cut off from the people").

The SP, 4QLev^d, and the LXX of Lev 17:4 contain a large plus that is missing in the MT as well as in 11QpaleoLev^a.[2] The plus specifies the types of sacrifice for which the slaughtered animal is to be brought (in the following parallel columns, the plus is represented by the SP, but the LXX and 4QLev^d contain a comparable plus):[3]

---

1. See Lev 1:2; 2:1, 4; 3:7; 7:13, 38; 22:18; etc. קרבן is the most general word for sacrifice in the Hebrew Bible; see, e.g., Ludwig Koehler and Walter Baumgartner, *The Hebrew and Aramaic Lexicon of the Old Testament* (Leiden: Brill, 2001).
2. Note that Targum Onqelos, Targum Pseudo-Jonathan, and the Vulgate also follow the MT.
3. The Göttingen LXX reads in v. 4: καὶ ἐπὶ τὴν θύραν τῆς σκηνῆς τοῦ μαρτυρίου μὴ ἐνέγκῃ ὥστε ποιῆσαι αὐτὸ εἰς ὁλοκαύτωμα ἢ σωτήριον κυρίῳ δεκτὸν εἰς ὀσμὴν εὐωδίας, καὶ ὃς ἂν σφάξῃ ἔξω καὶ ἐπὶ τὴν θύραν τῆς σκηνῆς τοῦ μαρτυρίου μὴ ἐνέγκῃ αὐτὸ ὥστε προσενέγκαι δῶρον κυρίῳ ἀπέναντι τῆς σκηνῆς κυρίου, καὶ λογισθήσεται τῷ ἀνθρώπῳ

Lev 17:1–4 MT

וידבר יהוה אל־משה לאמר
דבר אל־אהרן ואל־בניו ואל כל־בני ישראל ואמרת אליהם זה הדבר אשר־
צוה יהוה לאמר
איש איש מבית ישראל אשר ישחט שור או־כשב או־עז במחנה או אשר
ישחט מחוץ למחנה
ואל־פתח אהל מועד לא הביאו
להקריב קרבן ליהוה לפני משכן יהוה דם יחשב לאיש ההוא דם שפך
ונכרת האיש ההוא מקרב עמו

[1] Yhwh spoke to Moses: [2] "Speak to Aaron and his sons and to all the people of Israel and say to them, 'This is what Yhwh has commanded. [3] If anyone of the house of Israel slaughters an ox or a lamb or a goat in the camp, or slaughters it outside the camp, [4] and does not bring it to the entrance of the tent of meeting, to present (it) as an offering to Yhwh before the tabernacle of Yhwh, he shall be held guilty of bloodshed; he has shed blood, and he shall be cut off from the people.'"

Lev 17:1–4 SP

וידבר יהוה אל־משה לאמר
דבר אל־אהרן ואל־בניו ואל כל־בני ישראל ואמרת אליהם זה הדבר אשר־
צוה יהוה לאמר
איש איש מבית ישראל אשר ישחט שור או־כשב או־עז במחנה או אשר
ישחט מחוץ למחנה
ואל־פתח אהל מועד לא הביאו
<u>לעשות אתו עלה או שלמים ליהוה לרצונכם</u>
<u>לריח ניחח וישחטהו בחוץ</u>
<u>ואל פתח אהל מועד לא הביאו</u>
להקריבנ קרבן ליהוה לפני משכן יהוה דם יחשב לאיש ההוא דם שפך
ונכרת האיש ההוא מקרב עמו

ἐκείνῳ αἷμα· αἷμα ἐξέχεεν, ἐξολεθρευθήσεται ἡ ψυχὴ ἐκείνη ἐκ τοῦ λαοῦ αὐτῆς. Only part of the text is preserved in 4QLev^d (... עלה [או] שלמים ליהוה לרצונכם ל[ריח ...) but it is evident that this text contains a plus similar to what we find in the LXX and the SP. As noted by Armin Lange (*Die Handschriften biblischer Bücher von Qumran und den anderen Fundorten* [vol. 1 of *Handbuch der Textfunde vom Toten Meer*; Tübingen: Mohr Siebeck, 2009], 71), when we consider the number of shared variants, 4QLev^d stands closest to the LXX and furthest from the MT. Nevertheless, it contains some variants against the LXX as well.

¹ Yhwh spoke to Moses: ² "Speak to Aaron and his sons and to all the people of Israel and say to them, 'This is what Yhwh has commanded. ³ If anyone of the house of Israel slaughters an ox or a lamb or a goat in the camp or slaughters it outside the camp ⁴ and does not bring it to the entrance of the tent of meeting, <u>to make it a burnt offering or a peace offering to Yhwh, at your own will, for a sweet-smelling savor, and (who) slaughters it outside, and does not bring it to the entrance of the tent of meeting</u> to present it as an offering to Yhwh before the tabernacle of Yhwh, he shall be held guilty of bloodshed; he has shed blood, and he shall be cut off from the people.'"

Although the plus is exceptionally well supported by the witnesses of different textual traditions, it is likely that the MT is more original and that the plus is a reading that was occasioned by a later expansion. This is suggested by the following considerations.

The plus contains additional and more-detailed information about the sacrifices, and thereby its content goes beyond the shorter text represented by the MT. Because the original text refers to only the offerings in general, several editors who had a special interest in the details of sacrifices would have been tempted to specify what להקריב קרבן meant. Burnt and peace offerings, some of the most typical types of animal offerings, would have been a logical addition. It should be further noted that the following text in Lev 17:5 (שלמים) and 17:8 (עלה) refers to the offerings mentioned in the plus. These verses may thus have inspired the addition to v. 4. Moreover, the actual instruction on the peace offerings of the Holiness Code in Lev 19:5 contains the phrase שלמים ליהוה לרצונכם ("a peace offering to Yhwh, at your own will"), which is identical to the phrase in the plus of Lev 17:4. It would thus appear that the author behind the plus was also looking at the main legislation of the Holiness Code concerning this offering.[4]

An additional argument for regarding the plus as a later addition is that with it the text contains disturbing and awkward repetitions. The last sentence before the plus (ואל־פתח אהל מועד לא הביאו), "and does not

---

4. The general tendency to increase emphasis on sacrifices and their details is particularly evident when we compare Chronicles with its source in 1–2 Kings. Some expansions of this type are also witnessed by documented evidence. An expansion to similar effect can be found, for example, in 1 Esd 5:51–52 vs. Ezra 3:5, discussed in this volume (see ch. 13). A later editor in the tradition of 1 Esd 5:51–52 added the Sabbath sacrifices to a list of various sacrifices, while the MT preserves the more original reading.

bring it to the entrance of the tent of meeting") is repeated verbatim at the end of the plus. It is improbable that an original author would have created such a confusing text that repeats an extensive section but that effectively adds only two words of meaningful content, עלה ("burnt offering") and שלמים ("peace offering"). If the original author had intended to include a reference to these offerings, it is unlikely that he would have separated the word קרבן ("offering") from the specific offerings and introduced it separately after the specific offerings are already mentioned. In other words, it is illogical that the specific offerings mentioned first are followed by a reference to offerings in general. Furthermore, after the reference to עלה ("burnt offering") and שלמים ("peace offering") the word קרבן ("offering") and the whole phrase להקריב קרבן ליהוה ("to present as an offering to Yhwh") becomes entirely irrelevant. The sentence להקריב קרבן ליהוה is effectively replaced by לעשות אתו עלה או שלמים ליהוה ("to make it a burnt offering or a peace offering to Yhwh"). Consequently, the extensive repetition creates confusion in the whole passage.

It is more probable that we are dealing with a resumptive repetition (*Wiederaufnahme*) here. This editorial technique is often assumed in literary criticism and is also used as an argument for possible expansions.[5] The reason for the repetition was the editor's attempt to return to the older text after the expansion. In some cases this would conceal the expansion, because the text would then logically continue from where it left off before the expansion. In Lev 17:4 the technique was applied rather mechanically and created a stylistically awkward passage, because such a large section was repeated and the expansion was relatively short.[6] The repetition is too long in relation to the added material.

An alternative explanation of the plus would be its omission in the proto-MT, which can be divided into two possibilities: an intentional

---

5. See, e.g., Uwe Becker, *Exegese des Alten Testaments* (3d ed.; UTB 2664; Tübingen: Mohr Siebeck, 2011), 58. The principle was originally introduced by Curt Kuhl, "Die 'Wiederaufnahme'—ein literarkritisches Prinzip?" *ZAW* 64 (1952): 1–11. Note that the technique was already recognized in nineteenth-century scholarship. See, e.g., August Dillmann, *Die Bücher Numeri, Deuteronomium und Josua* (2d ed.; Leipzig: S. Hirzel, 1886), 281, 308, 465.

6. It should be noted that only the last sentence of the repetition is verbatim, while the sentence אשר ישחט מחוץ למחנה ("who slaughters it outside the camp") is repeated freely and in an abbreviated form in the plus as follows: וישחטהו בחוץ ("and slaughters it outside").

omission and an unintentional one. Both of them can be excluded for the following reasons.

It would be difficult to find a motive for an intentional omission, because the plus does not contain anything theologically or otherwise offensive that could have triggered an omission. An intentional omission of the disturbing repetitions (which also calls for an explanation; see below) could potentially be possible for the repeated elements, but it is unlikely that the later editor would have omitted the reference to the burnt and peace offerings as well. A later editor who attempted to polish unnecessary roughness and repetition of the text—there is documented evidence for such editorial processes in some parts of the Hebrew Bible[7]—would not have intervened in the content in such a way that he left out significant information. Consequently, an intentional omission in the MT can be excluded as an improbable alternative.

It is also unlikely that we are dealing with an unintentional omission in the proto-MT caused by a homoioteleuton.[8] Although an unintentional omission is technically possible, the extensive repetition is so disturbing and the content of the plus is so clearly a digression from the main focus of the passage that they far outweigh the assumption of an unintentional omission. It would also be quite a coincidence that an unintentional lapse of the eye made the passage much clearer than what we can read in the SP, LXX, and 4QLev[d]. Moreover, one would still have to explain the reason for the disturbing repetition.

Of the three different possibilities to explain the variant readings, the weight of the evidence tips the balance toward assuming that the MT rep-

---

7. The tendency to level out some roughness and repetitions in the older text can be seen, for example, in the LXX and Alpha text of Esther as well as in 1 Esdras in relation to the MT of Ezra-Nehemiah. The older text of Esther and Ezra had become repetitive, probably because of earlier additions, and therefore some later editors sought to make the text more readable. In the case of Ezra-Nehemiah and Esther there is documented evidence for this technique, but it is reasonable to assume that similar editorial changes were made in other parts of the Hebrew Bible as well where we do not have similarly extensive textual evidence.

8. "Homoioteleuton" means that the endings (of a sentence or line) are similar or identical (cf. "homoiarchon," which refers to similar beginnings). In an omission caused by homoioteleuton a copyist would have omitted part of the text because after copying the first ending, due to the eye skipping to the text following the second, identical ending the copyist would accidentally leave out part of the text.

resents the most original text and that the plus is a later addition. This assumption has also been supported by many scholars since early research.[9]

1.2. Results and Methodological Consequences

The textual evidence in Lev 17:1–4 is a prime example of additions that took place in the transmission of the Hebrew Bible. The text was expanded by editors who had a particular perspective, different from that of the older text, and who made additions irrespective of the passage's original idea. In this case, the addition also introduced a disturbing repetition. The editor was focused on the specific sacrifices and was not primarily concerned about the consequences of his editing for the consistency of the text. Because the original text referred to an ox, lamb, and goat being slaughtered, he wanted to emphasize that these animals were to be offered as a burnt or a peace offering.[10] It is probable that similar additions were made throughout the Pentateuch (as well as other books) for centuries, during periods that are mainly not represented by empirical evidence. It is only in exceptional cases that such additions can be observed and reconstructed on the basis of comparing different witnesses. The textual evidence preserves mainly some of the latest additions that were made to the texts, while the older editorial activity has to be determined by other means, namely literary criticism.

---

9. Thus, among many others, August Knobel and August Dillmann, *Die Bücher Exodus und Leviticus* (2d ed.; KeHAT; Leipzig: S. Hirzel, 1880), 536–37; Bruno Baentsch, *Exodus, Leviticus, Numeri* (HKAT 1.2; Göttingen: Vandenhoeck & Ruprecht, 1903), 389; Klaus Grünwaldt, *Das Heiligkeitsgesetz Leviticus 17–26: Ursprüngliche Gestalt, Tradition und Theologie* (BZAW 271; Berlin: de Gruyter, 1999), 25. Alfred Bertholet (*Leviticus* [KHC 3; Tübingen: Mohr Siebeck, 1901], 59) considers both alternatives as potentially possible but regards the MT as more probably original. Many commentators ignore the variant reading altogether and follow the MT. Thus, among many others, Erhard S. Gerstenberger, *Leviticus* (trans. D. W. Stott; OTL; Louisville: Westminster John Knox Press, 1996), 234–37; trans. of *Das dritte Buch Mose: Leviticus* (ATD 6; Göttingen: Vandenhoeck & Ruprecht, 1993).

10. Although the Holiness Code or the priestly texts in general are not specific about this—these animals can be used for other offerings as well (see Lev 22:23, 27)—this editor seems to have emphasized the burnt and peace offerings. In Leviticus these offerings alone are otherwise not emphasized. For example, in Lev 9:22 they are accompanied by the sin offerings. Perhaps the closest parallels are to be found in Exod 20:24 and 32:5, both of which refer only to these offerings. However, it is difficult to establish any specific link between the addition and these passages.

Leviticus 17:4 is important because the resulting text in the SP, LXX, and 4QLev^d would—even without the MT—strongly suggest that the text was edited. The awkward repetition would lead the critical scholar to suspect that this text was not written by a single author and that an editor must be behind some section of the text. This scholar would possibly suspect an editorial seam at the points of the disturbing repetition. Further support for the suspicion would be provided by the information that digresses from the main theme of the passage. It would suggest that the repetitions enclose the added text. Since handbooks of literary-critical methodology refer to resumptive repetition (*Wiederaufnahme*) as an editorial technique,[11] the critic's suspicion would be corroborated further. The final confirmation would come from the control text, the so-called *Gegenprobe*, which looks at the resulting text without the suspected addition. The resulting text should be functional and, ideally, be clearer and more fluent than with the suspected addition. In Lev 17:4 this would certainly be the case. This example unequivocally shows that the technique of resumptive repetition was in fact used by editors.

It stands to reason that literary criticism would have a very good chance of reconstructing the older text of Lev 17:4, as now represented by the MT, solely on the basis of the expanded texts in the SP, LXX, and 4QLev^d. In this case, it is even likely that one would be able to identify the addition in full, for, following the methodology, one would assume that the repeated element is duplicated and that everything in between was added later. This example thus corroborates that literary criticism is, to some extent, a viable method to reconstruct older literary layers. This method, if applied correctly, can lead to reliable results, at least in cases that are as clear as this example.

---

11. See above, n. 5.

2

An Expansion to the Passover Law: Leviticus 23:5–8 and Numbers 28:16–25 Compared

This chapter will illustrate how the law on the Passover festival of Lev 23:5–8 was expanded in Num 28:16–25. Rather than dealing with parallel textual witnesses of the same biblical passage, this example shows how a text was used as a source to form a new passage, both of which were eventually included in the same collection of books of the Pentateuch. Often the relationship of such passages is controversial or debatable, but here it is very likely that Lev 23:5–8 was the source for Num 28:16–25.[1] We are therefore on solid ground in determining how the text developed.

2.1. Five Versions of the Passover Law

Being part of passages on the festivals and their legislation, Lev 23:5–8 and

---

1. Many scholars since early research have assumed that Num 28–29 represents an expansion to the festival calendar in Lev 23 (e.g., Bruno Baentsch, *Exodus, Leviticus, Numeri* [HKAT 1.2; Göttingen: Vandenhoeck & Ruprecht, 1903], 640; Heinrich Holzinger, *Numeri* [KHC 4; Tübingen and Leipzig: J.C.B. Mohr, 1903], 140–41; Carl Steuernagel, *Lehrbuch der Einleitung in das Alte Testament* [Tübingen: J.C.B. Mohr, 1912], 168–69; Klaus Grünwaldt, *Das Heiligkeitsgesetz Leviticus 17–26* [BZAW 271; Berlin: de Gruyter, 1999], 287). However, some scholars (e.g., George Buchanan Gray, *A Critical and Exegetical Commentary on Numbers* [ICC; Edinburgh: T&T Clark, 1903], 403–4; Israel Knohl, *The Sanctuary of Silence* [Minneapolis: Fortress, 1995], 19–23) have suggested that Lev 23 could be based on Num 28 or that both are dependent on a lost version of the festival calendar, but at least in view of the Passover law discussed here, this seems unlikely. The assumption that Num 28:16–25 is directly dependent on Lev 23:5–8 provides a good explanation for the differences between these laws. Clearly, the relationships of the other parallel laws in Lev 23 and Num 28–29 should be determined separately. For further discussion, see, e.g., Andreas Ruwe, *"Heiligkeitsgesetz" und "Priesterschrift"* (FAT 26; Tübingen: Mohr Siebeck, 1999), 32 (n. 166).

Num 28:16-25 provide laws that regulate the Passover. In fact, the Pentateuch contains five different versions of the Passover law: Exod 23:15(18);[2] Exod 34:18, 25; Deut 16:1-8; Lev 23:5-8; and Num 28:16-25. Because there is a literary connection between the versions and it is possible to determine their chronological relationship, they provide significant information about the development and transmission of texts dealing with laws in the Pentateuch.[3] They show how the law in question developed over centuries and what kinds of changes were made to it by later editors. In the earliest stages, the Passover was seen as an essentially agricultural festival, but calendric considerations and its connection to the memory of the exodus later replaced its agricultural character. For the latest authors, sacrificial considerations are central. Our interest here lies in the relationship between Lev 23:5-8 and Num 28:16-25 because it provides the clearest and most illustrative example of the development of the laws in question. The other relationships between the Passover laws are much more complicated and also disputed. In most of the other cases, the revision of the older law(s) was much more extensive than in our example.[4]

2.2. The Use of Leviticus 23:5-8 in Numbers 28:16-25

The author of Num 28:16-25 used Lev 23:5-8 as the main source, and there is no evidence to assume that he used the other Passover laws as well.

---

2. Although Exod 23:18 is not part of the actual Passover law, the author of Deut 16 evidently used this verse to create his own version of the Passover law.

3. Although our interest here lies in the relationship between Lev 23:5-8 and Num 28:16-25, a few notes about the earlier literary development of the Passover festival are necessary. Exod 23:15(18) may be the oldest version of the law, although some scholars have assumed that Exod 34:18, 25 could be older. The Deuteronomistic features of the passage in Exod 34:11-26 could suggest that Exod 34:18 is younger (the opposite direction of development has been suggested by Jörn Halbe, *Das Privilegrecht Jahwes* [FRLANT 114; Göttingen: Vandenhoeck & Ruprecht, 1975], 447-49). Although the relationship between Exod 34:18, 25 and Deut 16:1-8 is debated, the other chronological relationships between the laws are less controversial. Lev 23:5-8 is clearly younger than Exod 23:15; 34:18, 25; and Deut 16:1-8, while Num 28:16-25 is directly dependent on Lev 23:5-8.

4. The revision of Exod 23:15(18) in Exod 34:18, 25 is an exception in this respect. The author of Exod 34:18, 25 has adopted nearly every word of Exod 23:15(18). Deut 16:1-8 and Lev 23:5-8 used their sources as resource material that could be changed rather freely.

LEVITICUS 23:5–8 AND NUMBERS 28:16–25

Numbers 28:16–25 follows Lev 23:5–8 rather faithfully, but the festival was developed toward a temple-oriented sacrificial occasion led by the priests. Because of the extensive parallels, the comparison of the passages is illustrative of the textual changes that took place in the Hebrew Bible:

Lev 23:5–8

בחדש הראשון בארבעה עשר לחדש <u>בין הערבים</u> פסח ליהוה
ובחמשה עשר יום לחדש
הזה חג <s>המצות ליהוה</s> שבעת ימים מצות <u>תאכלו</u>
ביום הראשון מקרא־קדש <s>יהיה לכם</s>
כל־מלאכת עבדה לא תעשו
והקרבתם אשה ליהוה
שבעת ימים
ביום השביעי מקרא־קדש
כל־מלאכת עבדה לא תעשו

⁵ In the first month, on the fourteenth of the month, <u>at twilight</u>, there shall be a Passover offering to Yhwh. ⁶ And on the fifteenth day of this month is the festival <s>of unleavened bread of Yhwh</s>: seven days <u>you shall eat</u> unleavened bread. ⁷ On the first day <s>you shall have</s> a holy convocation: You shall not work at your occupations. ⁸ You shall present Yhwh's fire offerings for seven days. On the seventh day is a holy convocation: you shall not work at your occupations.

Num 28:16–25

ובחדש הראשון בארבעה עשר <u>יום</u> לחדש פסח ליהוה
ובחמשה עשר יום לחדש הזה חג שבעת ימים מצות <u>יאכל</u>
ביום הראשון מקרא־קדש כל־מלאכת עבדה לא תעשו
והקרבתם אשה עלה ליהוה
<u>פרים בני־בקר שנים ואיל אחד ושבעה כבשים בני שנה תמימם יהיו לכם</u>
<u>ומנחתם סלת בלולה בשמן שלשה עשרנים לפר ושני עשרנים לאיל תעשו</u>
<u>עשרון עשרון תעשה לכבש האחד לשבעת הכבשים</u>
<u>ושעיר חטאת אחד לכפר עליכם</u>
<u>מלבד עלת הבקר אשר לעלת התמיד תעשו את־אלה</u>
<u>כאלה תעשו ליום שבעת ימים לחם אשה ריח־ניחח ליהוה על־עולת התמיד</u>
<u>יעשה ונסכו</u>
וביום השביעי מקרא־קדש <u>יהיה לכם</u> כל־מלאכת עבדה לא תעשו

¹⁶ In the first month, on the fourteenth <u>day</u> of the month there shall be a Passover offering to Yhwh. ¹⁷ And on the fifteenth day of this month

is a festival: seven days shall unleavened bread be eaten. ¹⁸ On the first day is a holy convocation: You shall not work at your occupations. ¹⁹ You shall present Yhwh's fire offerings, <u>a burnt offering: two young bulls, one ram, and seven male lambs a year old; see that they are without blemish.</u> ²⁰ <u>Their grain offering shall be of choice flour mixed with oil: three-tenths of an ephah shall you offer for a bull, and two-tenths for a ram;</u> ²¹ <u>one-tenth shall you offer for each of the seven lambs;</u> ²² <u>also one male goat for a sin offering, to make atonement for you.</u> ²³ <u>You shall offer these in addition to the burnt offering of the morning, which belongs to the regular burnt offering.</u> ²⁴ <u>In the same way you shall offer daily,</u> for seven days, <u>the food of a fire offering, a pleasing odor to Yhwh; it shall be offered in addition to the regular burnt offering and its drink offering.</u> ²⁵ <u>And</u> on the seventh day <u>you shall have</u> a holy convocation: you shall not work at your occupations.

The literary connection is undeniable, but the most prominent difference between the passages is the expansive sacrificial legislation in Num 28:19–24. Whereas the source text in Lev 23:5–8 only generally refers to the fire offerings that the Israelites should make during the seven days of the Passover festival, Num 28:19–24 contains detailed instructions and additional information on the exact offerings of the festival. The addition specifies which animals should be offered, how many of each one there should be, and which offerings are acceptable, as well as which grain and other additional offerings should be made in connection with the main offerings. Although the expansion may be more closely related to Ezek 45:21–25,[5] the increase of detail is in line with the general tendency in the priestly legislation to increase attention and detail in matters concerning the temple cult, priests, and offerings. A similar development, where later editors focus on offerings and related issues, can be discerned in other parts of the Hebrew Bible as well.[6]

The large expansion also shows how an expansion could technically be made in relation to an older text. The author of Num 28:16–25 followed

---

5. It is not possible to solve the potentially very complicated relationship between Ezek 45:21–25 and Num 28:19–24, but it is probable that both passages reflect similar conceptions about the festival, and they are very closely related in comparison with the other Passover laws of the Pentateuch.

6. As a comparison, the older editions of Ezra-Nehemiah pay little heed to the temple, priests, and offerings, whereas many of the later editors emphasize these themes. For the development of the text and further discussion, see Juha Pakkala, *Ezra the Scribe* (BZAW 347; Berlin: de Gruyter, 2004), 267–74, and ch. 13 in this volume.

the source text rather faithfully until the beginning of Num 28:19 (≈ Lev 23:8), and then he added his expansion inside a sentence of the source text. The sentence והקרבתם אשה ליהוה שבעת ימים ("You shall present Yhwh's fire offerings for seven days") of the source text was completely preserved, but it was split up in Num 28 so that the time frame of the offerings (שבעת ימים, "seven days") was placed in the middle of the expansion. The example shows how a sentence in the source text could be split up so that in the new text parts of the old sentence are placed several verses apart from their original main sentence.

Lev 23:8

וְהִקְרַבְתֶּם אִשֶּׁה לַיהוָה שִׁבְעַת יָמִים

Num 28:19–24

וְהִקְרַבְתֶּם אִשֶּׁה עֹלָה לַיהוָה
פרים בני־בקר שנים ואיל אחד ושבעה כבשים בני שנה תמימם יהיו לכם ומנחתם סלת בלולה בשמן שלשה עשרנים לפר ושני עשרנים לאיל תעשו עשרון עשרון תעשה לכבש האחד לשבעת הכבשים ושעיר חטאת אחד לכפר עליכם מלבד עלת הבקר אשר לעלת התמיד תעשו את־אלה כאלה תעשו לַיּוֹם שִׁבְעַת יָמִים לחם אשה ריח־ניחח ליהוה על־עולת התמיד יעשה ונסכו

Another interesting difference between the two laws is the name of the festival. Whereas Lev 23:6 uses the term חג המצות ליהוה ("festival of unleavened bread of Yhwh"), Num 28:17 refers to the festival as simply a חג ("festival") without any specific name. It is probable that the name was intentionally omitted in Num 28:16–25, because there are distinctive differences between the names of the festival in the other passages that deal with the Passover as well. In fact, none of the five laws fully agree with each other in this respect. Exodus 23:15, 18 refers to only "the feast of unleavened bread" (חג המצות), whereas Exod 34:25 additionally refers to "the feast of the Passover" (חג הפסח). The author of Deut 16:1–8 further changed the name to "the Passover of Yhwh" (פסח ליהוה). In other words, the laws disagree about the name of the festival, and this confusion could be the reason why Num 28:17 does not use any specific name for this day but refers to it as merely "the festival."[7]

---

7. According to Gray, *Numbers*, 404, the reason for the omission may be the ten-

There are several further minor differences between the passages. There seems to be a peculiar difference between the commandments to have a holy convocation. Whereas Lev 23:7 adds יהיה לכם ("you shall have") to the commandment in relation to its parallel in Num 28:18, in the second occurrence of the commandment, Num 28:25 adds the same words, while Lev 23:8 omits them. It is difficult to determine which of the readings is more original, for the words may have been relocated for stylistic reasons. A related difference is found in Lev 23:6 and Num 28:17: For the תאכלו ("you shall eat") of Lev 23:6, Num 28:17 has יאכל (*niphal*, "shall be eaten"). Numbers 28:16 also adds the word יום ("day"). Although the word is not absolutely necessary in the context, it may be an accidental omission in Lev 23:5 because the following verse 6 includes the word in a similar context (ובחמשה עשר יום לחדש, "And on the fifteenth day of the month"; cf. בארבעה עשר לחדש, "on the fourteenth of the month").

At least one of the plusses in Lev 23:5–8 in relation to Num 28:16–25 may be an addition that was inserted after Lev 23:5–8 was used as a source for Num 28:16–25: בין הערבים ("at twilight") in Lev 23:5 is probably a clarifying addition, because its intentional omission by the author of Num 28:16 would be improbable, and there is also no obvious reason for an accidental omission. Although the exact meaning of בין הערבים is unclear,[8] it seems to define the precise time when the Passover offering should be made. In the more original text, which in this case is represented by Num 28:16, the Passover offering should be made anytime during the day, while Lev 23:5 is more specific. The addition was probably influenced by Exod 12:6 or Num 9:2–11, where the idea that the Passover offering should be made בין הערבים is also met.[9] Additions that provide more detailed information are typical in the Hebrew Bible, whereas the omission of such details, especially concerning the exact time of offering, would be exceptional and unmotivated. This case also shows how another related passage may have caused a harmonizing addition in Lev 23:5.

---

dency of Num 28 for "greater brevity," but in view of the other parallel sections, this is unlikely.

8. Literally it means "between the evenings," but most scholars assume that twilight is meant. See Ludwig Koehler and Walter Baumgartner, *The Hebrew and Aramaic Lexicon of the Old Testament* (Leiden: Brill, 2001), 877–78.

9. It should also be noted that the LXX of Num 9:5 lacks a parallel to בין הערבים ("at twilight"), which would seem to indicate that the specific time when the Passover offering should be made was secondarily added to several texts of the Hebrew Bible.

2.3. Difficulties of Reconstruction

It would not be easy to identify the large addition in Num 28:19–24, because it was made after a general reference to offerings. The general reference is logically followed by a list of more-detailed instructions. The addition does not particularly stand out from its context, because the following verses begin with a new subtheme, the holy convocation. In other words, because the expansion was made at a thematic juncture, it does not disturb its context. Because there are also no grammatical or thematic tensions, a literary critic could not find many arguments for assuming that we are dealing with an expansion in Num 28:19–24.

We have seen that the sentence והקרבתם אשה ליהוה שבעת ימים ("You shall present Yhwh's fire offerings for seven days") of Lev 23:8 was split up in Num 28:19–24. In this case it would also be very difficult, if not impossible, to reconstruct the source text on the basis of Num 28:16–25 alone. Because שבעת ימים ("[for] seven days") was very well integrated to its new context, we would have few tools to reconstruct the source, did we not possess the source text as well.

2.4. Results and Methodological Consequences

The comparison between Lev 23:5–8 and Num 28:16–25 shows how an earlier text was expanded in the course of its textual transmission. This is an exemplary case where the empirical evidence would seem to fit very well with the typical model of an expansion, assumed in source- and redaction-critical approaches. A considerable amount of detail was added, and the expansion also develops the text in a new and specific direction. In Num 28:16–25 the sacrificial aspect of the law in question was considerably expanded in comparison with the source, Lev 23:5–8. If we did not possess the source, the thematic difference could reveal to the careful source critic that we are dealing with an expansion. Nevertheless, the source critic would not be able to provide many arguments for this suspicion. Moreover, the passage also suggests that it would be difficult to separate every part of the source from the expansion. In particular, the phrase שבעת ימים ("[for] seven days") was separated from its original context in a way that would probably preclude a correct reconstruction.

3
FROM GLOSSES TO LARGER EXPANSIONS: THE MASORETIC TEXT OF NUMBERS 13–14 COMPARED WITH THE SEPTUAGINT AND THE SAMARITAN PENTATEUCH

Within the books of the Pentateuch, the textual history of Num 13–14 is of particular interest since these chapters contain several verses where the major textual witnesses differ substantially. There are good reasons to assume that, in most cases, the differences are the result of late editorial changes. It seems that these changes are indicative of the importance and theological weight of this story within the larger narrative of the Pentateuch.[1]

An illustrative example is the transition from Num 13 to 14. In the textual history of Num 13:33, a verse that lies at the junction of these chapters, two different changes are documented that attest to the possible range of late editorial processes. Regarding the direction of the textual development of this verse, the MT probably represents a textual stage later than that of the LXX, but earlier than the form represented by the SP.

3.1. THE LXX PROVIDES EVIDENCE FOR A GLOSS IN NUMBERS 13:33 MT

The LXX text of Num 13:33, the last verse of the chapter, is shorter than the MT text of this verse. The words בני ענק מן הנפלים ("the Anakites from the Nephilim") of the MT have no counterpart in the oldest Greek ver-

---

[1]. Horst Seebass, *Numeri 10,11–22,1* (vol. 2 of *Numeri*; BKAT 4.2; Neukirchen-Vluyn: Neukirchener Verlag, 2003), 82. Key passages in the Hebrew Bible are often the most edited ones, as several successive later editors wanted to leave their imprint on them (e.g., 2 Kgs 23).

sion.[2] The missing passage can be found only in Greek manuscripts that represent a later textual development.[3] These manuscripts probably attest to a Greek version that was secondarily expanded and harmonized after the textual tradition represented by the MT.

Num 13:33 MT

ושם ראינו את הנפילים
<u>בני ענק מן הנפלים</u>
ונהי בעינינו כחגבים
וכן היינו בעיניהם

And there we saw the Nephilim, <u>the Anakites from the Nephilim,</u> and we were in our own eyes as locusts, and so we were in their eyes.

Num 13:33 LXX

καὶ ἐκεῖ ἑωράκαμεν τοὺς γίγαντας καὶ ἦμεν ἐνώπιον αὐτῶν ὡσεὶ ἀκρίδες, ἀλλὰ καὶ οὕτως ἦμεν ἐνώπιον αὐτῶν.

And there we saw the giants; and we were before them as locusts, yea, even so we were before them.

Even without the knowledge of the textual tradition represented by the LXX* one could surmise that here we could be dealing with a marginal gloss. The verse is understandable without the words בני ענק מן הנפלים ("the Anakites from the Nephilim"). The shorter version is also easier to read, since these words form a kind of parenthesis that is only loosely integrated into the syntactical structure:[4] ושם ראינו את הנפילים [בני ענק מן הנפלים] ונהי בעינינו כחגבים ("And there we saw the Nephilim, [the Anakites from the Nephilim,] and we were in our own eyes as locusts"). Another conspicuous detail that speaks for a secondary supplement is the disturbing repetition of הנפלים ("the Nephilim").

---

2. John William Wevers, ed., *Numeri* (vol. 3.1 of *Septuaginta: Vetus Testamentum Graecum*; Göttingen: Vandenhoeck & Ruprecht, 1982), 183–84.

3. These manuscripts represent the so-called *Mehrheitstext*; among them is the Hexaplaric version where the passage is marked with the asterisk sign; see ibid., 184.

4. George Buchanan Gray, *A Critical and Exegetical Commentary on Numbers* (ICC; Edinburgh: T&T Clark, 1903), 151.

The phrase בני ענק מן הנפלים ("the Anakites from the Nephilim") identifies the Nephilim seen by the Israelite spies with the Anakites, another people of the former inhabitants of the promised land. While the Nephilim are mentioned nowhere else in the entire narrative, the Anakites are mentioned earlier in ch. 13 as ילדי הענק ("the children of [the] Anak"; vv. 22, 28), the inhabitants of Hebron (v. 22). The term "Nephilim," which is met only here and in Gen 6:4 in the Hebrew Bible, provides a rationale for the explanatory gloss since the mythical giants of primeval origin, or Nephilim, play no further role in the context of Num 13–14. When they are identified with the Anakite populace of Hebron, mentioned in the preceding text, the motif of the giants in Num 13:33 is connected more closely with the context.[5]

The minus in the LXX* empirically corroborates the assumption that the MT contains an addition in this verse. There is no unequivocal reason why the additional words would have been secondarily omitted, either in the Greek translation or in its Hebrew *Vorlage*.[6] An intentional omission is improbable, since the plus is not theologically or otherwise problematic. As for the awkward style of the longer Hebrew text, the Greek translator could have easily created a smooth Greek sentence in which the parenthesis is syntactically well integrated into the sentence.[7] It is also unlikely that he would have left out the reference to the Anakites, which connects "the Nephilim" with the context. To be sure, one could alternatively assume that the plus was mistakenly omitted by scribal haplography because of the repetition of הנפילים ("the Nephilim"): [הַנְּפִילִים [בני ענק מן הַנְּפִלִים ("the Nephilim [the Anakites from the Nephilim]"). Although this alternative cannot completely be excluded, the simplest explanation for the shorter Greek version is that this text goes back to a Hebrew *Vorlage* that did not yet contain this addition.[8]

---

5. Martin Noth, *Numbers: A Commentary* (OTL; London: SCM, 1968), 107.

6. An omission in the LXX is assumed by Roland Kenneth Harrison, *Numbers: An Exegetical Commentary* (The Wycliffe Exegetical Commentary; Grand Rapids: Baker Book House, 1992), 210, but he gives no reason for this assumption.

7. Another difference between Num 13:33 MT and LXX could be due to a stylistic facilitation by the Greek translator. Instead of the strange phrase ונהי בעינינו כחגבים ("and we were in *our own* eyes as locusts") the LXX has the more natural καὶ ἦμεν ἐνώπιον αὐτῶν ὡσεὶ ἀκρίδες ("and we were before *them* as locusts").

8. E.g., Philip J. Budd, *Numbers* (WBC 5; Waco, Tex.: Word, 1984), 141; Seebass, *Numeri 10,11–22,1*, 83; Ludwig Schmidt, *Das vierte Buch Mose: Numeri 10,11–36,13* (ATD 7.2; Göttingen: Vandenhoeck & Ruprecht, 2004), 36 n. 38.

The gloss does not use the term ילדי הענק ("the children of [the] Anak"), which occurs earlier in the chapter (vv. 22, 28), but speaks of בני ענק ("the sons of Anak," or "the Anakites"). The latter term can also be found in Deut 9:2, and a similar term, בני ענקים ("the Anakites"), is used in Deut 1:28 and 9:2 as well. It is therefore probable that the editor who inserted this addition was influenced by the language of Deuteronomy. Moreover, it can be assumed that the editor intended to assimilate the spy narrative of Num 13–14 with its parallel in Deut 1, since in Deut 1:28 the Anakites are mentioned among the inhabitants of the promised land.

3.2. A Larger Plus in Numbers 13:33 SP

Another textual variant that points to more substantial editing can be found in the SP. Compared to the MT, this textual tradition has a large plus in Num 13:33. After the preceding speech of the spies that ends in Num 13:33 and before the weeping of the people in Num 14:1, the additional text mentions how the people complained about their fate and how Moses addressed them in order to reject this complaint.

Num 13:33–14:1 MT

ושם ראינו את הנפילים בני ענק מן הנפלים ונהי בעינינו כחגבים וכן היינו בעיניהם
ותשא כל העדה ויתנו את קולם ויבכו העם בלילה ההוא

[33] "And there we saw the Nephilim, the Anakites from the Nephilim, and we were in our own eyes as locusts, and so we were in their eyes."
[1] And all the congregation lifted up their voice, and cried; and the people wept that night.

Num 13:33–14:1 SP

ושם ראינו את הנפילים בני ענק מן הנפלים ונהי בעינינו כחגבים וכן היינו בעיניהם
וירגנו בני ישראל באהליהם ויאמרו בשנאת יהוה אתנו הוציאנו מארץ מצרים לתת אתנו ביד האמרי להשמידנו אנה אנחנו עלים ואחינו המיסו את לבבנו לאמר עם גדול ורם ממנו ערים גדלות ובצרות בשמים וגם בני ענקים ראינו שם ויאמר משה לבני ישראל לא תערצון ולא תיראון מהם יהוה אלהיכם ההלך לפניכם הוא ילחם לכם ככל אשר עשה אתכם במצרים לעיניכם ובמדבר אשר ראית אשר נשאך יהוה אלהיך כאשר ישא איש את

NUMBERS 13–14

בנו בכל הדרך אשר הלכתם עד באכם עד המקום הזה ובדבר הזה אינכם
מאמינים ביהוה אלהיכם ההלך לפניכם בדרך לתור לכם מקום להחנתכם
באש לילה להראתכם בדרך אשר תלכו בה וענן יומם
ותשא כל העדה ויתנו את קולם ויבכו העם בלילה ההוא

33 "And there we saw the Nephilim, the Anakites from the Nephilim, and we were in our own eyes as locusts, and so we were in their eyes."

And the Israelites grumbled in their tents and said, "It is because Yhwh hates us that he has brought us out of the land of Egypt, to hand us over to the Amorites to destroy us. Where are we headed? Our brothers have made our hearts melt by saying, 'The people are stronger and taller than we; the cities are large and fortified up to heaven, and we also saw there the Anakites!'" And Moses said to the Israelites, "Have no dread or fear of them. Yhwh your God, who goes before you, is the one who will fight for you, just as he did for you in Egypt before your very eyes, and in the wilderness, where you saw how Yhwh your God carried you, just as one carries a child, all the way that you traveled until you reached this place. But in spite of this, you have no trust in Yhwh your God, who goes before you on the way to seek out a place for you to camp, in fire by night, and in the cloud by day, to show you the route you should take."

¹ And all the congregation lifted up their voice, and cried; and the people wept that night.

The additional passage has a close parallel in Deut 1:27–32. Numbers 13:33 SP follows Deut 1:27–32 almost word for word. Apart from some different spellings, only minor differences can be observed: In Deut 1, Moses addresses the Israelites with the second-person plural (ותרגנו באהליכם, "And you grumbled in your tents"), and, since he is speaking all the time, the first-person singular is used (ואמר אלכם, "And I said to you"), while in Num 13:33 SP the equivalent phrases use the third person (וירגנו בני ישראל באהליהם, "And the Israelites grumbled in their tents"; ויאמר משה לבני ישראל, "And Moses said to the Israelites").

Deut 1:27–32 MT

ותרגנו באהליכם ותאמרו בשנאת יהוה אתנו הוציאנו מארץ מצרים לתת
אתנו ביד האמרי להשמידנו אנה אנחנו עלים אחינו המסו את לבבנו לאמר
עם גדול ורם ממנו ערים גדלת ובצורת בשמים וגם בני ענקים ראינו שם
ואמר אלכם לא תערצון ולא תיראון מהם יהוה אלהיכם ההלך לפניכם הוא
ילחם לכם ככל אשר עשה אתכם במצרים לעיניכם ובמדבר אשר ראית
אשר נשאך יהוה אלהיך כאשר ישא איש את בנו בכל הדרך אשר הלכתם
עד באכם עד המקום הזה ובדבר הזה אינכם מאמינים ביהוה אלהיכם ההלך

לפניכם בדרך לתור לכם מקום לחנתכם באש לילה לראתכם בדרך אשר
תלכו בה ובענן יומם

²⁷ And you grumbled in your tents and said, "It is because Yhwh hates us that he has brought us out of the land of Egypt, to hand us over to the Amorites to destroy us. ²⁸ Where are we headed? Our brothers have made our hearts melt by saying, 'The people are stronger and taller than we; the cities are large and fortified up to heaven, and we also saw there the Anakites!'"

²⁹ And I said to you, "Have no dread or fear of them. ³⁰ Yhwh your God, who goes before you, is the one who will fight for you, just as he did for you in Egypt before your very eyes, ³¹ and in the wilderness, where you saw how Yhwh your God carried you, just as one carries a child, all the way that you traveled until you reached this place. ³² But in spite of this, you have no trust in Yhwh your God, ³³ who goes before you on the way to seek out a place for you to camp, in fire by night, and in the cloud by day, to show you the route you should take."

It lies beyond doubt that the plus in the SP of Num 13:33 is secondary.[9] The additional text seems to have been inserted in an attempt to harmonize the passage with Deut 1:27–32. This was done by a rather mechanical technique of copying so that the donor text of Deut 1:27–32 was, with the exception of the minor changes noted above, adopted verbatim. Nevertheless, the insertion of the additional text is a substantial editorial alteration of Num 13–14 by which the narrative was aligned more closely with Deut 1. This militates against the common assumption that in the late stages of the literary history of the biblical texts substantial changes were no longer made. It is particularly noteworthy that there is evidence of such changes in the Pentateuch from a time, probably in the last two centuries BCE, when the textual traditions of the proto-MT and the SP developed separately.

This editorial alteration must have taken place after the marginal gloss בני ענק מן הנפלים ("the Anakites from the Nephilim"), unattested by the LXX*, was inserted into Num 13:33. This is suggested by the fact that the SP includes the gloss, along with the MT. Accordingly, the MT would attest to a stage of the textual development that lies between the LXX* and the SP. Significantly, both the gloss and the larger expansion have the tendency

---

9. Thus, e.g., Budd, *Numbers*, 141; Harrison, *Numbers*, 210; Seebass, *Numeri 10,11–22,1*, 83.

of assimilating Num 13-14 with Deut 1. It is probably no coincidence that the Anakites are also mentioned in the expansion that is attested by the SP (parallel to Deut 1:28). The editor who inserted the parallel of Deut 1:27-32 into the SP of Num 13:33 could have been inspired by the gloss in Num 13:33 that refers to the Anakites.

3.3. Other Expansions in the Textual History of Numbers 13-14

Both textual alterations in Num 13:33 are not isolated phenomena in the context of the spy narrative of Num 13-14. In the textual history of these chapters there are also other instances where the text was secondarily aligned with the Deuteronomic version of the narrative. In several cases more or less substantial additions were made following Deut 1. This editorial process is mostly attested by the SP, but it can also be seen, in part, in the LXX and the Peshitta, the ancient Syriac translation. The following chart gives an overview of these changes.

LXX	SP	Peshitta	Parallel to
	+ between Num 12:16 and 13:1		Deut 1:20-23a
	+ between Num 13:33 and 14:1		Deut 1:27-32
+ in Num 14:23			Deut 1:39
		+ in Num 14:31	Deut 1:39
	+ in Num 14:40		Deut 1:42
	+ in Num 14:45		Deut 1:44
+ in Num 14:45	+ in Num 14:45		Deut 1:45a

This chart illustrates that the harmonizations with Deuteronomy took place in three different textual traditions. The plusses in Num 14:23 and 45 are met only in the LXX, the plus in Num 14:31 only in the Peshitta, and repeated plusses only in the SP. The existence of independent harmonizations in three different textual traditions from a relatively late period implies that harmonizations were frequent in the transmission of the Pentateuch. It should be noted that these changes primarily took place at a rather late stage of the textual development. Harmonizations should thus also be assumed in those periods of textual transmission from which documented or textual evidence is lacking. Here one should further add that this phenomenon is by no means restricted to Num 13–14. Many successive editors and copyists were apparently comparing parallel passages within the Pentateuch, Deuteronomy often influencing other parts of this collection of books.[10]

Apart from larger expansions, the textual history of Num 13–14 also provides evidence for some minor changes similar to the addition of the gloss in Num 13:33 MT.[11] In contrast to this case, the other small expansions seem to have been made mainly in the textual traditions of the LXX and the SP.

In Num 13:29b, both the LXX and the SP have a small plus when compared with the MT. While the MT mentions three peoples that lived in the land before its conquest by the Israelites, the LXX and the SP speak about four peoples: καὶ ὁ Χετταῖος <u>καὶ ὁ Εὐαῖος</u> καὶ ὁ Ἰεβουσαῖος καὶ ὁ Ἀμορραῖος / והחתי <u>והחוי</u> והיבוסי והאמרי ("the Hittite, and the Hivite, and the Jebusite, and the Amorite"). In all likelihood, this plus is the result of a secondary addition that is in line with other lists of the former inhabitants of the land that recurrently mention the "Hivites" (e.g., Exod 3:8, 17; Deut 7:1).

Another plus shared by the LXX and the SP in comparison with the MT can be found in Num 14:12. According to the MT, Yhwh says that he intends to make of Moses a great nation, while both the LXX and the SP additionally mention the house of Moses's father: καὶ ποιήσω σὲ <u>καὶ τὸν οἶκον τοῦ πατρός σου</u> / ואעשה אתך <u>ואת בית אביך</u> ("I will make you <u>and the house of your father</u>"). This is probably an interpretive addition by which the Levite ancestors of Moses were secondarily included in the divine plan.

The formula about Yhwh's mercy that occurs in Num 14:18 is attested by both the LXX and the SP in a slightly expanded version: Κύριος μακρόθυμος καὶ πολυέλεος <u>καὶ ἀληθινός</u>, ἀφαιρῶν ἀνομίας καὶ ἀδικίας <u>καὶ ἁμαρτίας</u> / יהוה ארך אפים ורב חסד <u>ואמת</u> נשא עון ופשע <u>וחטאה</u> ("Yhwh is slow to anger, and abundant in steadfast love <u>and faithfulness</u>, forgiving iniquity and transgression <u>and sin</u>"). The additional words are parallel to

---

10. Here one should mention, for example, the probability that the Sinai pericope in Exod 21–23 and Deuteronomy, both effectively dealing with the giving of the law, have been harmonized during the transmission of the texts even though this harmonization is mostly not documented in textual witnesses.

11. See Seebass, *Numeri 10,11–22,1*, 82–84.

Exod 34:6-7, and therefore it can be assumed that the plusses were secondarily inserted in order to align the text more closely with Exod 34.

In the SP of Num 14:23, the formula about the divine gift of the land is, compared to the MT, expanded with an additional infinitive clause: הארץ אשר נשבעתי לאבתם לתת להם ("the land that I swore to their fathers to give to them"). The plus לתת להם ("to give to them") accords with the usual form of this formula, especially in the book of Deuteronomy (Deut 1:8; 6:10, etc.). Thus it is probable that the SP of Num 14:23 was secondarily assimilated with the Deuteronomic version of this formula.

To be sure, all these cases represent only minor changes that do not affect the meaning of the text very much, but they, nevertheless, attest to a kind of editorial activity by which the text was, albeit cautiously, modified and interpreted. It is significant that in three of these cases the LXX and the SP attest to the same textual tradition, sharing a secondary addition. This means that these changes cannot have been made by the Greek translator but must have been part of the Hebrew *Vorlage* of the LXX. As a consequence, they are probably of pre-Samaritan origin.

Regarding the methodology of reconstructing the development of the Hebrew Bible, these small changes are an important phenomenon that needs to be recognized in literary or redaction criticism. If we possessed only the witnesses where these changes are already included, it would be difficult, if not impossible, to identify the additions and thus reconstruct the earlier versions. The addition of והחוי ("and the Hivites"), ואת בית אביך ("and the house of your father"), or ואמת ("and faithfulness"), for example, left virtually no trace in the resulting text. In other words, they caused no syntactical, stylistic, or thematic tensions, and therefore we would have no criteria for detecting them without the evidence of the MT. There is no reason why such changes should not have taken place during the earlier stages of the literary history in times from which documented evidence is not preserved. We should therefore avoid the claim or assumption that literary- or redaction-critical approaches would be able to reconstruct earlier stages of the textual development in every detail.

3.4. Results and Methodological Consequences

The textual history of Num 13–14 attests to several cases of late editorial activity. The text of the spy narrative was changed by virtue of a substantial number of smaller and larger expansions. All of these changes show a clear interpretive tendency. In several cases, the expansion assimilates or harmonizes the narrative more closely with its parallel in Deut 1. This editorial process, as a whole, took place mainly in textual traditions other than the (proto-)MT. Since most of the changes can be found in the SP—but in part also in the LXX—the MT seems to attest to a relatively early stage of the textual development. It seems that there was less freedom to alter the proto-MT during the time in which these three textual traditions developed independently. However, one should not deduce from this an a priori preference for the MT. The case of Num 13:33 LXX* shows that the MT is the result of late editing as well so that each case has to be independently investigated. The possibility that the MT contains a less original reading than another witness should always be taken into consideration.

At the same time, it should be noted that the documented evidence covers only the latest stages of the textual development. There is no reason to assume that similar changes could not have taken place during earlier stages of the textual development as well. Considering the gradually increasing authority and holiness of the text, it is probable that the editorial processes were even more radical in the earlier stages of the development of the texts.

Regarding the methodology of reconstructing the literary history, two kinds of additions can be observed in these chapters: First, there are some small additions that left virtually no trace in the resulting texts. The possibility that such changes were made needs to be taken into account, although, without documented evidence, we have, in practice, no means to identify and reconstruct them. Second, there are other cases where it is possible to detect additions even without empirical evidence from textual witnesses. For instance, if we possessed only the MT of Num 13:33, we could deduce from inner-textual arguments that this text contains an addition concerning the Anakites, and if we possessed only the SP of this passage, we would be able to determine that the long parallel with Deut 1 might have been inserted only secondarily. In consequence, attempts to reconstruct earlier stages of the literary development are not futile, although in view of the present example, it is unlikely that scholarship would be able to reconstruct every detail of the earlier forms of the texts.

4
LATE ADDITIONS OR EDITORIAL SHORTENING? JOSHUA 20 IN THE MASORETIC TEXT AND THE SEPTUAGINT

4.1. INTRODUCTION

Joshua 20 discusses the cities of refuge and cases of an accidental slayer. There are substantial differences between the MT and the LXX; in parts of the text the MT contains extensive plusses in relation to the Greek tradition. The textual differences are reflected in differing concepts about the cities of refuge. From the comparison between the MT and the LXX it can be deduced that substantial editorial alterations took place in the history of this chapter, although it is not evident which version is more original and which developed from the other. At first glance, the LXX seems to provide evidence for the assumption that the MT is the result of large secondary additions, but there are also good arguments that the minuses in the LXX could mainly go back to substantial editorial shortening.

4.2. THE TEXTUAL EVIDENCE: A LONG AND A SHORT VERSION OF JOSHUA 20

Joshua 20 can be divided into two parts. In the first part (vv. 1–6), Yhwh commissions Joshua (v. 1) to remind the Israelites about establishing cities of refuge (v. 2) and to explain what the function of these cities is (vv. 3–6). The second part (vv. 7–9) records that the Israelites established six cities of refuge: three west of the Jordan (v. 7) and three east (v. 8). A brief summary repeats what the purpose of these cities was (v. 9).

The main differences between the MT and the LXX are found in the first part, where the MT contains a large plus in vv. 4–6 in relation to the Greek text of Codex Vaticanus and some other manuscripts (e.g., the majuscules N and Θ and the minuscule b_2). These Greek witnesses probably preserve the original Greek translation.¹ The rest of the Greek manuscripts represent a textual form that has been harmonized after the textual tradition represented by the MT, but this is clearly a secondary development.

Josh 20:1–6 MT

וידבר יהוה אל יהושע לאמר
דבר אל בני ישראל לאמר תנו <u>לכם</u> את ערי המקלט אשר דברתי אליכם ביד משה
לנוס שמה רוצח מכה נפש בשגגה <u>בבלי דעת</u> והיו לכם למקלט מגאל הדם
<u>ונס אל אחת מהערים האלה ועמד פתח שער העיר ודבר באזני זקני העיר ההיא את דבריו ואספו אתו העירה אליהם ונתנו לו מקום וישב עמם
וכי ירדף גאל הדם אחריו ולא יסגרו את הרצח בידו
כי בבלי דעת הכה את רעהו ולא שנא הוא לו מתמול שלשום</u>
וישב בעיר ההיא
עד עמדו לפני העדה למשפט
<u>עד מות הכהן הגדול אשר יהיה בימים ההם</u>
אז ישוב הרוצח ובא אל עירו ואל ביתו
אל העיר אשר נס משם

¹ And Yhwh spoke to Joshua, saying, ² "Speak to the Israelites and say to them, 'Appoint <u>for you</u> the cities of refuge, of which I spoke to you through Moses, ³ so that a slayer may flee there who kills a person without intent, <u>without knowledge</u>; and they shall be for you a refuge from the avenger of blood. ⁴ <u>And he shall flee to one of these cities and shall stand at the entrance of the gate of the city and speak in the ears of the elders of that city, and they shall take him into the city and give him a place, and he shall dwell with them.</u> ⁵ <u>And if the avenger of blood is in pursuit, they shall not deliver the slayer into his hand, because without knowledge he killed his neighbor, and he hated him not before.</u> ⁶ And he shall dwell in that city until he stands before the congregation for judgment, <u>until the death of the high priest who shall be in those days</u>; then

---

1. Thus also *BHS* and the LXX edition of Rahlfs (Alfred Rahlfs and Robert Hanhart, eds., *Septuaginta* [2nd ed.; Stuttgart: Deutsche Bibelgesellschaft, 2006]), as well as A. Graeme Auld, *Joshua: Jesus Son of Nauē in Codex Vaticanus* (Septuagint Commentary Series; Leiden: Brill: 2005), 202; and Cornelis den Hertog, "Jesus: Josue / Das Buch Josua," in *Septuaginta Deutsch: Erläuterungen und Kommentare zum griechischen Alten Testament* (ed. Martin Karrer and Wolfgang Kraus; Stuttgart: Deutsche Bibelgesellschaft, 2011), 1:649.

the slayer shall return home and enter his town and his house, his city from whence he fled.'"

Josh 20:1–6 LXX*

¹ Καὶ ἐλάλησεν κύριος τῷ Ἰησοῖ λέγων ² Λάλησον τοῖς υἱοῖς Ισραηλ λέγων Δότε τὰς πόλεις τῶν φυγαδευτηρίων, ἃς εἶπα πρὸς ὑμᾶς διὰ Μωυσῆ, ³ φυγαδευτήριον τῷ φονευτῇ τῷ πατάξαντι ψυχὴν ἀκουσίως, καὶ ἔσονται ὑμῖν <u>αἱ πόλεις</u> φυγαδευτήριον, <u>καὶ οὐκ ἀποθανεῖται ὁ φονευτὴς</u> ὑπὸ τοῦ ἀγχιστεύοντος τὸ αἷμα, ⁶ ἕως ἂν καταστῇ ἐναντίον τῆς συναγωγῆς εἰς κρίσιν.

¹ And the Lord spoke to Joshua, saying, ² "Speak to the Israelites and say to them, 'Give the cities of refuge, of which I spoke to you through Moses, ³ a refuge to the slayer who has smitten a person unintentionally, and <u>the cities</u> shall be for you a refuge, <u>and the slayer shall not be killed</u> by the avenger of blood, ⁶ until he stands before the congregation for judgment.'"

As for the major plusses in the MT in vv. 3–6, it is not obvious which version, the MT or the LXX*, is more original. There are two basic alternatives to explain the development from one version to the other. Either the LXX* preserves a more original version of the chapter, which was then secondarily expanded in the proto-MT, or the proto-MT was deliberately shortened in the Greek translation or its Hebrew *Vorlage*. Both theories have found advocates in scholarship (see below).

4.3. Inconsistencies in the MT and a Coherent Version in the LXX*

The versions differ not only in length but also in conceptual consistency. While the shorter LXX* unfolds a coherent concept of the cities of refuge, the MT shows considerable tensions, even logical contradictions.

A major problem in the MT concerns the procedure of how the case of an accidental slayer, who has taken refuge in one of these cities, is resolved. According to v. 4, the slayer shall state his case before the elders of the city at the gate, and "they shall take him into the city and give him a place, and he shall dwell with them" (ואספו אתו העירה אליהם ונתנו לו מקום וישב עמם). This implies that the case is decided when the elders take the slayer into the city. The same concept is presupposed in v. 5, since according to this verse the elders are not allowed to deliver the slayer to the avenger: כי בבלי דעת הכה את רעהו ולא שנא הוא לו מתמול שלשום ("because without knowledge he killed his neighbor, and he hated him not before"; v. 5b). According to v. 6, however, the decisive trial is conducted only later, when the congregation of the people gathers for judgment: עד עמדו לפני העדה למשפט ("until he stands before the congregation for judgment").

To be sure, one could argue that the final decision of the case is suspended until the trial before the congregation. This would imply the possibility that the elders made a false decision that could be corrected later by the congregation. However, the wording of v. 5 does not fit to this theory. This verse presupposes that the elders make the *final* decision on how to deal with the slayer. Thus, one can ask with Alexander Rofé, "What room is there for an additional trial before the assembly?"[2] Verse 6 seems to refer to a concept different from that of vv. 4–5.

Another contradiction is related to the period of dwelling that is envisaged in vv. 4 (וישב עמם, "and he shall dwell with them") and 6 (וישב בעיר ההיא עד עמדו לפני העדה למשפט, "And he shall dwell in that city until he stands before the congregation for judgment"). As Michael Fishbane states, "Verse 6 hardly repeats v. 4, since the inquest of v. 4 ends with the incorporation of the killer into the city, whereas v. 6 would seem to indicate a period of settlement *until* the inquest."[3]

Verse 6 contains further problems. The double temporal preposition עד ("until") is stylistically awkward and causes a problem within the internal logic of the law.

Josh 20:6 MT

וישב בעיר ההיא עד עמדו לפני העדה למשפט
עד מות הכהן הדגול אשר יהיה בימים ההם
אז ישוב הרוצח ובא אל עירו ואל ביתו אל העיר אשר נס משם

And he shall dwell in that city until he stands before the congregation for judgment, until the death of the high priest who shall be in those days; then the slayer shall return home and enter his town and his house, his city from whence he fled.

---

2. Alexander Rofé, "Joshua 20: Historico-Literary Criticism Illustrated," in *Empirical Models for Biblical Criticism* (ed. Jeffrey H. Tigay; Philadelphia: University of Pennsylvania Press, 1985), 136.

3. Michael Fishbane, "Biblical Colophons, Textual Criticism and Legal Analogies," *CBQ* 42 (1980): 445 (italics original).

Since it cannot be assumed that the high priest regularly dies at the date of the trial, the two prepositions עד ("until") would appear to refer to two different dates.[4] The slayer shall live in the city of refuge until he stands trial before the congregation, but it is only when the high priest dies that he is allowed to return to the place where he originally lived. This leads to the question: What happens between the trial and the death of the high priest? The text seems to imply that the slayer has to return to the city of refuge after the trial, but it is peculiar that the text does not say this explicitly.

Regarding these problems concerning the logic of the law, it is very likely that the MT merges different concepts of how to proceed with a slayer who seeks protection from the avenger in a city of refuge. According to one concept, the elders of the city of refuge decide whether to admit the refugee to the city or not (v. 4). If he is admitted, the case is decided that he is in fact an accidental slayer (v. 5), and he finds a new home in this city (v. 4b). According to the other concept, any person who flees from an avenger can enter a city of refuge and find temporary protection there (v. 3), until the case is decided in a trial before the congregation (v. 6aα*: עד עמדו לפני העדה למשפט, "until he stands before the congregation for judgment").

That the slayer's return to his original home depends on the death of the high priest, as suggested in parts of v. 6, further complicates the issue. This idea might be related to the first concept, where the elders of the city decide the case, since this concept implies that the slayer has to settle in the city of refuge (v. 4).[5] Yet, it is also possible that this motif is more closely connected with the second concept, since v. 4 seems to speak of a permanent settlement that is not limited by the potential death of the high priest.

Compared to the evident tensions between two different concepts in the MT, the original Greek text would seem to be much more coherent, for this version contains only the second concept, where the congregation decides the case. All references to the elders of the cities of asylum (vv. 4–5) as well as to the death of the high priest (v. 6aβb) are missing in the original Greek version.

---

4. One could expect that only *if the high priest dies* the case has to be restated before the congregation, but the text does not say this; cf. ibid.

5. At least this is assumed in most theories; cf., e.g., Rofé, "Joshua 20," 136; and Ludwig Schmidt, "Leviten- und Asylstädte in Num. xxxv und Jos. xx; xxi 1–42," *VT* 52 (2002), 103–21, esp. 107–8.

4.4. The Literary Horizon of Joshua 20 MT/LXX*

Joshua 20:1–6 is closely connected with two texts of the Pentateuch. They may give a clue as to what is taking place in Josh 20. The second concept of Josh 20:1–6, where the congregation makes the decision, is in accordance with Num 35:11–12. This becomes evident when we compare these two passages.

Josh 20:2–6

תנו לכם את ערי המקלט ...
לנוס שמה רוצח מכה נפש בשגגה ...
והיו לכם למקלט מגאל הדם ...
עד עמדו לפני העדה למשפט

[2] Appoint for you the cities of refuge ... [3] so that a slayer may flee there who kills a person without intent ... ; and they shall be for you a refuge from the avenger of blood. [6] ... until he stands before the congregation for judgment.

Num 35:11–12

והקריתם לכם ערים ערי מקלט תהיינה לכם ונס שמה רצח מכה נפש בשגגה והיו לכם הערים למקלט מגאל ולא ימות הרצח עד עמדו לפני העדה למשפט

[11] And you shall select for you cities, cities of refuge shall be for you, and the slayer who kills a person without intent shall flee there. [12] And the cities shall be for you a refuge from the avenger, so that the slayer may not die, until he stands before the congregation for judgment.

In addition to the evident literary relationship between Num 35 and Josh 20, the latter contains words and phrases that are known from the law on the cities of refuge in Deut 19. These parallels or similarities are met in Josh 20:4–5 MT, while they are missing in the LXX* version.

Josh 20:4–5 MT

ונס אל אחת מהערים האלה ...
וכי ירדף גאל הדם אחריו ...

כי בבלי דעת הכה את רעהו
ולא שנא הוא לו מתמול שלשום

⁴ And he shall flee to one of these cities ...
⁵ And if the avenger of blood is in pursuit, ...
because without knowledge he killed his neighbor,
and he hated him not before.

Deut 19:4–6

... הוא ינוס אל אחת הערים האלה ...
פן ירדף גאל הדם אחרי הרצח ...
... אשר יכה את רעהו בבלי דעת ...
... כי לא שנא הוא לו מתמול שלשום

⁵ ... he shall flee to one of these cities ...
⁶ lest the avenger of blood pursue the slayer ...
⁴ ... someone who kills his neighbor without knowledge ...
⁶ ... because he hated him not before.

However, the death of the high priest, which is mentioned in the MT version of Josh 20:6, has no parallel in Deut 19, while this motif is found in Num 35:25–28.

Josh 20:6 MT

עד עמדו לפני העדה למשפט
עַד־מוֹת הַכֹּהֵן הַגָּדוֹל אשר יהיה בימים ההם
אז יָשׁוּב הרוצח ובא אל עירו ואל ביתו
אל העיר אשר נס משם

Until he stands before the congregation for judgment, until the death of the high priest who shall be in those days, then the slayer shall return home and enter his town and his house, his city from whence he fled.

Num 35:25–28

והצילו העדה את הרצח מיד גאל הדם והשיבו אתו העדה אל עיר מקלטו
אשר נס שמה וישב בה עד מות הכהן הגדל ...
כי בעיר מקלטו ישב עַד־מוֹת הַכֹּהֵן הַגָּדֹל ואחרי מות הכהן הגדל יָשׁוּב
הרצח אֶל ארץ אחזתו

> ²⁵ And the congregation shall rescue the slayer from the avenger of blood, and the congregation shall send him to the city of his refuge, whither he was fled, and he shall dwell there until the death of the high priest...,
> ²⁸ because in the city of his refuge he shall dwell until the death of the high priest, but after the death of the high priest the slayer shall return to the land of his possession.

Num 35:25–28 explains what happens between the trial before the congregation and the death of the high priest—an explanation that is missing but one would expect in Josh 20:6 MT. According to Num 35:25–28, the congregation shall bring the slayer back to the city of refuge, and there he shall live until the high priest dies.

4.5. Does the LXX* Provide Evidence for Late Expansions in the Proto-MT?

The shorter Greek text could be explained as a witness of an earlier version of the chapter. The LXX* would thus go back to a Hebrew *Vorlage* that predated the proto-MT,[6] and the substantial plusses of the MT would be the result of later editorial activity, influenced by Deut 19 and Num 35:25–28. Several scholars advocate this theory.[7] They postulate that the older version of Josh 20, represented by the LXX*, would have been in line with Num 35:9–15, since this version represents only the concept that the slayer finds temporary protection in a city of refuge until his case is decided in a trial before the congregation. The content of Josh 20:9 seems to corroborate that the short version of vv. 1–6 is the original one, since v. 9, also in its MT version, corresponds exclusively to the LXX* version of vv. 1–6.

---

6. Cf. den Hertog, "Jesus," 649.

7. J. Alberto Soggin, *Joshua: A Commentary* (OTL; London: SCM, 1972), 197; James Maxwell Miller and Gene M. Tucker, *The Book of Joshua* (CBC; Cambridge: Cambridge University Press, 1974), 156; Fishbane, "Biblical Colophons," 443–46; Rofé, "Joshua 20," 141–44; Enzo Cortese, *Josua 13–21: Ein priesterschriftlicher Abschnitt im deuteronomistischen Geschichtswerk* (OBO 94; Fribourg: Universitätsverlag, 1990), 20, 80; Richard D. Nelson, *Joshua: A Commentary* (OTL; Louisville, Ky.: Westminster John Knox, 1997), 228; Auld, *Joshua*, 202. This theory of the history of Joshua 20 is presented in the chapter "Textual and Literary Criticism" in the textbook of Emanuel Tov, *Textual Criticism of the Hebrew Bible* (3d ed.; Minneapolis: Fortress, 2012), esp. 296.

Josh 20:9

אלה היו ערי המועדה לכל בני ישראל ... לנוס שמה כל מכה נפש בשגגה
ולא ימות ביד גאל הדם עד עמדו לפני העדה

These were the cities designated for all the Israelites ... that anyone who killed a person without intent could flee there, so that he shall not die by the hand of the avenger of blood, until he stands before the congregation.

Reconstructed *Vorlage* of Josh 20:3, 6 LXX*

לנוס שמה רוצח מכה נפש בשגגה והיו לכם למקלט ולא יומת הרצח מגאל
הדם ... עד עמדו לפני העדה למשפט

³ So that a slayer may flee there who kills a person without intent; and they shall be for you a refuge, so that the slayer shall not be killed by the avenger of blood ... ⁶ until he stands before the congregation for judgment.

This concept would have been secondarily altered by means of the large plusses in the proto-MT of vv. 4–6, which added the role of the elders (vv. 4–5) and the death of the high priest as the date when the slayer is allowed to return to his hometown (v. 6).

Although a longer text is commonly assumed to contain secondary additions, the theory that the LXX* preserves an older version of Josh 20:1–6 faces a major obstacle related to the logic of vv. 4–6. It is difficult to explain why an editor would have ascribed to the city elders the role of the judges, as mentioned in v. 4, *after* the older text had already stated that the case is decided by the congregation, not by the elders (v. 6: עד עמדו לפני העדה למשפט, "until he stands before the congregation for judgment").⁸ This would mean that an editor deliberately marginalized the trial before the congregation even though this trial is in accordance with the law of Num 35:9–15. In addition, vv. 4–5 do not refer to the decisive communal trial, which would be very peculiar if these verses were added later to the original form of vv. 1–6*. Because of these problems with the alleged priority of the LXX*, an alternative explanation for the differences between the MT and the LXX* should be tested.

---

8. Cf. Schmidt, "Leviten- und Asylstädte," 106.

4.6. The LXX* as Witness of an Intentionally Shortened Version?

Several scholars, such as Martin Noth, reject the priority of the shorter Greek text and propose that the plusses of vv. 3–6* were deliberately omitted in the textual tradition represented by the LXX*.[9] These omissions could have been made either by an editor of the Hebrew *Vorlage* of the LXX or, perhaps less probably, by the Greek translator.

According to this theory, the reason for the substantial omissions would have been the internal tensions and the logical incoherence of the proto-MT. An editor of the *Vorlage* of the LXX or the Greek translator would have sought to align Josh 20 much more closely with Num 35:9–15 by omitting all parts of Josh 20 that do not accord with this law. A major argument that speaks for this assumption is related to the motif of the elders in Josh 20:4–5 MT. In Num 35:9–15, the elders of the city of refuge are not mentioned at all, while the trial before the congregation is presented as decisive (v. 12b). With respect to this pentateuchal law, an editor (or the translator) could have wanted to suppress all references to the elders in Joshua 20 and thus omitted Josh 20:4–5, 6* MT, because in these verses the judgment of the elders is presented as crucial for deciding the case.

While such an editorial alteration is well imaginable, this theory faces a problem in another respect. It would remain unclear why in the course of the omissions of vv. 4–5, 6* the reference to the death of the high priest in v. 6b should have been omitted as well. This could be an important counterargument, since the law of Num 35:25–28 provides a clear rationale for this motif. In other words, if an editor (or the translator) shortened the text of Josh 20:1–6 in order to align it closer to Num 35, why would he also omit the reference to the death of the high priest, a motif that *is* included in another section of Num 35, namely, in vv. 25–28?

---

9. Martin Noth, *Das Buch Josua* (2d ed.; HAT 7; Tübingen: Mohr Siebeck, 1953), 127; Volkmar Fritz, *Das Buch Josua* (HAT 7; Tübingen: Mohr Siebeck, 1994), 201–3; Schmidt, "Leviten- und Asylstädte," 105–8; Horst Seebass, *Numeri 22,2–36,13* (vol. 3 of *Numeri*; BKAT 4.3; Neukirchen-Vluyn: Neukirchener Verlag, 2007), 426; thus implicitly also Ernst Axel Knauf, *Josua* (ZBK; Zürich: Theologischer Verlag, 2008), 170–71.

4.7. A Possible Solution: Editorial Shortening in the LXX* and a Late Addition in the MT

The comparison of Josh 20:6 MT with Josh 20:6 LXX* could provide a solution for this problem. The LXX* of Josh 20:6, which is much shorter than the MT, could attest to the fact that in this verse the death of the high priest was originally not mentioned at all. As demonstrated above, there is no reason why this motif would have been secondarily omitted, since it is in accordance with Num 35. The shorter text of the LXX* may in most parts of vv. 1–6 go back to secondary shortening, but in the case of v. 6 the LXX* may attest to the original form. This proposal resolves the weaknesses of a clear-cut assumption that one of the versions is secondary throughout the passage. According to the theory proposed here, the motif of the high priest would have been added to the proto-MT *after* the shortened version of Josh 20:1–6 LXX* had been created.

With this model all differences between the MT and the LXX* can be explained. The version of the LXX* would mainly go back to an editorial attempt to align the text closely with the law of Num 35:9–15. In the case of v. 6, however, the shorter version of the LXX* would attest to a text in which the reference to the death of high priest was not yet included.

Josh 20:3–6 MT

לנוס שמה רוצח מכה נפש בשגגה בבלי־דעת והיו לכם למקלט מגאל הדם
ונס אל אחת מהערים האלה ...
וישב בעיר ההיא עד עמדו לפני העדה למשפט
[עד מות הכהן הגדול אשר יהיה בימים ההם אז ישוב הרוצח ובא אל עירו
ואל ביתו אל העיר אשר נס משם]

³ So that a slayer may flee there who kills a person without intent, ~~without knowledge;~~ and they shall be for you a refuge from the avenger of blood. ⁴ ~~And he shall flee to one of these cities~~ ... ⁶ ~~And he shall dwell in that city~~ until he stands before the congregation for judgment, [until the death of the high priest who shall be in those days; then the slayer shall return home and enter his town and his house, his city from whence he fled.]

Josh 20:3–6 LXX*

³ φυγαδευτήριον τῷ φονευτῇ τῷ πατάξαντι ψυχὴν ἀκουσίως, καὶ ἔσονται ὑμῖν αἱ πόλεις φυγαδευτήριον, καὶ οὐκ ἀποθανεῖται ὁ φονευτὴς ὑπὸ τοῦ ἀγχιστεύοντος τὸ αἷμα, ⁶ ἕως ἂν καταστῇ ἐναντίον τῆς συναγωγῆς εἰς κρίσιν.

³ A refuge to the slayer who has smitten a person unintentionally, and <u>the cities</u> shall be for you a refuge, <u>and the slayer shall not be killed</u> by the avenger of blood, ⁶ until he stands before the congregation for judgment.

Joshua 20:4–5 MT would have been omitted because, as demonstrated above, these verses do not fit with the concept of Num 35 according to which the congregation decides the case. The differences between v. 3 LXX* and MT can be explained accordingly: The phrase בבלי דעת ("without knowledge") is also found in v. 5, and therefore it is related to the concept according to which the elders, and not the congregation, decide the case. A secondary omission of this phrase in the LXX* of v. 3 (or its *Vorlage*) is therefore easily understandable. On the other hand, the plusses in v. 3 LXX* (αἱ πόλεις ... καὶ οὐκ ἀποθανεῖται ὁ φονευτής, "<u>the cities</u> ... <u>and the slayer shall not be killed</u>") are similar to Num 35:12 (והיו לכם הערים למקלט מגאל ולא ימות הרצח, "And <u>the cities</u> shall be for you a refuge from the avenger, <u>so that the slayer shall not die</u>") and can therefore be explained as assimilations to this law. The opening phrase of v. 6 (וישב בעיר ההיא, "And he shall dwell in that city") would have been omitted as well, since this phrase seems to be connected with the concept of vv. 4–5 and becomes syntactically and logically unnecessary when these verses are omitted. The end of v. 6, however, has to be explained differently, since, as demonstrated above, a secondary omission is improbable in this case. The reference to the death of the high priest as the moment when the slayer is allowed to return home (Josh 20:6αβb) would have been added to the proto-MT after the version of the LXX* had been created. According to this theory, the oldest version of vv. 1–6αα is found in the MT, while in these verses the LXX* attests to a younger literary stage caused by shortening. In v. 6αβb, however, the plus in the MT is secondary, added independently of the textual tradition represented by the LXX*.

4.8. Results and Methodological Consequences

Joshua 20 provides evidence of substantial editorial changes. This is reflected in the two versions of the MT and the LXX*, which differ considerably. The differences have to be seen as the result of deliberate editorial decisions regarding the judicial content. The text was changed to such an extent that the concept of the case of the slayer was substantially altered.

The editorial processes that took place in this chapter seem to have been rather complex. The two conventional theories proposed in scholarship may explain some aspects of the text, but they also face considerable difficulties. It seems that a simple and one-sided solution is not sufficient in this case. The third theory proposed above seeks to resolve the difficulties of both theories. It implies that the short text of the LXX* is mainly the result of substantial omissions but in part also attests to a text that was in fact shorter than the MT.

If the minuses in the LXX* go back mainly to editorial shortening, as proposed, the reason for this shortening must have been the contradiction between vv. 4–5 and the law of Num 35:9–15. The fact that Joshua, according to Josh 20:4–5, told the people a judicial concept that is in such obvious contrast with the Mosaic instruction of Num 35 seems to have been intolerable.[10] Therefore an editor of the Hebrew *Vorlage* of the LXX* (or, perhaps less probably, the Greek translator[11]) removed this contradiction by omitting all passages that are not in agreement with Num 35. In addition, he inserted small plusses in v. 3 that accord with Num 35:12. After the separation between the two textual traditions, the reference to the death of the high priest that accords with Num 35:25–28 was added to the proto-Masoretic version in v. 6.

It is significant that such substantial alterations took place rather late, which is implied by the fact that their outcome is documented in the textual witnesses. These changes must have taken place after the divergence of the *Vorlage* of the LXX* from the proto-Masoretic textual tradition, probably in the last two or three centuries BCE. We should note, however, that the documented evidence covers only the last stages of the literary history of this chapter. It is probable that other editorial changes were made in

---

10. The relation to Deut 19 did not cause a comparable problem because this text does not explicitly say how and by whom the case of the accidental slayer is finally decided. The instructions of Josh 20:4–5 may have developed in relation to Deut 19, but they go beyond this text, since the elders of the city of refuge are not mentioned in Deut 19. In a harmonistic perspective, the instructions of Num 35 can be combined with Deut 19.

11. This question cannot be resolved here, since it would need a full analysis of the Greek Joshua in relation to the Hebrew. It seems, however, that it is more probable that the changes were made by an editor of the Hebrew *Vorlage*, since the Greek translation of Joshua is generally very precise and tries to reflect even details of the Hebrew wording. Thus, most differences between the LXX and the MT, which occur quite often, attest to a Hebrew *Vorlage* of the LXX considerably different from the proto-MT; cf. Wolfgang Kraus and Martin Karrer, eds., *Septuaginta Deutsch: Das griechische Alte Testament in deutscher Übersetzung* (Stuttgart: Deutsche Bibelgesellschaft, 2009), 218.

earlier periods. The inner-textual tensions in Josh 20:3–6 MT indicate a complex process of literary growth, although this process is, apart from the latter parts of v. 6 MT, not documented in differing textual witnesses.

One further aspect can be observed. If only one of the two different versions were preserved, it would be next to impossible to know of the existence of the other version. It can be doubted that, if we possessed only the MT, we would be able to conclude that there also existed an abbreviated version of the chapter. And if we knew only the LXX* version, it would be impossible to conclude that there had also existed a longer version within which two different concepts of the matter are merged. In consequence, Josh 20 shows that, even during the late stages of the textual transmission, two different versions of the same text existed side by side. In the case of Josh 20 it is obvious that both versions were transmitted further, while we may assume that in many cases different versions that once existed are lost.

5
A Qumran Manuscript as Evidence of an Addition in the Masoretic Text: Judges 6:7–10

In an ideal case a theory about the literary growth of a text is corroborated by the evidence of textual witnesses in which the postulated older version is still preserved. A striking example is found in Judg 6. A theory about the history of this chapter was widely accepted before the discovery of a manuscript from Qumran that confirmed the theory. In other words, a literary-critical reconstruction was later corroborated by empirical evidence.

5.1. The Context of Judges 6:7–10

The sixth chapter of the book of Judges begins with an extensive description of the suffering of the Israelites at the hands of the Midianites (6:1–6). The very beginning of this description states that the suffering of the Israelites was caused by their sin, which is the standard reason given in other passages in Judges as well (cf. 2:11–15; 3:7–8, 12–14; 4:1–3; 10:6–9; 13:1). Judges 6:1 reads: ויעשו בני ישראל הרע בעיני יהוה ("The Israelites did evil in the eyes of Yhwh"), but it does not clarify what exactly is meant by "evil in the eyes of Yhwh." The reader has to infer from the preceding passages what kind of sin the Israelites may have committed (cf. Judg 2:11–13 and 3:7, where the "evil in the eyes of Yhwh" is defined as worship of the Baals and Asherim).

The following passage in Judg 6:7–10, however, gives an unequivocal definition of this sin. Yhwh sends an anonymous prophet to the Israelites, who explains why they have to suffer so much. His speech clarifies what sin they have committed.

Judg 6:7–10

ויהי כי זעקו בני ישראל אל יהוה על אדות מדין
וישלח יהוה איש נביא אל בני ישראל ויאמר להם כה אמר יהוה אלהי
ישראל אנכי העליתי אתכם ממצרים ואציא אתכם מבית עבדים
ואצל אתכם מיד מצרים ומיד כל לחציכם ואגרש אותם מפניכם ואתנה
לכם את ארצם
ואמרה לכם אני יהוה אלהיכם לא תיראו את אלהי האמרי אשר אתם
יושבים בארצם ולא שמעתם בקולי

⁷ And when the Israelites cried to Yhwh on account of the Midianites, ⁸ Yhwh sent a prophet to the Israelites; and he said to them: "Thus says Yhwh, the God of Israel: 'I led you up from Egypt and brought you out of the house of slavery; ⁹ and I delivered you from the hand of Egypt, and from the hand of all who oppressed you, and drove them out before you and gave you their land; ¹⁰ and I said to you: "I am Yhwh your God; you shall not fear the gods of the Amorites, in whose land you live!" But you have not listened to my voice.'"

By fearing "the gods of the Amorites," the Israelites broke the first commandment (Exod 20:3 // Deut 5:7), which the prophet quotes in a modified form (in v. 10a), and also their promise not to abandon Yhwh, a promise they gave immediately before Joshua's death (Josh 24:16–18). After the speech of the prophet, the scene suddenly breaks off. It is not related how the Israelites reacted to the oracle, and the prophet disappears.

The text proceeds with a new scene that introduces Gideon, the son of Joash, the Abiezrite (6:11–24). In this scene the messenger of Yhwh calls Gideon to "deliver Israel from the hand of Midian" (6:14). Prior to this call, Gideon addresses the messenger by lamenting Israel's oppression (6:13).

Judg 6:13

בי אדני ויש יהוה עמנו ולמה מצאתנו כל זאת ואיה כל נפלאתיו אשר ספרו
לנו אבותינו לאמר הלא ממצרים העלנו יהוה ועתה נטשנו יהוה ויתננו בכף
מדין

But lord, if Yhwh is with us, why has all this happened to us? And where are all his wonderful deeds that our ancestors recounted to us, saying, "Did not Yhwh bring us up from Egypt?" But now Yhwh has cast us off and given us into the hand of Midian.

It seems that Gideon takes no notice of the prophetic words in Judg 6:7–10. His lament completely ignores that his question "why has all this happened to us?" has already been specifically addressed by the prophet: the Israelites have to suffer because they did not listen to Yhwh, who prohibited them from fearing the gods of the Amorites. The entire call narrative of Judg 6:11–24 does not refer to this explanation, and it seems to be unaware of the preceding speech of the prophet.

5.2. Judges 6:7–10 as a Late Addition

Because of the problems described above, most scholars agree that the text about the anonymous prophet is a rather late addition. This theory was already argued in the nineteenth century.[1] The scene is only loosely connected with the context and can easily be taken out without disturbing the narrative. It is not said where and under what circumstances the prophet spoke, and the prophet remains anonymous. The narrative elements are reduced to a minimum, which indicates that the sole purpose of this episode is to comment on the situation from a theological perspective. As already noted, this theological comment is also not presupposed in the ensuing call narrative of Judg 6:11–24.

Taking all these consideration together leads to the conclusion that the scene with the prophet in vv. 7–10 was, in all likelihood, secondarily added. This fictitious figure already answers in advance the theological question raised by Gideon's lament (6:13):[2] indeed, Yhwh delivered the Israelites from Egypt, and he also delivered them from the Amorites, who

---

1. E.g., Julius Wellhausen, *Die Composition des Hexateuchs und der historischen Bücher des Alten Testaments* (3d ed.; Berlin: Georg Reimer, 1899), 214; Wolfgang Richter, *Die Bearbeitungen des "Retterbuches" in der deuteronomischen Epoche* (BBB 21; Bonn: Peter Hanstein, 1964), 97–109; Timo Veijola, *Das Königtum in der Beurteilung der deuteronomistischen Historiographie: Eine redaktionsgeschichtliche Untersuchung* (AASF 198; Helsinki: Academia Scientiarum Fennica, 1977), 44; Richard D. Nelson, *The Double Redaction of the Deuteronomistic History* (JSOTSup 18; Sheffield: JSOT Press, 1981), 47–53; J. Alberto Soggin, *Judges* (OTL; London: SCM, 1987), 110–12; Erhard Blum, "Der kompositionelle Knoten am Übergang von Josua zu Richter," in *Deuteronomic Literature* (ed. M. Vervenne and J. Lust; BETL 133; Leuven: University Press, 1997), 195–97; Walter Groß, *Richter* (Freiburg: Herder, 2009), 370.

2. Andreas Scherer, *Überlieferungen von Religion und Krieg: Exegetische und religionsgeschichtliche Untersuchungen zu Richter 3–8 und verwandten Texten* (WMANT 105; Neukirchen-Vluyn: Neukirchener, 2005), 164.

oppressed them, and even gave them their land (6:9). Because the Amorite gods are still a religious lure for Israel, Yhwh specifically has prohibited the Israelites from fearing them. The Israelites, however, have not obeyed this prohibition, which explains their suffering. This theological concept mainly refers to Joshua's farewell speech and Israel's promise not to abandon Yhwh in Josh 24 (see esp. vv. 8, 15–18). Apart from this reference, the speech of the prophet is modeled after 1 Sam 10:18–19.[3]

5.3. External Evidence: A Qumran Manuscript without Judges 6:7–10

Judges 6:7–10 is attested in all major witnesses, and thereby the literary-critical theory that assumed these verses to be an addition was originally developed on the basis of inner-textual arguments. However, a Qumran manuscript from Cave 4, consisting of a single fragment (4Q49 = 4QJudg^a),[4] presents a version of Judg 6 that coincides exactly with this theory, first presented half a century before the discovery of the manuscript: the entire section of the anonymous prophet is missing in this textual witness.

4QJudg^a

כי הם [ומקניהם יעלו ואהליהם וגמליהם יבאו כדי] אַרבה לרב ולהם אֵ[ין
מספר וי]באו בא[רץ לשחתה
וידל ישראל מאד מפני מדין [ויזעקו בני יש[ראל אל] יהוה
] ויבא מלאך יהוה וישב תחת האלה אשר בעפרה [אשר ליואש האביעזרי
וג]דעון בנו חבט חטים בגת להניס מפני מדין[

[5] For they [and their livestock would come up, and their tents and their camels, they would come as] thick as locusts, and they [could not be counted; so they] came in the la[nd to waste it. [6] Thus Israel was greatly impoverished because of Midian;] and the Israe[lites] cried out [to] Yhwh. [[11] And the angel of Yhwh came and sat under the oak at Ophrah,]

---

3. E.g., Veijola, *Königtum*, 41–43; Reinhard Müller, *Königtum und Gottesherrschaft: Untersuchungen zur alttestamentlichen Monarchiekritik* (FAT 2.3; Tübingen: Mohr Siebeck, 2004), 171–73.

4. Edited by Julio C. Trebolle Barrera in Eugene Ulrich et al., eds., *Qumran Cave 4.IX: Deuteronomy to Kings* (DJD 14; Oxford: Clarendon, 1995), 161–64 and pl. XXXVI; see also Eugene Ulrich, ed., *The Biblical Qumran Scrolls: Transcriptions and Textual Variants* (Leiden: Brill, 2010), 255.

which belonged to Joash the Abiezrite, as Gi[deon, his son, was beating out wheat in the wine press to hide it from the Midianites.]

Although 4QJudgᵃ is a small and damaged fragment of a scroll (only other small parts of Judg 6 are preserved on this fragment), it lies beyond doubt that v. 11 follows immediately after v. 6. There is no space for vv. 7–10. After the description of Israel's suffering from the Midianite raids (vv. 1–6), the text continues with the scene of Gideon's call as Israel's savior (vv. 11–24). 4QJudgᵃ reads as a concise beginning of the Gideon narrative, and there is nothing to indicate that something is missing. Thus, 4QJudgᵃ can be regarded as empirical evidence for the theory that the speech of the prophet is a very late addition. Or, in the words of the manuscript's editor Julio Trebolle Barrera: "4QJudgᵃ can confidently be seen as an earlier literary form of the book than our traditional texts."[5]

The textual evidence may give us some guidelines for dating the addition. Apart from the MT, the speech of the prophet in Judg 6:7–10 is also attested by the LXX, the translation of which in the case of Judges may be dated to the second or first centuries BCE.[6] The Qumran manuscript was written by "a late Hasmonean or early Herodian book hand from c. 50–25 BCE."[7] Although the addition may be older than this manuscript, it is apparent that we are dealing with a very late editorial intervention.

5.4. Counterarguments

Some scholars have tried to refute this manuscript evidence by stressing that 4QJudgᵃ is too small a fragment to prove an intentional expansion.[8] They argue that the omission of Judg 6:7–10 in the Qumran manuscript could be due either to a scribal error[9] or to "a certain flexibility or liberty of

---

5. Ulrich et al., *Qumran Cave 4.IX*, 162.

6. See Wolfgang Kraus and Martin Karrer, eds., *Septuaginta Deutsch: Das griechische Alte Testament in deutscher Übersetzung* (Stuttgart: Deutsche Bibelgesellschaft, 2009), 243.

7. Ulrich et al., *Qumran Cave 4.IX*, 161.

8. Natalio Fernández Marcos, "The Hebrew and Greek Text of Judges," in *The Earliest Text of the Hebrew Bible: The Relationship between the Masoretic Text and the Hebrew Base of the Septuagint Reconsidered* (ed. Adrian Schenker; SBLSCS 52; Atlanta: Society of Biblical Literature, 2003), 1–16, esp. 15.

9. Richard S. Hess, "The Dead Sea Scrolls and Higher Criticism of the Hebrew Bible: The Case of 4QJudgᵃ," in *The Scrolls and the Scriptures: Qumran Fifty Years after*

the scribes in moving paragraphs, inserting and omitting sections for their own purposes, be they liturgical or other kinds of readings."[10] Moreover, structural observations allegedly show that Judg 6:7–10 forms an integral part of the Gideon cycle and the book of Judges as a whole.[11] In addition, stylistic and content-related factors supposedly prove the early origin of Judg 6:7–10.[12] In particular, it has been argued by Alexander Rofé that the divine prohibition of fearing the gods of the Amorites in whose land the Israelites dwell (לא תיראו את אלהי האמרי אשר אתם יושבים בארצם; v. 10) must have been "intimated *in the Land* after the settlement. It was not given to Moses, nor contained in the Torah." Rofé concludes that this concept cannot be of late or Deuteronomistic origin, since Deuteronomists or later authors would have "attributed all divine laws to the Mosaic legislation."[13]

These arguments are of different weight. A scribal mistake causing the omission of Judg 6:7–10 is not very probable, because there are no textual features that could explain why such an error should have happened here.[14] It would also be quite a coincidence if a scribal lapse had cut off a separate scene exactly on its seams. An intentional omission is theoretically possible, but the theological weight of the prophet's oracle speaks clearly against it.[15] This theological comment on the situation of Israel's suffering is well in

---

(ed. Stanley E. Porter and Craig A. Evans; JSPSup 26; Sheffield: Academic Press, 1997), 124–25; Natalio Fernández Marcos, ed., *Judges* (vol. 7 of *Biblia Hebraica: Quinta editione*; Stuttgart: Deutsche Bibelgesellschaft, 2011), 65*–66*.

10. Fernández Marcos, "Hebrew and Greek Text of Judges," 5.

11. Robert H. O'Connell, *The Rhetoric of the Book of Judges* (VTSup 63; Leiden: Brill, 1996), 147 n. 178; Yairah Amit, *The Book of Judges: The Art of Editing* (Biblical Interpretation Series 38; Leiden: Brill, 1999), 249–51.

12. Thus Alexander Rofé ("Studying the Biblical Text in the Light of Historico-Literary Criticism: The Reproach of the Prophet in Judg 6:7–10 and 4QJudg[a]," in *The Dead Sea Scrolls in Context: Integrating the Dead Sea Scrolls in the Study of Ancient Texts, Languages and Cultures* [ed. Armin Lange, Emanuel Tov, and Mathias Weigold; VTSup 140; Leiden: Brill, 2011], 111–23), who, on the one hand, admits that Judg 6:7–10 is an addition but, on the other hand, tries to prove that it is of pre-Deuteronomic-Deuteronomistic origin. He explains the minus in 4QJudg[a] as the result of a scribal parablepsis.

13. Ibid., 119; emphasis original.

14. Armin Lange, *Die Handschriften biblischer Bücher von Qumran und den anderen Fundorten* (vol. 1 of *Handbuch der Textfunde vom Toten Meer*; Tübingen: Mohr Siebeck, 2009), 204.

15. *Pace* O'Connell, *Rhetoric*, 147 n. 178, who assumes that the scribe of 4QJudg[a]

line with the theological profile of the entire book, since it elaborates that the Israelites were punished because they left Yhwh, which accords with Judg 2:11–15; 3:7–8; and 10:6–16. One would have to explain why this comment that is not theologically or otherwise problematic should have been omitted intentionally. It is much more probable that such a theological explanation was added later and that 4QJudg[a] attests to an older version of Judg 6.[16] Structural observations that allegedly prove the unity of the text are not cogent, because they explain only that its final form has some logic. The compositional unity cannot thus be proven, especially considering the clear inner-textual tensions between the speech of the prophet and Gideon's call, as demonstrated above. It should also be noted that the structural argument is a hypothetical construct, while 4QJudg[a] provides us with a textual witness dated to 50–25 BCE.

Finally, stylistic and content-related arguments are scarcely strong enough to prove an early origin of this passage. The supposed contradiction between the prohibition of Judg 6:10 and the Deuteronomistic concept of Mosaic legislation is a circular argument, since it is based on an assumption that would have to be proved. It assumes that in late periods it would have been impossible to write such a text, and in particular, to quote a divine prohibition in Judg 6:10 related to the situation after the settlement (לא תיראו את אלהי האמרי אשר אתם יושבים בארצם, "you shall not fear the gods of the Amorites, in whose land you live!"). To be sure, the exact wording of this prohibition is not found in the Pentateuch, but it cannot be denied that its essence is in accordance with the first commandment. In addition, Judg 6:10 refers to Joshua's admonition in Josh 24:14–15, and both passages are part of prophetic speeches (cf. כה אמר יהוה אלהי ישראל, "Thus says Yhwh, the God of Israel," in Josh 24:2 and Judg 6:8); as such they are presented as divinely inspired oracles. It is difficult to see why these oracles would conflict with the Deuteronomistic concept of the Mosaic legislation. In contrast, both Josh 24:2–15 and Judg 6:7–10 are related to the style and concepts of Deuteronomy and Deu-

---

did not want to confront his readers with the hard words of the prophet. Sometimes it has been argued that the scene could have been left out for liturgical purposes because in the MT it is framed by two *petuchot*; thus Hess, "Dead Sea Scrolls and Higher Criticism," 125–27; Fernández Marcos, "Hebrew and Greek Text of Judges," 5–6; see also idem, *Judges*, 65*–66*. However, it is difficult to see why liturgical considerations would necessitate the omission of such a theologically crucial text.

16. Lange, *Handschriften*, 204–5.

teronomism. For instance, Joshua's admonition to fear Yhwh (Josh 24:14) closely resembles the Mosaic admonition of Deut 6:13, and the prophetic speech of Judg 6:7–10 ends with the formulaic phrase ולא שמעתם בקולי ("But you have not listened to my voice"), which is closely related to Deut 28:15. Thus, Judges 6:7–10 can be called a "Deuteronomistically inspired" text.[17] As noted by Eugene Ulrich, "It seems inconceivable that 4QJudg^a would still preserve in the first century BCE, against all other witnesses, a seventh-century pre-DtrH text. It is, rather, far more likely that the short text as in 4QJudg^a was the dominant text during the early Second Temple period, and that this deuteronomistically inspired insertion in MT and LXX is part of the late, widespread, developmental growth at the hands of numerous scribes seen in many biblical books."[18] The Qumran manuscript would not only be evidence of a late addition but also provide significant evidence for the discussion about the nature of Deuteronomism and its continuous impact on this book.

5.5. How Was the Addition Inserted into the Older Text?

The addition of Judg 6:7–10 shows some of the technical means by which editors inserted additions into older texts. In order to introduce a new scene, Yhwh's sending of the prophet, the editor repeated most of the last sentence of the preceding text (v. 6b).

Judg 6:6–8

וידל ישראל מאד מפני מדין ויזעקו בני ישראל אל יהוה
ויהי כי זעקו בני ישראל אל יהוה על אדות מדין
וישלח יהוה איש נביא אל בני ישראל

⁶ Thus Israel was greatly impoverished because of Midian; and the Israelites cried out to Yhwh. ⁷ <u>And when the Israelites cried to Yhwh on account of the Midianites,</u> ⁸ <u>Yhwh sent a prophet to the Israelites.</u>

---

17. Eugene Ulrich, "Deuteronomistically Inspired Scribal Insertions into the Developing Biblical Texts: 4 QJudg^a and 4QJer^a," in *Houses Full of All Good Things: Essays in Memory of Timo Veijola* (ed. Juha Pakkala and Martti Nissinen; Publications of the Finnish Exegetical Society 95; Helsinki: The Finnish Exegetical Society, 2008), 490–94.

18. Ibid., 492–93.

With this repetition and the clause of v. 7b, the editor emphasized that Yhwh's sending of the prophet was a reaction to Israel's cry. The repetition of parts of the preceding text in v. 6b was used to introduce a new passage as a theological commentary to the older text. This technique is often assumed in literary criticism as a potential indication of a later expansion. By repeating a phrase of the older text, an editor seeks to connect an addition with the older text.[19]

Because the repetition causes a redundancy, some textual witnesses, like the Greek manuscript of Codex Vaticanus,[20] present a smoother transition from v. 6 to v. 8 by omitting v. 7a (the same text is attested by some medieval Hebrew manuscripts).[21]

Judg 6:6–8 Codex Vaticanus

⁶ καὶ ἐπτώχευσεν Ισραηλ σφόδρα ἀπὸ προσώπου Μαδιαμ, καὶ ἐβόησαν οἱ υἱοὶ Ισραηλ πρὸς κύριον ⁷ ἀπὸ προσώπου Μαδιαμ. ⁸ καὶ ἐξαπέστειλεν κύριος ἄνδρα προφήτην πρὸς τοὺς υἱοὺς Ισραηλ.

⁶ Thus Israel was greatly impoverished because of Midian; and the Israelites cried out to Yhwh ⁷ on account of the Midianites. ⁸ And Yhwh sent a prophet to the Israelites.

However, this omission is clearly secondary, since an isolated addition of v. 7a ("when the Israelites cried to Yhwh") in the MT and the rest of the ancient manuscripts would not be easy to explain. It should be further noted that the tendency to present a smoother text often hints at a tension in the older version. In our case, the LXX reading thus confirms that the MT contains a textual problem.

---

19. See the classic article of Curt Kuhl, "Die 'Wiederaufnahme'—ein literarkritisches Prinzip?," *ZAW* 64 (1952), 1–11; and Wolfgang Richter, *Exegese als Literaturwissenschaft: Entwurf einer alttestamentlichen Literaturtheorie und Methodologie* (Göttingen: Vandenhoeck & Ruprecht, 1971), 70–72. To be sure, Judg 6:7 is no typical example for this technique, because in most cases the last phrase of the preceding older text was repeated *at the end of the addition*. Such a case is found, for instance, in 1 Kgs 6:11–14; see ch. 8.

20. See Ulrich, *Biblical Qumran Scrolls*, 255.

21. Ulrich et al., *Qumran Cave 4.IX*, 162.

5.6. Results and Methodological Consequences

In a methodological perspective, Judg 6:7–10 is a very important case, since a manuscript find from Qumran later corroborated an older literary-critical reasoning about the growth of the text. This shows that the literary- and redaction-critical methods have, in some cases, produced reliable theories. In this case, the literary-critical theory conformed exactly to the manuscript evidence, which shows that the method has the potential to identify a later addition in full.

Two further outcomes concerning the methods of reconstructing the history of a text can be deduced. Firstly, content-related tensions between a passage and its contexts need to be taken seriously when the coherence of a passage is investigated. If a text is clearer without a passage that causes tensions with its surroundings, one should raise the question whether we are dealing with a secondary expansion. The tensions should be used as an argument for assuming an expansion. In addition, repetitions or doublets of entire phrases need to be explained. It is unlikely that the original author repeats a sentence without a reason. If no such reason can be found, one should consider the possibility that a repetition is related to editorial techniques of inserting an expansion. Secondly, if we observe in the textual history a tendency by some textual witnesses to create a smoother version of a passage, one has to consider the possibility that it was triggered by a redundancy, such as an unnecessary repetition, in an older version.

6
A Secondary Omission in the Masoretic Text of 1 Samuel 10:1

If one textual witness contains a plus in relation to another witness, there are often good reasons to assume the priority of the *lectio brevior*, "the shorter reading." Accordingly, this is one of the classic rules of textual criticism. It is easy to imagine that such expansions were secondarily inserted in order to explain earlier texts or to comment on them.[1] Although rarely acknowledged, there are exceptions to this rule. There is evidence of cases where a plus in a textual witness is not an expansion but represents the original text so that the parallel to the plus was secondarily omitted in another witness, either by mistake or by intention.[2]

A case of an omission can be found in 1 Sam 10:1. A detailed analysis of this verse provides good reasons to assume that an original reading was secondarily omitted in the proto-MT and that this reading is preserved in the LXX. While it is possible that the omission was due to a scribal mistake, it is perhaps more probable that it attests to a case of editorial shortening.

6.1. The Textual Phenomenon: A Large Plus Attested by Several Textual Traditions

In the first narrative about Saul's appointment as king (1 Sam 9:1–10:16), a short verse in the MT describes how Samuel anointed Saul (1 Sam 10:1). In this verse the LXX contains a large plus in relation to the MT.[3]

---

1. See chs. 5 (Judg 6:7–10), 6 (1 Sam 10:27–11:1), and 8 (1 Kgs 6:11–14).

2. See the substantial critique of the rule of *lectio brevior* by Emanuel Tov, *Textual Criticism of the Hebrew Bible* (3d ed.; Minneapolis: Fortress, 2012), 277–79.

3. *BHS* incorrectly places the plus after יהוה. The correct position is shown in *BHK*.

1 Sam 10:1 MT

ויקח שמואל את פך השמן ויצק על ראשו וישקהו ויאמר הלוא כי משחך
יהוה על נחלתו לנגיד

And Samuel took the flask of oil, and poured it upon his head, and kissed him, and said: "Is it not that Yhwh has anointed you over his inheritance as a leader?"

1 Sam 10:1 LXX

καὶ ἔλαβεν Σαμουηλ τὸν φακὸν τοῦ ἐλαίου καὶ ἐπέχεεν ἐπὶ τὴν κεφαλὴν αὐτοῦ καὶ ἐφίλησεν αὐτὸν καὶ εἶπεν αὐτῷ Οὐχὶ <u>κέχρικέν σε κύριος εἰς ἄρχοντα ἐπὶ τὸν λαὸν αὐτοῦ, ἐπὶ Ισραηλ; καὶ σὺ ἄρξεις ἐν λαῷ κυρίου, καὶ σὺ σώσεις αὐτὸν ἐκ χειρὸς ἐχθρῶν αὐτοῦ κυκλόθεν. καὶ τοῦτό σοι τὸ σημεῖον</u> ὅτι ἔχρισέν σε κύριος ἐπὶ κληρονομίαν αὐτοῦ εἰς ἄρχοντα·

And Samuel took the vial of oil, and poured it upon his head, and kissed him, and said: "<u>Did the Lord</u> not <u>anoint you as a leader over his people, over Israel? And you shall rule over the people of the Lord, and you shall save them from the hand of their enemies all around. And this shall be the sign for you</u> that the Lord has anointed you over his inheritance as a leader."

The plus resembles phrases in 1 Sam 9:16–17, a passage that describes how Yhwh commissioned Samuel to anoint Saul as king.

1 Sam 9:16–17

ומשחתו לנגיד על עמי ישראל והושיע את עמי מיד פלשתים ...
זה יעצר בעמי

[16] And you shall anoint him to be a leader over my people Israel; and he shall save my people from the hand of the Philistines ... [17] He it is who shall rule over my people.

Based on the wording of this passage, it is possible to reconstruct the Hebrew text that was probably the *Vorlage* of 1 Sam 10:1 LXX.[4]

---

4. Thus *BHK* and, e.g., Karl Budde, *Die Bücher Samuel* (KHC 8; Tübingen: J.C.B. Mohr, 1902), 66.

הלוא <u>משחך יהוה</u>	Οὐχὶ κέχρικέν σε κύριος
<u>לנגיד על עמו על ישראל</u>	εἰς ἄρχοντα ἐπὶ τὸν λαὸν αὐτοῦ, ἐπὶ Ισραηλ;
<u>ואתה תעצר בעם יהוה</u>	καὶ σὺ ἄρξεις ἐν λαῷ κυρίου,
<u>ואתה תושיענו</u>	καὶ σὺ σώσεις αὐτὸν
<u>מיד איביו מסביב</u>	ἐκ χειρὸς ἐχθρῶν αὐτοῦ κυκλόθεν.
<u>וזה לך האות</u>	καὶ τοῦτό σοι τὸ σημεῖον
כי משחך יהוה	ὅτι ἔχρισέν σε κύριος
על נחלתו לנגיד	ἐπὶ κληρονομίαν αὐτοῦ εἰς ἄρχοντα.

Reconstructed Hebrew *Vorlage* of 1 Sam 10:1 LXX

<u>Has Yhwh not anointed you
as a leader over his people, over Israel?
And you shall rule over the people of Yhwh,
and you shall save them
from the hand of their enemies all around.
And this shall be the sign for you</u>
that Yhwh has anointed you
over his inheritance as a leader.

This plus is also attested by *some* Old Latin witnesses[5] and the Vulgate. Thus, the attestation of the longer version by ancient manuscripts is rather broad, which provides a first argument for the priority of this version.

However, according to the text-critical rule *lectio brevior potior* ("the shorter reading is the stronger one") we would have to assume that the plus is nevertheless a later addition. One could argue that the plus was secondarily inserted on the basis of 1 Sam 9:16–17 or as a harmonization toward this passage. In other words, the more original version, attested by the MT, would have contained only the rather short remark about Yhwh's anointing of Saul, and a later editor would have added phrases parallel to Yhwh's instruction for Samuel in 1 Sam 9:16–17. This theory is advocated by several scholars.[6]

---

5. E.g., Codex Vindobonensis and the Napoli codex.

6. Carl Friedrich Keil, *Die Bücher Samuels* (Biblischer Commentar über das Alte Testament 2.2; Leipzig: Dörfling und Franke, 1864), 71–72 n. 1; Arnold B. Ehrlich, *Josua, Richter, I. u. II. Samuelis* (vol. 3 of *Randglossen zur hebräischen Bibel*; 1910; repr.,

6.2. A Grammatical Argument against the Shorter Version of the MT

A close comparison between the short and the long versions of 1 Sam 10:1 reveals, however, that the priority of the plus is also corroborated by inner-textual indications. Firstly, the shorter MT contains a rather unusual wording in the phrase הלוא כי משחך יהוה על נחלתו לנגיד ("*Is it not that* Yhwh has anointed you over his inheritance as a leader?"). The expression הלוא ("Is it not ... ?"), a common opening of a rhetorical question,[7] is followed immediately by כי ("that").[8] This is otherwise found only once in the Hebrew Bible (2 Sam 13:28: הלוא כי אנכי צויתי אתכם, "*Is it not that* I commanded you?"). To be sure, the paucity of parallels might be coincidental, especially since the expression הלוא כי ("Is it not that ... ?"), as it is used in 2 Sam 13:28, seems to be "a good Hebrew expression," as noted by Samuel Rolles Driver.[9]

However, the longer text of 1 Sam 10:1, attested by the LXX, the Old Latin witnesses, and the Vulgate, does not contain this expression at all. According to the probable Hebrew *Vorlage* of the LXX, as presented above, it uses the parallel to the Hebrew conjunction כי in a completely different position and with a different syntactical function. In this version the word כי probably connected the clause משחך יהוה ("Yhwh has anointed you")

Hildesheim: Georg Olms, 1968), 201; Hans Joachim Stoebe, *Das erste Buch Samuelis* (KAT 8.1; Gütersloh: Mohn, 1973), 197; A. H. van Zyl, *I Samuël* (2 vols.; POut; Nijkerk: G. F. Callenbach, 1988–89), 1:139; Dominique Barthélemy, ed., *Critique textuelle de l'Ancien Testament* (4 vols.; OBO 50; Fribourg: Éditions Universitaires; Göttingen: Vandenhoeck & Ruprecht, 1982–2005), 1:163 (although "non sans hésitation"); Stephen Pisano, *Additions or Omissions in the Books of Samuel: The Significant Pluses and Minuses in the Massoretic, LXX and Qumran Texts* (OBO 57; Fribourg: Éditions Universitaires; Göttingen: Vandenhoeck & Ruprecht, 1984), 169 (while admitting "the possibility for omission of the plus").

7. E.g., Gen 13:9; 20:5; 31:15.

8. On this phenomenon see Paul Joüon and Takamitsu Muraoka, *A Grammar of Biblical Hebrew* (2nd repr. of 2nd ed.; SubBi 27; Rome: Gregorian & Biblical Press, 2009), §161j, who also refer to the similar opening of a rhetorical question with הכי.

9. Samuel Rolles Driver, *Notes on the Hebrew Text and the Topography of the Books of Samuel* (Oxford: Clarendon, 1913), 78; see also Pisano, *Additions or Omissions*, 168, who points out that in 2 Sam 13:28 "the expression is passed over in silence by all [i.e., other textual witnesses] and therefore, presumably, is an acceptable Hebrew construction."

with the preceding וזה לך האות ("And this shall be the sign for you"):[10] וזה לך האות כי משחך יהוה ("And this shall be the sign for you that Yhwh has anointed you"). The meaning of this sentence is clarified in what follows. Samuel predicts that Saul will encounter several people who will act in a certain way on his way home (1 Sam 10:2–6). These predictions are soon fulfilled (10:9b–13), and, according to 10:7, these "signs" (10:7, 9) show the divine approval of Samuel's anointing of Saul. Thus, the final sentence of the long text of 1 Sam 10:1 (וזה לך האות כי משחך יהוה על נחלתו לנגיד, "And this shall be the sign for you that Yhwh has anointed you over his inheritance as a leader") makes good sense in its immediate context.

A further consideration suggests that the plus was probably not secondarily added. If this were the case, it would be necessary to assume that an editor tore the original expression הלוא כי ("Is it not that … ?") apart in order to introduce another rhetorical question and to add three sentences, the last one of which uses the remaining word כי ("that") in a completely different position and in a different sense.

Reconstructed Hebrew *Vorlage* of 1 Sam 10:1 LXX

הלוא משחך יהוה לנגיד על עמו על ישראל ואתה תעצר בעם יהוה ואתה
תושיענו מיד איביו מסביב
וזה לך האות כי משחך יהוה על נחלתו לנגיד

Has Yhwh not anointed you as a leader over his people, over Israel? And you shall rule over the people of Yhwh, and you shall save them from the hand of their enemies all around. And this shall be the sign for you that Yhwh has anointed you over his inheritance as a leader.

To insert such an expansion exactly between הלוא ("Is it not … ?") and כי ("that") would be rather unnatural regarding the given syntax. It would be even more so if the phrase הלוא כי ("Is it not that … ?") was in fact "a good Hebrew expression." In other words, it would remain unclear why the editor did not leave the original rhetorical question הלוא כי משחך יהוה

---

10. This Hebrew text is the only possible equivalent of the Greek καὶ τοῦτό σοι τὸ σημεῖον ὅτι ἔχρισέν σε κύριος. Although the Hebrew *Vorlage* remains hypothetical, it is highly probable that the Greek text reflects this Hebrew wording, in particular regarding the syntactical function of כי in this sentence: The words משחך יהוה must have been connected with the preceding clause, and this is only possible with the word כי ("that").

על נחלתו לנגיד ("Is it not that Yhwh has anointed you over his inheritance as a leader?") intact and add the three sentences that connect the passage with 1 Sam 9:16–17 after this rhetorical question.

If a secondary expansion is assumed, the following text could be expected instead:

הלוא כי משחך יהוה על נחלתו לנגיד ואתה תעצר בעם יהוה ואתה תושיענו
מיד איביו מסביב וזה לך האות כי משחך יהוה לנגיד על עמו על ישראל

Is it not that Yhwh has anointed you over his inheritance as a leader? <u>And you shall rule over the people of Yhwh, and you shall save them from the hand of their enemies all around. And this shall be the sign for you that Yhwh has anointed you as a leader over his people, over Israel.</u>

These considerations provide another argument for the priority of the plus. Thus, the theoretical probability that the short MT is original should not be regarded as very high. Many commentators thus argue for the priority of the plus, and the plus is even accepted in many modern Bible translations.[11]

6.3. Possible Reasons for the Omission

Most of the scholars who advocate the priority of the plus assume that the omission may be the result of an unintentional scribal lapse. They explain that it would have been caused by haplography or parablepsis. In this case a scribe would have jumped from the first משחך יהוה to the second משחך יהוה, thus mistakenly skipping a substantial part of the text.[12]

---

11. E.g., Julius Wellhausen, *Der Text der Bücher Samuelis* (Göttingen: Vandenhoeck und Ruprecht, 1871), 72–73; Paul Dhorme, *Les Livres de Samuel* (Paris: Librairie Victor Lecoffre, 1910), 82; Driver, *Books of Samuel*, 78; Hans Wilhelm Hertzberg, *Die Samuelbücher* (ATD 10; Göttingen: Vandenhoeck & Ruprecht, 1956), 57; P. Kyle McCarter Jr., *1 Samuel* (AB 8; Garden City, N.Y.: Doubleday, 1980), 171; Ralph W. Klein, *1 Samuel* (WBC 10; Waco, Tex.: Word, 1983), 83; Walter Brueggemann, *First and Second Samuel* (Interpretation; Louisville, Ky.: John Knox, 1990), 74 (based on RSV); Walter Dietrich, *1 Sam 1–12* (Vol. 1 of *Samuel*; BKAT 8.1; Neukirchen-Vluyn: Neukirchener Verlag, 2010), 387; A. Graeme Auld, *I and II Samuel: A Commentary* (OTL; Louisville, Ky.: Westminster John Knox, 2011), 107, 109 (with discussion of both possibilities on p. 110). E.g., NEB, RSV, and NRSV, whereas the short text is given by KJV and ASV.

12. E.g., Budde, *Samuel*, 66; Dhorme, *Livres de Samuel*, 82; McCarter, *1 Samuel*, 171; Klein, *1 Samuel*, 83; Anneli Aejmelaeus, "How to Reach the Old Greek in

1 SAMUEL 10:1

Hypothetical Omission from *Vorlage* of 1 Sam 10:1 LXX

הלוא משחך יהוה לנגיד על עמו על ישראל ואתה תעצר בעם יהוה
ואתה תושיענו מיד איביו מסביב וזה לך האות
כי משחך יהוה על נחלתו לנגיד

~~Has Yhwh not anointed you as a leader over his people, over Israel? And you shall rule over the people of Yhwh, and you shall save them out of the hand of their enemies all around. And this shall be a sign for you~~ that Yhwh has anointed you over his inheritance as a leader.

This theory has an evident weakness, for it does not explain why the word כי ("that") was preserved in the MT when it logically would also have to have been skipped in the course of the haplography.[13] If the haplography was triggered by the repeated משחך יהוה ("Yhwh has anointed you"), we should expect that it resulted in the following text: הלוא משחך יהוה על נחלתו לנגיד ("Has Yhwh not anointed you over his inheritance as a leader?"). This would also provide a clearer sentence than what is now contained in the MT. In other words, it is difficult to see why a copyist who was distracted by the doubled משחך יהוה ("Yhwh has anointed you") should have jumped from הלוא to the word כי ("that"). The technical explanation is therefore not entirely convincing.

Alternatively, one could argue that the text was intentionally shortened due to considerations related to the content of the passage. This is suggested by the positive view of Saul's kingdom that is contained in the longer text. Here the prophet Samuel, in the name of Yhwh, commissions Saul to rule over the Israelites and to save them from their enemies. This call does not fit with Saul's rejection by Yhwh in the following chapters (see 1 Sam 13:13–14; 15:23, 26). In many texts that follow, Saul is depicted as a rather bad ruler over Yhwh's people. This tension between the positive view of Saul's kingdom in 1 Sam 10:1 and the negative description in the ensuing narrative could easily have caused an editor to omit the references to Saul's political leadership over Israel within Samuel's speech to Saul (1 Sam 10:1–8). To be sure, such a revision would not seem very system-

---

1 Samuel and What to Do with It," in *Congress Volume Helsinki 2010* (ed. Martti Nissinen; VTSup 148; Leiden: Brill, 2012), 191; Tov, *Textual Criticism*, 224.

13. Pisano, *Additions or Omissions*, 168; David Toshio Tsumura, *The First Book of Samuel* (The New International Commentary on the Old Testament; Grand Rapids: Eerdmans, 2007), 282.

atic, since the parallel passage in 1 Sam 9:16–17 was left intact.[14] However, one should not overlook that the two passages are not completely identical. According to 1 Sam 9:16 Saul has the task of saving Israel from the Philistines, while the long text of 1 Sam 10:1 speaks about Israel's "enemies all around," referring to a totality of enemies. The latter is, strictly speaking, a contradiction to Yhwh's speech in 1 Sam 9:16. This contradiction and the totality of the perspective in the longer text of 1 Sam 10:1 that does not fit with Saul's soon-following rejection might have triggered the omission. In addition, there are also other cases in 1 Samuel where rather isolated anti-Saulide changes in the proto-MT have probably taken place.[15] Consequently, it is possible to explain the shorter MT reading of 1 Sam 10:1 as a result of an isolated editorial alteration of the text. Considering the different alternatives discussed above, the weight of the evidence suggests that this theory is the most probable.

6.4. Results and Methodological Consequences

Although this case is not completely unambiguous, the priority of the plus provides the most probable explanation for the variant readings. The priority of the shorter MT remains a theoretical possibility, although a rather improbable one, since it implies an editorial technique by which a syntactically coherent phrase was torn apart without any obvious reason. In addition, the plus is attested by rather broad manuscript evidence, since it is found in more than one textual tradition: the LXX, some Old Latin witnesses, and the Vulgate. It is a different question whether the plus was omitted in the MT by mistake or by intention. Since the theory of a technical mistake has an evident weakness, the omission is best explained as an intentional editorial change caused by content-related considerations regarding the kingship of Saul.

Methodologically this case shows that a mechanical use of the text-critical rule *lectio brevior potior* is problematic. To be sure, many cases

---

14. This is stressed by Aejmelaeus, "How to Reach the Old Greek in 1 Samuel," 191, as a counterargument against an intentional omission.

15. A similar Saul-critical omission could be assumed in 1 Sam 13 MT, where the age of Saul at the time of his becoming king (1 Sam 13:1) seems to have been left out in the course of the textual history; also comparable is the tendentious change of יושע ("he was saved") in 1 Sam 14:47, attested by the LXX and one Old Latin witness, into ירשיע ("he acted wickedly") in the MT.

remain where the priority of a shorter version of a text is the most probable explanation, as many examples in other chapters of this volume show. Yet, the present example suggests that the possibility of secondary omissions should always be taken into consideration. In any case, it can be learned from 1 Sam 10:1 that textual plusses should be compared meticulously with the respective shorter texts. It is possible that some grammatical or content-related details are decisive for the question of which version is probably the more original one.

7
An Addition in a Qumran Manuscript as Evidence for the Continuous Growth of the Text: 1 Samuel 10:27–11:1

7.1. Introduction

After the appointment of Saul as king in 1 Sam 10, the MT and LXX versions of the following chapter move rather abruptly to the Ammonite siege of Jabesh-Gilead. 4QSam^a, however, contains three additional lines of text, making the transition more natural. This plus was also known, or so it seems, to Flavius Josephus. Although the first editor of the fragment explained the plus as an original piece of text lost in the MT and the LXX,[1] it is argued here that the passage is more likely a later addition in Deuteronomistic style, smoothing over the transition from one source to the other. The addition thus provides significant evidence for a later addition whose author imitated older style. The case at hand also shows that textual and literary criticism cannot be separated.

7.2. The Textual Evidence: A Long Plus in 4QSam^a and Josephus

In 1 Sam 10:17–25a Samuel presents the people's request for a king as their rejection of God. Nevertheless, Samuel gathers all the tribes, and Saul is selected to be king by lot. After this episode, 1 Sam 10:25b–27 tells us that Saul and all the people go home but that not everybody trusts the new king. Without further introduction, 1 Sam 11 MT then abruptly proceeds

---

1. Frank Moore Cross, "The Ammonite Oppression of the Tribes of Gad and Reuben: Missing Verses from 1 Samuel 11 Found in 4QSamuel^a," in *The Hebrew and Greek Texts of Samuel: 1980 Proceedings IOSCS—Vienna* (ed. Emanuel Tov; Jerusalem: Academon, 1980), 105–19.

to the Ammonite siege of Jabesh-Gilead. According to the LXX this happened "after about a month," which suggests that it has read ויהי כמחדש (while interpreting this as ויהי כְּמֵחדש) instead of MT's ויהי כמחריש ("and he was like someone who keeps silent," or "he held his peace").

1 Sam 10:27–11:1 MT

10:27 ובני בליעל אמרו מה ישענו זה ויבזהו ולא הביאו לו מנחה ויהי כמחריש
11:1 ויעל נחש העמוני ויחן על יבש גלעד ויאמרו כל אנשי יביש אל נחש
כרת לנו ברית ונעבדך

10:27 And worthless fellows said: "How would this one save us?" And they despised him and brought him no gift, but he held his peace.
11:1 And Nahash the Ammonite went up and besieged Jabesh-Gilead; and all the men of Jabesh said to Nahash: "Make a treaty with us, and we shall serve you."

1 Kgdms 10:27–11:1 LXX

10:27 καὶ υἱοὶ λοιμοὶ εἶπαν Τί σώσει ἡμᾶς οὗτος; καὶ ἠτίμασαν αὐτὸν καὶ οὐκ ἤνεγκαν αὐτῷ δῶρα.
11:1 Καὶ ἐγενήθη ὡς μετὰ μῆνα καὶ ἀνέβη Ναας ὁ Αμμανίτης καὶ παρεμβάλλει ἐπὶ Ιαβις Γαλααδ. καὶ εἶπον πάντες οἱ ἄνδρες Ιαβις πρὸς Ναας τὸν Αμμανίτην Διάθου ἡμῖν διαθήκην, καὶ δουλεύσομέν σοι.

10:27 And pestilent sons said: "How will this man save us?" And they despised him and brought him no gifts.
11:1 And it happened about a month later that Naas the Ammanite went up and besieged Jabis-Galaad; and all the men of Jabis said to Naas the Ammanite: "Make a treaty with us, and we shall serve you."

The abruptness of the transition to the passage on the siege of Jabesh is aggravated by the fact that King Nahash, contrary to the usual practice of the book of Samuel, is simply introduced as "Nahash the Ammonite." It is not until 1 Sam 12:12 that the MT and LXX reveal his title. It also remains unclear why he chose Jabesh-Gilead as his target and why the condition for a peace treaty was so harsh: Nahash stipulated that he would gouge out everyone's right eye. However, all these problems disappear in 4QSam[a].[2]

---

2. The Hebrew text is taken from the edition by Frank Moore Cross et al., *Qumran Cave 4.XII: 1–2 Samuel* (DJD 17; Oxford: Clarendon, 2005), 65–67.

1 SAMUEL 10:27–11:1

1 Sam 10:27–11:1 4QSamᵃ X, 4–10

4 [וילכו] [בני החיל א̇שר נגע יה[ו]ה בלבבם   vacat   ‎10:27בני בליעל א[מרו
  מ]ה̇ יושיענו[

5 [זה וי[ב̇זוהו ולוא הביאו לו מנחה   vacat   [   ]

6 [ונ]ח̇ש מלך בני ע̇מון הוא לחץ את בני גד ואת בני ראובן בחזקה ונקר להם
  כ]ול

7 [ע]י̇ן ימין ונתן אין [מושי]ע̇ ל[י]שראל ולוא נשאר איש בבני ישראל אשר
  בע̇[בר הירדן]

8 [אש]ר̇ ל[וא נ]ק̇ר לו נח̇[ש מלך] בני̇ ע̇[מ]ון כול עין ימין ו[ה]ן̇ שבעת
  אלפים איש

9   *supralinear, first hand*   ויהי כמו חדש ‎11:1ויעל נחש העמוני ויחן על יביש
9 [נצלו מיד] בנ̇י̇ עמון ויבאו אל [י]בש ג̇לעד ויאמרו כול אנשי יביש אל נחש
  מ̇[לך]

10 [בני עמון כרת] ל[נו ברית ונעבדך ‎2ויאמר א[ל]י̇ה[ם̇ נח̇ש̇ [העמוני בזאת
   אכרת לכם[

4 ... ¹⁰:²⁷ And worthless fellows s[aid:] "H[ow would this one save us?"]
5 [And th]ey despised him and brought him no gift.
6 [And Na]hash, king of the Ammonites, he grievously oppressed the Gadites and the Reubenites, and he gouged out a[ll] their right
7 [ey]es and allowed [I]srael no [deliver]er. No one was left of the Israelites ac[ross the Jordan]
8 [of wh]om Naha[sh, king] of the [Am]monites, had n[ot g]ouged out every right eye. But see, seven thousand men
9 [had escaped from] the Ammonites and had come to [Ja]besh-Gilead. And about a month later ¹¹:¹ Nahash the Ammonite went up and besieged Jabesh<-Gilead>; and all the men of Jabesh said to Nahash, ki[ng of the]
10 [Ammonites: "Make a treaty] with u[s, and we shall serve you." ...]

Flavius Josephus must have known a similar plus.³ However, his Μηνὶ δ' ὕστερον ("However, a month later") comes at the beginning rather than at

---

3. Josephus, *Ant.* 6.68–71 (B. Niese, ed., *Flavii Iosephi opera* [Berlin: Weidmann, 1885–95], 2:19–20: (68) Μηνὶ δ' ὕστερον ἄρχει τῆς παρὰ πάντων αὐτῷ τιμῆς ὁ πρὸς Ναάσην πόλεμος τὸν τῶν Ἀμμανιτῶν βασιλέα· οὗτος γὰρ πολλὰ κακὰ τοὺς πέραν τοῦ Ἰορδάνου ποταμοῦ κατῳκημένους τῶν Ἰουδαίων διατίθησι, μετὰ πολλοῦ καὶ μαχίμου

the end of the plus, and he does not mention the escape of the seven thousand men but simply suggests that after Nahash had dealt with Gad and Reuben, he moved on to the Gileadites.

7.3. The Plus as Evidence of Continuing Scribal Expansion and Revision of the Text

Even on the basis of the data given above, it is clear that the plus can best be explained as a later scribal addition. The following arguments favor this assumption.

1. There is nothing in the long text that could have triggered a haplographic omission.[4] As an interpolation, however, the plus fulfills a clear role: even though, as we shall see, it does not remove all problems, it eases the abrupt transition between 1 Sam 10 and 11, as it introduces Nahash in the proper way and explains the harshness of Nahash's condition for

---

στρατεύματος διαβὰς ἐπ' αὐτούς· (69) καὶ τὰς πόλεις αὐτῶν εἰς δουλείαν ὑπάγεται, ἰσχύι μὲν καὶ βίᾳ πρὸς τὸ παρὸν αὐτοὺς χειρωσάμενος, σοφίᾳ δὲ καὶ ἐπινοίᾳ πρὸς τὸ μηδ' αὖθις ἀποστάντας δυνηθῆναι τὴν ὑπ' αὐτῷ δουλείαν διαφυγεῖν ἀσθενεῖς ποιῶν· τῶν γὰρ ἢ κατὰ πίστιν ὡς αὐτὸν ἀφικνουμένων ἢ λαμβανομένων πολέμου νόμῳ τοὺς δεξιοὺς ὀφθαλμοὺς ἐξέκοπτεν. (70) ἐποίει δὲ τοῦθ', ὅπως τῆς ἀριστερᾶς αὐτοῖς ὄψεως ὑπὸ τῶν θυρεῶν καλυπτομένης ἄχρηστοι παντελῶς εἶεν. (71) καὶ ὁ μὲν τῶν Ἀμμανιτῶν βασιλεὺς ταῦτ' ἐργασάμενος τοὺς πέραν τοῦ Ἰορδάνου, ἐπὶ τοὺς Γαλαδηνοὺς λεγομένους ἐπεστράτευσε. English translation by Henry St John Thackeray and Ralph Marcus, *Jewish Antiquities, Books V–VIII* (vol. 5 of *Josephus*; LCL; London: Heinemann; Cambridge: Harvard University Press, 1934), 201: (68) However, a month later, he began to win the esteem of all by the war with Naas, king of the Ammanites. For this monarch had done much harm to the Jews who had settled beyond the river Jordan, having invaded their territory with a large and warlike army. (69) Reducing their cities to servitude, he not only by force and violence secured their subjection in the present, but by cunning and ingenuity weakened them in order that they might never again be able to revolt and escape from servitude to him; for he cut out the right eyes of all who either surrendered to him under oath or were captured by right of war. (70) This he did with intent—since the left eye was covered by the buckler—to render them utterly unserviceable. (71) Having then so dealt with the people beyond Jordan, the Ammanite king carried his arms against those called Galadenians.

4. Thus P. Kyle McCarter Jr. (*I Samuel* [AB 8; Garden City, N.Y.: Doubleday, 1980], 199), who defends the plus as original and suggests that "a scribe simply skipped an entire paragraph of his text" in "an extraordinary case of oversight." See below.

a peace treaty as well as his choice of Jabesh. There is, in other words, an evident motive for a scribe to add a plus.[5]

2. The differences between the plus in 4QSam[a] and the parallel in Josephus point to the fact that this was a recent addition of which the phrasing and positioning—before or after the temporal clause—were not yet completely fixed.[6]

3. The language of the plus is heavy and to some extent archaizing (rather than archaic), and it contains some late features. Thus the opening formula in l. 6, the *casus pendens* [ון]חֹשׁ מלך בני עַמוֹן taken up by the pronoun הוא and followed by a verbal rather than a nominal clause, is grammatically possible but unnecessary.[7] Stephen Pisano states that the

---

5. Cf. for this opinion Dominique Barthélemy, ed., *Critique textuelle de l'Ancien Testament* (4 vols.; OBO 50; Fribourg: Éditions Universitaires; Göttingen: Vandenhoeck & Ruprecht, 1982–2005), 1:170–71; Alexander Rofé, "The Acts of Nahash according to 4QSam[a]," *IEJ* 32 (1982): 129–33; and Stephen Pisano, *Additions or Omissions in the Books of Samuel: The Significant Pluses and Minuses in the Massoretic, LXX and Qumran Texts* (OBO 57; Fribourg: Éditions Universitaires; Göttingen: Vandenhoeck & Ruprecht, 1984), 95. See also Walter Dietrich, *1 Sam 1–12* (vol. 1 of *Samuel*; BKAT 8.1; Neukirchen-Vluyn: Neukirchener Verlag, 2010), 503–4.

6. Barthélemy, *Critique textuelle*, 1:171, followed by Pisano, *Additions or Omissions*, 95 with n. 22. The latter points to the case of the Song of Hannah in 1 Sam 2:1–10, which "appears to have been inserted in a slightly different place in MT, LXX and 4Q traditions." In a passage often misunderstood, Frank Moore Cross suggests explaining the position of the adverbial clause in Josephus as the result of vertical dittography in his supposed Hebrew *Vorlage*. Thus one would have found ויהי כמו חדש at the beginning and end of the plus. Cross adds that in such a text, the whole paragraph could have been lost through homoioteleuton. See Cross, "Ammonite Oppression," 110–11, and now also his new edition, Cross, *Qumran Cave 4.XII*, 66. This explanation does not account for Josephus's silence regarding the seven thousand refugees but rather accounts for the position of the temporal clause in Josephus and the loss of the whole plus in the MT. In my opinion, Josephus's text remains partly unexplained in this way, while there are easier ways of accounting for the difference between the MT and 4QSam[a] than the combination of vertical dittography (itself rather complicated) and haplography. Moreover, according to Eugene Ulrich (*The Qumran Text of Samuel and Josephus* [HSM 19; Chico, Calif.: 1978], 255–56), Josephus used a Greek Bible rather than a Hebrew one.

7. Reasons for this form of topicalization are emphasis or the wish to obtain clarity by allowing a grammatically complex part of the clause to stand on its own. See Bruce K. Waltke and M. O'Connor, *An Introduction to Biblical Hebrew Syntax* (Winona Lake, Ind.: Eisenbrauns, 1990), §4.7c; and Paul Joüon and Takamitsu Muraoka, *A Grammar of Biblical Hebrew* (2d repr. of 2d ed.; SubBi 27; Rome: Gregorian & Biblical Press,

designations בני גד and בני ראובן ("Gadites" and "Reubenites"), using the name of the tribe with בני ("sons of") are "curiously anachronistic."[8] This use is indeed highly infrequent in the book of Samuel: we find it only four times with the name of Benjamin and once with Judah.[9] With the word כול ("all, every") before עין ימין ("right eye") in l. 8, the author repeats the expression used in ll. 6–7, thus making the passage sound solemn and formulaic. However, the word כול in this position is both awkward and superfluous. As for l. 9 *supralinear*, Cross calls ויהי כמו חדש ("And about a month later") "a clearly archaic expression."[10] In fact, in Biblical Hebrew the word כמו is not unusual, but as a preposition its use is limited to poetry.[11] Here it is clearly out of place. It can best be explained as an archaizing feature, meant to solve the problem posed by the reading ויהי כמחדש that is behind the LXX's ὡς μετὰ μῆνα (and which is probably original, MT's ויהי כמחריש, "but he held his peace," being another solution to the same problem).[12]

2009), §156a. Here, however, the subject is already emphasized by its position, and the subject is not complex as in, for instance, Gen 30:30 or 34:21.

8. Pisano, *Additions or Omissions*, 97.

9. One finds בני בנימן ("Benjaminites") in 1 Sam 22:7; 2 Sam 2:25; 4:2; 23:29, and בני יהודה ("Judaites") in 2 Sam 1:18. Pisano adds that even the use of בני ישראל for the Israelites is relatively infrequent (Pisano, *Additions or Omissions*, 97).

10. Cross, "Ammonite Oppression," 113.

11. Thus already Karl Budde, *Die Bücher Samuel* (KHC 8; Tübingen: J.C.B. Mohr, 1902), 73 (in reply to a conjecture), followed by Barthélemy, *Critique textuelle*, 1:167, and Pisano, *Additions or Omissions*, 96, who also reject Cross's explanation on the basis of Ugaritic.

12. The problem is that after -כ other prepositions are usually elided. However, an exception to this rule is made for standing expressions like כבראשנה and כבתחלה; see Ludwig Koehler and Walter Baumgartner, *Hebräisches und aramäisches Lexikon zum Alten Testament* (3d ed.; Leiden: Brill, 1967–96), s.v. כ 4b. It seems that כמחדש and, in Gen 38:24 SP, כמשלשת חדשים (to be interpreted as כְּמְשֻׁלֶּשֶׁת) originally belonged to the latter category but were no longer seen that way at a later stage. Hence the MT offered כמחריש and משלש חדשים respectively (here מְשֻׁלָּשׁ is to be interpreted as a noun meaning "having reached the number three," "threefoldness"—a *hapax legomenon*; cf. Rashi *ad loc.* and Koehler and Baumgartner, *Lexikon*, s.v.). In short, contrary to Barthélemy (*Critique textuelle*, 1:166–68, 171–72; followed by Pisano, *Additions or Omissions*, 95–96), we see the *Vorlage* of the LXX as the more difficult reading, which has given rise to two different solutions. If one were to follow him and to accept the MT as original, one would have to assume a three-stage development: כמחריש > כמו חדש > כמחדש.

The word ‏ה[ן]‏ in l. 8 cannot be a masculine personal pronoun "they," as it is often translated.[13] In our translation we have chosen to consider it a deictic particle.[14] As such, the form ‏הן‏ is less widely used than ‏הנה‏, and therefore it fits the picture of a scribe who wants to make his text sound old and authentic. Alternatively, one could point to the use of ‏הן‏ in the sense of ‏אם‏, which—possibly under Aramaic influence—we find especially in late Biblical Hebrew and even later stages of the language. In that case, it may have been used here with ‏ו‏ concessively in the sense of "even though"[15] or "except."[16] Other forms betraying the late character of the text are the perfects with *waw* conjunctive in ll. 6–7 (‏ונקר‏ and ‏ונתן‏), unless one wants to read these with Cross as absolute infinitives,[17] and the item-adverbial use of ‏אין‏, which in the Hebrew Bible is found mainly in later texts and which became more usual in the Qumran texts.[18]

---

13. In the first place by the editor himself: Cross, *Qumran Cave 4.XII*, 67, note under "Reconstructed Variants." The word ‏הן‏ is used independently as a feminine plural pronoun in Mishnaic Hebrew; in Biblical Hebrew it occurs only as a bound morpheme. See Joüon and Muraoka, *Grammar*, §39a. Here one really needs a masculine form. A similar problem occurs in Job 24:5, where it is not necessary to assume a masculine pronoun ‏הן‏ either.

14. Thus also Dietrich, *1 Sam 1–12*, 501.

15. For this sense, see Koehler and Baumgartner, *Lexikon*, s.v. ‏אם‏ 7, where this use is compared with Arabic *wa'in* and Latin *etsi*.

16. "Except" is Rofé's rendering (without explanation): Alexander Rofé, "Midrashic Traits in 4Q51 (So-Called 4QSam^a)," in *Archaeology of the Books of Samuel: The Entangling of the Textual and Literary History* (ed. Philippe Hugo and Adrian Schenker; VTSup 132; Leiden: Brill, 2010), 75–88, esp. 80.

17. Cross discusses the problem of these forms, which is often overlooked, at length in "Ammonite Oppression," 108–9 (note, however, that the narrative use of absolute infinitives is very rare in the Hebrew Bible). See also Rofé, "Acts of Nahash," 133 n. 17. McCarter, *I Samuel*, 202, vocalizes the verbs as participles; in Biblical Hebrew, however, we would not expect participles for verbs summing up events in a historical narrative. To say the least, this use would be no less anachronistic than that of perfects with *waw* consecutive.

18. Waltke and O'Connor, *Syntax*, §39 n. 61, and Jean Carmignac, "L'emploi de la négation ‏אין‏ dans la Bible et à Qumran," *RevQ* 8 (1974): 407–13. It should be noted that the phrase is largely a reconstruction; of the crucial final *nun* of ‏אין‏ only inconclusive traces remain. Rofé ("Midrashic Traits," 80 n. 21) suggests returning to Cross's original proposal, which was to read ‏ונתן אי[ן מה ופחד] על‏ ("and he struck terror and dread"; cf. Exod 15:16; 1 Chr 14:17). He contends that the new reconstruction "sounds as a nice calque-translation from American English 'gave no savior,' but is not Hebrew, Biblical or post-Biblical, at all." This is probably too negative, given the expansion of

4. The plus would seem to be composed of several conventional motifs that could have been taken from elsewhere. As Alexander Rofé has indicated, "One cannot point out any original detail that could be known only by a pre-exilic author."[19] The enmity between Israel and Ammon, as well as the Ammonite land claims, are described in Judg 10–11; the presence of Gad and Reuben across the Jordan, in Num 32. The notion of foreign kings "oppressing" (לחץ) Israel is, according to Frank Moore Cross, a Deuteronomistic cliché.[20] It is even possible that the phrase is directly borrowed from Judg 4:3: והוא לחץ את בני ישראל בחזקה ("and he grievously oppressed the Israelites"). The number of seven thousand refugees is, as Cross also explains, a round number appropriate to the style of the narrative.[21]

5. Rofé points to a procedure typical of Second Temple texts, which duplicates or even multiplies an action of a character, transforming it into a constant trait of this hero or anti-hero.[22] Here, it seems that the addition intends to make Nahash the "gouger of eyes" par excellence. Rofé calls this procedure a midrashic feature, which is an appropriate characterization *only* if one defines "midrash" as a reediting of older stories to fit the taste and needs of new generations, that is, the way in which it is probably used in 2 Chr 13:22 and 24:27,[23] and the way in which Chronicles itself could be called a midrash. The addition of this paragraph is well within the limits of

---

the use of אין just mentioned, but it is clear that if one wants to maintain the new reconstruction, one has to accept a very late date for the passage.

19. Rofé, "Acts of Nahash," 131.

20. Cross, "Ammonite Oppression," 112, for whom this was rather an indication of authenticity, though he admitted that "such clichés are easily imitated."

21. Ibid.; cf. 1 Kgs 19:18; 2 Kgs 24:15.

22. Rofé, "Acts of Nahash," 131–32, and idem, "Midrashic Traits," 80.

23. Rofé, "Midrashic Traits," 76 with n. 5, explains the meaning of the verb דרש in this period as "to enquire, investigate," whereas "to interpret" would be a later development. Still, he uses the term "commentary" here, which is slightly misleading, as a commentary is a form of interpretation. It should be clear that the editorial work visible in 4QSam[a]—on which see also Rofé, "The Nomistic Correction in Biblical Manuscripts and Its Occurrence in 4QSam[a]," *RevQ* 14 (1989–90): 247–54—does not make it a commentary: it constitutes an updated version of the text itself, and that is how it was seen: a text very much like 4QSam[a] was used by the Chronicler for his composition. Given the later development and use of the term "midrash," we would rather avoid speaking of a *Midrash Sefer Shemuel* in regard to 4QSam[a] as Rofé does.

contemporary scribal tradition,[24] even though the duplication procedure may have become especially popular in later times.

In short, the plus can best be explained as an addition by a later scribe who wanted to resolve some of the problems posed by the sudden transition from 1 Sam 10 to 11, and who tried to fit his lines to the context using Deuteronomistic phrases as well as solemn and archaizing language. We can, however, take the argument one step further. Dominique Barthélemy and Pisano have pointed to the fact that there were several layers of redaction in the Deuteronomistic History.[25] Just as the later redaction of Jeremiah was characterized by Deuteronomistic additions, the plus discussed here could be part of a late redactional development not known to the MT or LXX.

As Julius Wellhausen has remarked regarding the LXX, textual developments usually take place where two versions of a story come together and to some extent are in conflict.[26] Now 1 Sam 11:1-11, 15 has indeed been recognized by the majority of modern commentators since Wellhausen as a separate story.[27] In addition to the problems in the transition between 1 Sam 10 and 11 mentioned above, there is the glaring problem of the fact that Saul has been made king in 1 Sam 10, whereas in 1 Sam 11:5 we learn that Saul—hardly befitting a king—is plowing the field behind the oxen when the news comes to his village. Nobody seems to take the trouble to warn him, as he hears it only on his return. Then, however, Saul takes action quickly, gathering an army and gaining a total victory over the Ammonites. According to this story, it is only now that Saul is made king (in 1 Sam 11:15).

Originally, 1 Sam 11's version of how Saul became king may have stood in relation to 1 Sam 9:1-10:16, whereas 1 Sam 10:17-25a and to some extent 1 Sam 12 continue the line of chs. 7 and 8. In the former version, Samuel is a rather unknown seer in Rama. In the latter he is a theocratic ruler, opposing kingship. The two stories of how Saul became king are

---

24. Cf. Zecharia Kallai, "Samuel in Qumrān: Expansion of a Historiographical Pattern (4QSamª)," *RB* 103 (1996): 581-91.

25. Barthélemy, *Critique textuelle*, 1:170; followed by Pisano, *Additions or Omissions*, 95.

26. Julius Wellhausen, *Die Composition des Hexateuchs und der historischen Bücher des Alten Testaments* (3d ed.; Berlin: Georg Reimer, 1899), 124 (in relation to Josh 8); cf. 236 (on 1 Sam 1).

27. Ibid., 240-43. Cf., e.g., very recently, Dietrich, *1 Sam 1-12*, 488-90, 492-501.

connected by the editorial verses 1 Sam 10:25b–27 and 11:12–14, which suggest that after the selection of Saul in 1 Sam 10 some opposition arose. Hence comes the need to *renew* the kingship, which allows the two stories to stand next to each other. However clever this editorial solution may be, there are obvious loose ends, and it is the further editorial intervention preserved by 4QSam[a] and Josephus that seeks to tie them together.

7.4. Could the Plus Be Original, After All?

A number of scholars have followed Cross and are convinced that the plus is original, or at least part of the earlier layer of Deuteronomistic redaction.[28] Emanuel Tov summarizes their case in his *Textual Criticism of the Hebrew Bible*, mentioning four arguments:[29]

1. The brutality of Nahash's approach in the MT, without any introduction, "seems to be out of order."
2. The title "king of the Ammonites" is lacking in the MT but appears in accordance with biblical custom in 4QSam[a].
3. The reading ויהי כמו חדש is "appropriate in the context of 4QSam[a]," whereas ויהי כמחריש in the MT is "contextually difficult though not impossible."
4. The plus was known to Josephus, who in several other instances also reflects a text identical to that of 4QSam[a].

In an earlier edition of this work, Tov mentions yet another argument: the idea that "in general, 4QSam[a] reflects a reliable text," while the MT "has many corruptions."[30] Though he has apparently retracted this argument now and already expressed reserve when mentioning it, it is important to review why this argument cannot be upheld before we deal with the first

---

28. Ulrich, *Qumran Text*, 166–70; McCarter, *I Samuel*, 199–200; Emanuel Tov, *Textual Criticism of the Hebrew Bible* (3d ed.; Minneapolis: Fortress, 2012), 311–13; Armin Lange, *Die Handschriften biblischer Bücher von Qumran und den anderen Fundorten* (vol. 1 of *Handbuch der Textfunde vom Toten Meer*; Tübingen: Mohr Siebeck, 2009), 219–20. Note that Lange still quotes Cross's first edition instead of the new edition and that he omits the final part as well as Josephus, *Ant.* 6.68.

29. Tov, *Textual Criticism*, 312–13.

30. Emanuel Tov, *Textual Criticism of the Hebrew Bible* (2d ed.; Minneapolis: Fortress; Assen: Royal Van Gorcum, 2001), 344.

four points. As Tov himself concedes, in agreement with Rofé, 4QSam^a does contain contextual changes.[31] Thus what might seem to be a corruption in the MT could equally well be a contextual change in 4QSam^a. But there is something else, also noted by Tov: one should be careful with generalizations. When one generalizes, one basically promotes a preference for a number of readings in a given manuscript—a preference that is based on internal considerations—by way of induction to a general preference, which is then applied as an external criterion to other instances by way of deduction.[32] In other words, one promotes a single witness to the status of "best manuscript." Now, there is indeed a sphere in which the authority of a manuscript can be invoked in this way, but this is a very narrow sphere. If no *stemma codicum*, a family tree of witnesses, can be established, the authority of a manuscript is indeed based on the evaluation of all readings where one can make a choice on the basis of internal considerations. But we can rely on the best manuscript thus established solely in instances where our judgment is helpless and no such considerations present themselves. It is a very last resort. Where judgment has scope, as in the case discussed in this chapter, there is no reason to take shelter here.[33]

Now let us return to Tov's four points. The last one, the fact that Josephus also knew the plus, is a typical external argument: the broadness of the attestation. Of course, the shorter reading is attested even more broadly, but the reason why Josephus is mentioned is clear: 4QSam^a is an important, ancient witness that often has better readings but also contains some contextual changes. Now, Josephus's support for the reading shows that it is not merely a fabrication of the scribe of 4QSam^a; it appears to have a wider currency. This wider currency, however, does not necessarily

---

31. See Rofé, "Nomistic Correction"; cf. now also Eugene Ulrich, "A Qualitative Assessment of the Textual Profile of 4QSam^a," in *Flores Florentino: Dead Sea Scrolls and Other Early Jewish Studies in Honour of Florentino García Martínez* (ed. Anthony Hilhorst et al.; JSJSup 122; Leiden: Brill, 2007), 147–61; and Donald W. Parry, "The Textual Character of the Unique Readings of 4QSam^a (4Q51)," in Hilhorst, *Flores Florentino*, 163–82.

32. Tov, *Textual Criticism*, 272–73.

33. See on this A. E. Housman, "The Editing of Juvenal: Preface of MDCCCCV," in *Collected Poems and Selected Prose* (ed. Christopher Ricks; Harmondsworth: Penguin, 1988), 395–402, esp. 399–400. The case at hand is one about which Housman would say: "To settle this case by appeals to the relative worth of MSS is to stand upon one's head: cases like this are the things by which the relative worth of MSS is settled"; see "From the Classical Papers: 24 Ovid," in Ricks, *Collected Poems*, 419.

make it an original reading. As Tov himself explains elsewhere, readings "should be judged only on the basis of their intrinsic value," as attestation is very much a matter of historical coincidence.[34] The fact that Josephus, as Tov indicates,[35] more often reflects a text identical to that of 4QSam[a] is an example of such coincidence: there must have been some form of interdependence between the text used by Josephus and the model of 4QSam[a]. The last blow to the Josephus argument is finally given by the fact that the position of the plus vis-à-vis the temporal clause is different in the two witnesses, showing, as we have seen above, that this was a recent addition, of which the phrasing and positioning were not yet completely fixed.

Tov's first three points are more relevant and in a way more interesting, as they show that the main ammunition of the defenders and attackers of the plus is basically the same. Textual criticism is a matter of reason and common sense. A textual critic tries to establish which reading may have given rise to other readings, but this is usually not a matter that can be established with certainty. The critic is after probabilities: what was the most likely course of the development of the text? The result is necessarily subjective, but it is the best we can do.

The brutality of Nahash's approach to Jabesh and the simple introduction of Nahash as "Nahash the Ammonite" in the MT, in combination with the fact that the longer text would seem to solve these issues, led us to follow the rules of *lectio difficilior probabilior* and *lectio brevior potior* above.[36] However, Tov rightly explains that one cannot apply these rules automatically.[37] A simple scribal error, such as an omission through homoioteleuton, may cause a difficult and short reading that has, of course, no claim to originality. In textual criticism there are no hard-and-fast rules, as every problem must be regarded as possibly unique.[38] *Lectio difficilior probabilior*, for instance, is a consideration that is sensible in many cases, as it is natural for a scribe to have the wish to present a readable and understandable text, but we should not apply it without thinking. Given the tendency among some scholars to defend any MT reading that is more difficult but not downright impossible as original, it is also understand-

---

34. Tov, *Textual Criticism*, 273–74.
35. Ibid., 313.
36. This is implicit in our first point, pages 82–83.
37. Tov, *Textual Criticism*, 275–81.
38. For this, see also A. E. Housman, "The Application of Thought to Textual Criticism," in Ricks, *Collected Poems*, 325–39.

able that Tov stresses the importance of a reading's appropriateness to its context.[39] Coming back to the brutality of Nahash and the simple way he is introduced, Tov defines these not just as difficulties, as we did, but as "out of order" and contrary to custom, respectively. This suggests that he feels that an author or editor could hardly be responsible for them. In his opinion these are readings that do not fit the context and therefore must be the result of an error. Hence his conclusion that the longer text, which does not have these problems, must be original.

We share Tov's opinion that the brutality of Nahash's approach to Jabesh and the incompleteness of his epithet are problematic. We think, however, that the abrupt transition between 1 Sam 10 and 11 may very well be the result of the earlier literary history of the passage (for which there is no documented evidence). In other words, the sudden brutality of Nahash and his incomplete epithet are not necessarily the result of an error; they could have found a place in this context as a result of an editorial development: the Deuteronomistic editor or editors, having solved the main issue of combining two election stories into one thread, may have left the text as we find it in the MT. He or they would not have sought to smooth out all the contradictions but left some that occasioned later scribes to change the text. This means that in our opinion, the *lectio difficilior probabilior* rule may very well apply in this case, after all. Even if one does not accept our appeal to the earlier literary history of the passage, however, it is possible to assume that the brutality of Nahash's approach was the original motif of the narrative of 1 Sam 11: it makes Saul's intervention even more impressive. Again, this suggests that Nahash's brutality could very well be considered befitting the context, even if a later scribe felt the need to provide a narratological rationale for it.

Thus we have to choose between two scenarios: either the plus was lost through scribal error, or it was added to resolve difficulties in the text, which might be the result of the combination of two conflicting accounts. What tips the scale in favor of the latter option is the fact that there is nothing in the longer text that could have triggered a haplographic omission. Although a scribal error is always possible, it is in this case much less probable than a later addition. The likelihood of the plus being original is further reduced by the different positions that the plus has in the two witnesses, the nature of the language used in it, the fact that it is composed

---

39. Tov, *Textual Criticism*, 281.

of conventional motifs that are found in other texts as well, and the growing attractiveness of the procedure of the duplication of the protagonist's action.

Tov's third point concerns the phrase ויהי כמחריש ("but he held his peace") in the MT, and ויהי כמו חדש ("And about a month later") in 4QSamᵃ as well as in the *Vorlage* of the LXX and Josephus. The former would be "contextually difficult though not impossible," whereas the latter is deemed "appropriate in the context of 4QSamᵃ." The first problem with this statement is that ויהי כמו חדש is considered the probable *Vorlage* of the LXX, even though he mentions in a footnote that ויהי כמחדש "would have been more appropriate."[40] The other two readings can be explained from ויהי כמחדש, as we have seen, and there can hardly be any doubt that ὡς μετὰ μῆνα reflects ויהי כמחדש rather than ויהי כמו חדש. Second, even if ויהי כמו חדש is appropriate in the context of 4QSamᵃ, this does not prove that the plus that constitutes a large part of this context is original. Third, though Tov is right in pointing out the importance of readings being appropriate to their context—not every possible reading can claim to be original—he seems to go too far when he says, "The quintessence of textual evaluation is the selection from among the different transmitted readings of the one that is the most appropriate to its context."[41] As the main goal for textual evaluation this is too vague. Moreover, it would amount to a reversal of the *lectio difficilior* rule, which, even if it cannot be applied automatically, remains a useful consideration. The goal of textual evaluation is rather to find the reading that, in the most natural way, explains the origin of the other readings.[42] Tov complains about this formula that it is "general to the point of being almost superfluous."[43] However, the fact that the formula refers to distinguishing original readings from a variety

---

40. Ibid., 313 n. 46. The comparison in this note with Gen 19:15 is incorrect, as כמו is used there as a temporal conjunction followed by a verbal clause, whereas it is a preposition in 1 Sam 11:1 4QSamᵃ.

41. Emanuel Tov, "The Relevance of Textual Theories for the Praxis of Textual Criticism," in *A Teacher for All Generations: Essays in Honor of James C. VanderKam* (ed. E. F. Mason et al.; JSJSup 153.1; Leiden: Brill, 2012), 1:34. See also Tov, *Textual Criticism*, 281.

42. *Utrum in alterum abiturum erat?* See Martin L. West, *Textual Criticism and Editorial Technique Applicable to Greek and Latin Texts* (Stuttgart: Teubner, 1973), 51–53; and Ronald S. Hendel, *The Text of Genesis 1–11: Textual Studies and Critical Edition* (New York: Oxford University Press, 1998), 7.

43. Tov, *Textual Criticism*, 280.

of secondary readings, including scribal errors, interpolations, deliberate alterations, and omissions, is not a disadvantage but the very nature of textual criticism.

7.5. Results and Methodological Consequences

We have seen that the plus before 1 Sam 11 in 4QSam^a is probably a sign of further literary growth of the historical books rather than an earlier part of the text that has been lost through scribal error. To some extent, later scribes took the liberty of continuing the editorial process, especially at the fault lines where different sources come together, such as in 1 Sam 10 and 11. One of the interesting things about this case is that the comparison between the MT and LXX on the one hand and 4QSam^a and Josephus on the other presents us with textual evidence for a literary development. This brings us to the issue of the distinction between textual and literary criticism.

Traditionally literary criticism has investigated the authenticity, uniformity, and, where applicable, literary growth of texts, whereas textual criticism deals with the copying and transmission of the final form of the text. Even before the discovery of the Qumran scrolls, the observation that the LXX could be based on a Hebrew text different from the MT brought up doubts regarding this distinction.[44] To what extent can textual criticism deal with changes of a literary nature? Interesting is, for instance, Marie-Joseph Lagrange's 1898 statement, of which one can still hear echoes in more recent scholarly discussion.[45] Looking at some of the differences between the MT and the LXX, he wonders whether one should consider them the work of copyists or of editors. His point of view is that a text form that was accepted by all to the extent that people decided to translate it should be seen as the final edition. On this basis, he calls all changes after the LXX the work of copyists, who are not working under divine inspiration. It is these changes

---

44. See Dominique Barthélemy, "L'enchevêtrement de l'histoire textuelle et de l'histoire littéraire dans les relations entre la Septante et le Texte Massorétique: Modifications dans la manière de concevoir les relations existant entre la LXX et le TM, depuis J. Morin jusqu'à E. Tov," in *De Septuaginta: Studies in Honour of John William Wevers on His Sixty-Fifth Birthday* (ed. Albert Pietersma and Claude Cox; Mississauga: Benben, 1984), 21–40.

45. Marie-Joseph Lagrange, "*Les sources du Pentateuque*," *RB* 7 (1898): 10–32, esp. 16–17.

that are the object of textual criticism. At the same time, Lagrange admits, however, that sometimes the copyists have taken such liberties that their changes actually belong to the domain of literary criticism. This makes him suggest that the distinction is rather a question of words: the main thing is the fact that major changes were still made at a very late stage. Thus, though Lagrange does distinguish between the work of editors, which belongs to literary criticism, and the work of copyists, which is the subject of textual criticism, he also stresses the relativity of the issue.

In Lagrange's statement, theology follows history: as the text was translated, it must have been considered final, and therefore later interventions cannot claim to be inspired. In the original point of view of Barthélemy and the other members of the committee executing the Hebrew Old Testament Text Project of the United Bible Societies (henceforth UBS Committee),[46] stabilization and canonization were likewise connected. Textual criticism in this view had to aim at the authentic state of the Bible, that is, "the state in which it is canonized."[47] They suggested a clear division of work, as it would be the task of textual analysis to establish the "most primitive text attested" (the beginning of the second stage of the development of the text), whereas literary-critical analysis should try to establish the "original texts" (belonging to the first stage).[48] In this view it was the process of canonization that led to literary stabilization, and thus to the end of the first stage and the beginning of the history of the final text.

However, some texts provided evidence to the UBS Committee that a clear-cut distinction between textual criticism and literary criticism runs into difficulties. While working on Jeremiah, Ezekiel, and Proverbs, where they discerned two different literary developments of the text, the committee felt unable to reconstruct the "most primitive text attested." Therefore, in these books they decided to follow the tradition of the MT regardless of whether it represented the "most primitive text attested" or not.[49]

---

46. The Hebrew Old Testament Text Project (HOTTP, 1976–85) of the United Bible Societies was to provide aid to Bible translators on some six thousand passages that had proved troublesome. Its final report has appeared in Barthélemy, *Critique textuelle*.

47. Ibid., 1:*77. On this, see the fundamental essay by Hermann-Josef Stipp, "Das Verhältnis von Textkritik und Literarkritik in neueren alttestamentlichen Veröffentlichungen," *BZ* 34 (1990): 16–37.

48. Barthélemy, *Critique textuelle*, 1:*69.

49. Ibid., 1:*70.

However, the UBS Committee noted similar but less prominent literary innovations in other books as well. It had to conclude that stabilization and adaptation were tendencies working at the same time and with the same goal of preserving the identity of the text, but with different results.[50] As the moment of canonization could therefore no longer be determined on the basis of the stabilization of the text, while external sources did not allow a dating either—it is as much a long-term process as the stabilization of the text—the UBS Committee felt it had to abandon its attempt to establish the "most primitive text attested."[51] As an alternative, the committee decided, for traditional and religious reasons, to focus for all books on the Masoretic tradition, taking the proto-MT at the end of the first century CE as its point of reference.[52] It basically redefined textual criticism as "applied scholarship," its goal being dependent on the various areas of application: text edition; scholarly, popular, or liturgical Bible translations; or scholarly commentaries. Only in the latter should the relation between the traditional received text and the other literary and textual traditions be analyzed.[53]

The fact that canonization and stabilization were progressive developments that took quite some time implies that a sharp boundary between the two stages of literary and textual development cannot be drawn. The UBS Committee admits this, while on the other hand it maintains a division between textual criticism and literary criticism. This is visible in the principles of the *Biblia Hebraica Quinta* (*BHQ*), which is based on the committee's views.[54] The editors of the *BHQ* maintain that some textual data can be evaluated only with the methods of literary criticism, as they reflect a literary form of the book different from the MT. In the *BHQ* such

---

50. Ibid., 1:*95.

51. It is important to mention this, as in spite of the committee's clear discussion of the matter, the idea of a distinction between the canonical and precanonical manuscript evidence keeps coming up in recent publications; see, for instance, George J. Brooke, "The Qumran Scrolls and the Demise of the Distinction between Higher and Lower Criticism," in *New Directions in Qumran Studies: Proceedings of the Bristol Colloquium on the Dead Sea Scrolls* (ed. Jonathan G. Campbell, William John Lyons, and Lloyd K. Pietersen; London: T&T Clark, 2005), 26–42, esp. 31.

52. Barthélemy, *Critique textuelle*, 1:*107–11.

53. Ibid., *111–14.

54. See the editorial committee's general introduction in Adrian Schenker et al., eds., *General Introduction and Megilloth* (vol. 18 of *Biblia Hebraica: Quinta editione*; Stuttgart: Deutsche Bibelgesellschaft, 2004), xii, xvii.

details are not judged text-critically but are marked as "lit," meaning literary variants.

The question remains, when is a variant literary and when is it textual? The UBS and *BHQ* committees are not specific about this, but we could refer to Emanuel Tov, who discusses this issue from his point of view. Tov's working hypothesis in the second edition of his *Textual Criticism of the Hebrew Bible* was that "large-scale differences displaying a certain coherence were created at the level of the literary growth of the books by persons who considered themselves actively involved in the literary process of composition."[55] Though this sentence has not made it into the third edition, the criteria to distinguish literary variants from textual ones in this latest version of his handbook are still based on quantity (large-scale differences)[56] and quality (shared features or tendencies).[57] In Tov's opinion, small differences that do not form a pattern should be seen as created by "copyists-scribes" rather than by "authors/editors-scribes."[58] They would therefore belong to the area of textual criticism rather than literary criticism.

The criterion just formulated reminds us of Lagrange. The latter, however, saw the boundary at the moment of translating the text into Greek, and he admitted that later developments, though by definition textual, could actually belong to literary criticism. In the second edition of his handbook, Tov would seem to have been slightly more rigid. At that stage he contended that textual criticism had to aim at the literary composition that had been accepted as authoritative by Jewish tradition. The object of textual criticism was to reconstruct the "final authoritative copy."[59] In this earlier view, literary developments that took place before the final copy were relevant: these earlier editions of the text, such as the *Vorlagen* of the LXX, were considered authoritative in certain communities. However, he considered literary developments after the final copy irrelevant, as they would not be able to contribute to the literary and textual analysis of the final copy.[60]

In the opinion of the authors of the present volume the establishment by the UBS Committee and by Tov of the proto-MT as the point of refer-

---

55. Tov, *Textual Criticism* (2d ed.), 314.
56. Tov, *Textual Criticism*, 284.
57. Ibid., 325.
58. For the terminology, see ibid., 240, 283–84.
59. Tov, *Textual Criticism* (2d ed.), 177–79.
60. Ibid., 316–17. In the first edition, Tov also considered literary developments before the final copy irrelevant; see the discussion in ibid., 177–78.

ence or even the goal of textual criticism is based on practical, traditional, and religious grounds. Though eminently defendable within synagogue and church, this choice is eventually not satisfactory from a historical and scholarly point of view. It promotes one form of the text as more important than others on other than historical grounds, and it draws an artificial borderline between a stage of composition and a stage of transmission. The truth is, as the committee and Tov admit, that over a very long time these activities overlapped. Any approach that tries to reduce the text history to a two-stage model is therefore likely to fail. Given the fact that the way the text was reworked before the proto-MT is similar to the way this was done after, as Lagrange already recognized,[61] Tov's earlier decision not to deal with later expansions and editing is arbitrary.

In the meantime, Tov has published the third edition of his handbook, in which he gives up the exclusion of later literary developments. This is a major step forward. Moreover, he now also speaks of the finished composition or, for some books, a "series of consecutive determinative (original) editions" as the goal of textual criticism, thus fully abandoning the focus on the MT.[62] However, his point of view that the assumption of consecutive editions implies that these texts should not be subjected to text-critical judgment, an idea also reflected in *BHQ*'s approach to "lit" variants, creates several new problems.

1. The term "edition" comes with a number of associations that appear to be invalid. Thus we cannot be certain that the *Vorlagen* of the LXX were actually edited and published as an edition that was supposed to supersede earlier editions. The word "edition" suggests a purpose-oriented and coherent process, and we cannot be sure at all that this ever took place. As Zipora Talshir remarks: "The confrontation of revisions with their extant sources shows that revisers can hardly be accused of being systematic."[63]

---

61. See also Arie van der Kooij, "Textual Criticism of the Hebrew Bible: Its Aim and Method," in *Emanuel: Studies in the Hebrew Bible, Septuagint, and Dead Sea Scrolls in Honor of Emanuel Tov* (ed. Shalom M. Paul et al.; VTSup 94; Leiden: Brill, 2003), 729–39, esp. 731.

62. Tov, *Textual Criticism*, 167–69.

63. Zipora Talshir, "The Contribution of Diverging Traditions Preserved in the Septuagint to Literary Criticism of the Bible," in *VIII Congress of the International Organization for Septuagint and Cognate Studies, Paris 1992* (ed. Leonard Greenspoon and Olivier Munnich; SBLSCS 41; Atlanta: Scholars Press, 1995), 38.

Coherence or a clear tendency as a criterion for literary variants is therefore problematic.

2. The one clear example of a coherent and purposeful edition is the SP. However, as we have seen in chs. 1 and 3, the changes that answer to Tov's quantitative criterion happen to belong to the *Vorlage* of the SP and not to the coherent Samaritan edition. It is therefore also hard to maintain the scale of the differences as a criterion for literary variants.

3. The gradual differences between the MT, LXX, 4QSam^a, and Josephus suggest that the revising of texts happened much more frequently and haphazardly than the limited number of editions now accepted suggests,[64] and that the choice of a certain text for copying or translation purposes was much more based on what was accidentally available at a given time and place.

4. Tov himself admits that the distinction between textual and literary variants is hard to draw in practice. He calls this "a worrying aspect of post-modern textual criticism."[65]

5. The idea that literary variants cannot be judged is incorrect. There is no reason suddenly to deny the linear development that Tov assumes in most cases when he is evaluating readings as a textual critic. Moreover, interpolations and changes of wording have always been part of textual criticism.[66] The rules *lectio brevior potior* and *lectio difficilior probabilior* have actually been formulated mainly in view of these. Postmodernism has changed our attitude to such changes. Housman could still refer to an original reading as "the truth," and he mentions the fact that some called a manuscript with few interpolations "sincere."[67] He already criticized the latter use for its moral implications, and we no longer use such terms, as we have come to appreciate the importance of later developments of the text. But this does not mean that we cannot try to figure out which variant was earlier and which was later, or how one reading could have given rise

---

64. See also Karel van der Toorn, *Scribal Culture and the Making of the Hebrew Bible* (Cambridge, Mass.: Harvard University Press, 2007).

65. Tov, *Textual Criticism*, 324–26.

66. Brooke, "Qumran Scrolls," 28–29 with n. 12, makes a caricature of textual criticism, and in particular the search for the original text, when he says that it assumes that the vast majority of variants are the results of errors or misunderstandings. His reference to Housman's "Application of Thought" is taken out of context: intentional changes are discussed further on. See also West, *Textual Criticism*, 32.

67. Housman, "Application of Thought," 329, 331–32.

to the other. Our appreciation for later forms of the text, including the MT, should not make us abandon the study of its earlier stages and possible origin.[68]

With Stipp and Van der Kooij, we would therefore conclude that it is best to consider all available data.[69] We are in the luxurious position that for a certain period, we have textual data for literary developments. These data often allow us to establish a relative chronology, on the basis of which we can sketch the literary and textual development of the composition. Even though the earliest attainable stage is for us no longer the *only* truth, it remains relevant to search for it, as this is the starting point of all later development, and the stage that is the basis for the investigation of possible earlier literary development. Though from a theoretical point of view textual criticism deals with the transmission of the text and literary criticism with its literary development, for the period where transmission and composition overlap, these two methodologies share the same data and also the main instruments: reason and common sense. Therefore they cannot be separated.

---

68. Against Brooke, "Qumran Scrolls," 33–35, who, in a reasoning that we cannot follow, argues that if we accept his view and give up the quest for the original form of the text, we gain the ability to discern that in many instances the MT is actually not the most original form of the text.

69. Hermann-Josef Stipp, "Verhältnis"; idem, "Textkritik – Literarkritik – Textentwicklung: Überlegungen zur exegetischen Aspektsystematik," *ETL* 66 (1990): 143–59; Arie van der Kooij, "Textual Criticism of the Hebrew Bible," 730–31; idem, "Textual Criticism," in *The Oxford Handbook of Biblical Studies* (ed. Judith M. Lieu and J. W. Rogerson; Oxford: Oxford University Press, 2008), 579–90, esp. 583–84.

8
THE SEPTUAGINT PROVIDES EVIDENCE OF A LATE ADDITION IN THE MASORETIC TEXT: 1 KINGS 6:11–14

8.1. INTRODUCTION

Although the MT is a witness of high quality, it contains many readings that are probably secondary in relation to the text of other witnesses, the LXX in particular. The most conspicuous examples of such differences between the MT and the LXX are found throughout the book of Jeremiah,[1] but one can also find secondary readings of the MT in other parts of the Hebrew Bible. Many of these readings are not due to scribal mistakes but go back to deliberate changes that give insight into the late stages of editorial activity. Among them are not only marginal glosses and minor corrections of single words and phrases but some larger expansions as well. A clear case can be found in 1 Kgs 6. In this passage the comparison between the MT and the LXX shows that Deuteronomistic and priestly phraseology were added at a very late stage in the development of the text.

8.2. THE CONTEXT OF 1 KINGS 6:11–14 AND A THEORY OF LITERARY GROWTH

The account of the building of the temple in 1 Kgs 6 consists mainly of architectural descriptions. The text explains in detail how the structure of the temple was built and how its rich interior was crafted. However, the chapter also contains one paragraph that belongs to a completely different genre. Between the description of the building's outer structure (vv. 2–10) and the description of its interior (vv. 15–36), vv. 11–13 quote a divine oracle to Solomon.

---

1. See ch. 10.

THE SEPTUAGINT PROVIDES EVIDENCE OF A LATE ADDITION

1 Kgs 6:11–13

ויהי דבר יהוה אל שלמה לאמר
הבית הזה אשר אתה בנה אם תלך בחקתי ואת משפטי תעשה ושמרת את
כל מצותי ללכת בהם והקמתי את דברי אשר דברתי אל דוד אביך
ושכנתי בתוך בני ישראל ולא אעזב את עמי ישראל

[11] And the word of Yhwh came to Solomon: [12] "As for this house that you are building, if you will walk in my statutes, obey my ordinances, and keep all my commandments by walking in them, then I will establish my word with you, which I spoke to David your father. [13] And I will dwell among the Israelites and will not forsake my people Israel."

This oracle is only loosely connected to the surrounding text. It interrupts the architectural descriptions that are found before and afterward. These descriptions make no reference to the oracle and can be fully understood without knowledge of its content. In effect, the oracle is a disturbing digression in its immediate context. Thus, there is good reason to assume that the oracle was secondarily inserted into the account.[2] An additional argument is provided by the fact that, immediately after the oracle, a passage from the preceding text is resumed almost verbatim.

1 Kgs 6:9–15

ויבן את הבית ויכלהו ויספן את הבית גבים ושדרת בארזים
ויבן את היצוע על כל הבית חמש אמות קומתו ויאחז את הבית בעצי ארזים
ויהי דבר יהוה אל שלמה לאמר
הבית הזה אשר אתה בנה ...
ויבן שלמה את הבית ויכלהו
ויבן את קירות הבית מביתה בצלעות ארזים ...

[9] And he built the house and finished it. And he roofed the house with beams and planks of cedar. [10] He built the structure against the whole house, each story five cubits high, and supported the house with cedar beams.

---

2. E.g., Immanuel Benzinger, *Die Bücher der Könige* (KHC 9; Freiburg i. B.: Mohr Siebeck, 1899), 34; Martin Noth, *I Könige 1–16* (vol. 1 of *Könige*; BKAT 9.1; Neukirchen-Vluyn: Neukirchener Verlag, 1968), 118; J. Robinson, *The First Book of Kings* (Cambridge: Cambridge University Press, 1972), 76.

¹¹ And the word of Yhwh came to Solomon: ¹² "As for this house that you are building ... "
¹⁴ So Solomon built the house and finished it. ¹⁵ And he built the walls of the house on the inside with cedar boards ...

This phenomenon can be explained as a resumptive repetition (*Wiederaufnahme*), an editorial technique often assumed in literary and redaction criticism.³ It is probable that the editor who inserted the oracle also repeated the phrase of v. 9a after the addition. This was done in order to resume the text preceding the oracle and thus to connect the added passage more closely with the original context.⁴

8.3. Empirical Evidence for an Older Version in 1 Kings 6:10–15 LXX

The literary-critical arguments presented above are corroborated by empirical evidence. Several manuscripts of the LXX, among them Codex Vaticanus and the Lucianic group,⁵ do not contain vv. 11–14, while these

---

3. The technique was originally discussed by Curt Kuhl, "Die 'Wiederaufnahme'— ein literarkritisches Prinzip?" *ZAW* 64 (1952): 1–11.

4. E.g., Charles F. Burney, *Notes on the Hebrew Text of the Books of Kings: With Introduction and Appendix* (Oxford: Clarendon, 1903), 68; James A. Montgomery, *A Critical and Exegetical Commentary on the Books of Kings* (ed. Henry Snyder Gehman; ICC; Edinburgh: T&T Clark, 1967), 147.

According to Volkmar Fritz (*Das erste Buch der Könige* [ZBK 10.1; Zürich: Theologischer Verlag, 1996], 70–71) and Mordechai Cogan (*1 Kings: A New Translation with Introduction and Commentary* [AB 10; New York: Doubleday, 2001], 240), vv. 9b–10 were also secondarily inserted after v. 9a. This is in fact possible, since these passages give some additional architectural details only after the note about the completion of the temple. However, the *Wiederaufnahme* of v. 9a in v. 14 seems to be related to the addition of vv. 11–13, since these verses are missing in the LXX*, but vv. 9b–10 are attested in the LXX* (see below). Thus, if vv. 9b–10 are not original, they must have been added earlier than vv. 11–14. In this case, the *Wiederaufnahme* refers not simply to the last passage that occurs prior to the addition (i.e., v. 10b, which contains only an architectural detail) but to the last main statement that is found prior to the addition.

5. For Vaticanus, see Alan England Brooke, Norman McLean, and Henry St. John Thackeray, eds., *I and II Kings* (vol. 2.2 of *The Old Testament in Greek: According to the Text of Codex Vaticanus, Supplemented from Other Uncial Manuscripts, with a Critical Apparatus Containing the Chief Ancient Authorities for the Text of the Septuagint*; Cambridge: Cambridge University Press, 1930), 225; Alfred Rahlfs and Robert Hanhart, eds., *Septuaginta* (2d ed.; Stuttgart: Deutsche Bibelgesellschaft, 2006), 640. For

verses are attested in the rest of the LXX manuscripts. It is reasonable to assume that the shorter LXX version represents the original LXX, while the longer one is the result of a harmonization with the MT.

In the shorter LXX version of the chapter, the description of the outer structure of the temple (vv. 2–10) is immediately followed by the description of its interior (vv. 15–36). The oracle of vv. 11–13 and the repetition of the phrase about the completion of the building (v. 14) are lacking.

1 Kgs 6:9–15 LXX

⁹ καὶ ᾠκοδόμησεν τὸν οἶκον καὶ συνετέλεσεν αὐτόν· καὶ ἐκοιλοστάθμησεν τὸν οἶκον κέδροις. ¹⁰ καὶ ᾠκοδόμησεν τοὺς ἐνδέσμους δι' ὅλου τοῦ οἴκου, πέντε ἐν πήχει τὸ ὕψος αὐτοῦ, καὶ συνέσχεν τὸν ἔνδεσμον ἐν ξύλοις κεδρίνοις. ¹⁵ καὶ ᾠκοδόμησεν τοὺς τοίχους τοῦ οἴκου διὰ ξύλων κεδρίνων ...

⁹ So he built the house and finished it; and he made the ceiling of the house with cedars. ¹⁰ And he built the partitions through all the house, each five cubits high, and enclosed each partition with cedar boards.
¹⁵ And he built the walls of the house with cedar boards ...

1 Kgs 6:9–15 MT

ויבן את הבית ויכלהו ויספן את הבית גבים ושדרת בארזים
ויבן את היצוע על כל הבית חמש אמות קומתו ויאחז את הבית בעצי ארזים
ויהי דבר יהוה אל שלמה לאמר
הבית הזה אשר אתה בנה אם תלך בחקתי ואת משפטי תעשה ושמרת את כל מצותי ללכת בהם
והקמתי את דברי אתך אשר דברתי אל דוד אביך
ושכנתי בתוך בני ישראל ולא אעזב את עמי ישראל
ויבן שלמה את הבית ויכלהו
ויבן את קירות הבית מביתה בצלעות ארזים...

⁹ And he built the house and finished it. And he roofed the house with beams and planks of cedar. ¹⁰ He built the structure against the whole house, each story five cubits high, and supported the house with cedar beams.

---

the Lucianic group, see Natalio Fernández Marcos and José Ramón Busto Saiz, eds., *1–2 Reyes* (vol. 2 of *El texto antioqueno de la Biblia griega*; TECC 53; Madrid: Instituto de Filología, 1992), 17 (note that the verses are counted differently: v. 10 MT = v. 15 LXX and v. 15 MT = v. 16 LXX).

¹¹ <u>And the word of Yhwh came to Solomon:</u> ¹² <u>"As for this house that you are building, if you will walk in my statutes, obey my ordinances, and keep all my commandments by walking in them, then I will establish my word with you, which I spoke to David your father.</u> ¹³ <u>And I will dwell among the Israelites and will not forsake my people Israel."</u>
¹⁴ <u>So Solomon built the house and finished it.</u> ¹⁵ And he built the walls of the house on the inside with cedar boards …

The short text of the original LXX probably preserves an older stage of the literary history than does the MT. It is unlikely that the minus in the LXX is the result of the translation process, since it would be difficult to explain why the translator skipped these verses. It is more probable that vv. 11–14 were already lacking in the Hebrew *Vorlage* of the LXX. The divine oracle and the repeated passage about the completion of the temple seem to have been inserted only after the pre-MT diverged from the shared textual tradition with the *Vorlage* of the LXX.

There are no clear arguments that point in the opposite direction. Nothing speaks for a secondary omission in the *Vorlage* of the LXX. There are no apparent technical reasons that would have caused a scribe to skip such a substantial passage by mistake. A deliberate omission is also highly improbable, since the oracle of vv. 11–13 contains a statement of considerable theological weight. Since this statement is in accordance with other biblical traditions (see below), there is no reason why a later editor would have omitted it because of its content. In sum, there are good reasons to assume that the oldest text of the LXX provides empirical evidence of a secondary addition in the proto-MT.[6] This evidence points to a rather late stage of the literary development, since the *Vorlage* of the original LXX probably did not include the addition.

---

6. Montgomery, *Books of Kings*, 147; Frank H. Polak, "The LXX Account of Solomon's Reign: Revision and Ancient Recension" in *X Congress of the International Organization for Septuagint and Cognate Studies Oslo, 1998* (ed. Bernard A. Taylor; SBLSCS 51; Atlanta: Scholars Press, 2001), 145. Ernst Würthwein, *Die Bücher der Könige: 1. Kön. 1–16* (ATD 11.1; Göttingen: Vandenhoeck & Ruprecht, 1977), 65, takes only vv. 11–13 as secondary while assuming that v. 14 (and not v. 9) was part of the original source.

8.4. The Literary Horizon of the Addition and Its Phraseology

It is evident that the oracle of 1 Kgs 6:11–13 refers back to the famous oracle of Nathan and, in particular, to the promise of an eternal dynasty that is included in this oracle. The connection with 2 Sam 7:13 is apparent: הוא יבנה בית לשמי וכננתי את כסא ממלכתו עד עולם ("He shall build a house for my name, and I will establish the throne of his kingship forever").[7] Despite the connection, 1 Kgs 6:11–13 may not be very closely linked to this promise, for the phraseology differs.[8] The motif of obedience to the commandments and the promise of divine presence among the people seem to refer to other textual and theological traditions.

The phrases that mention the condition of obedience to the divine commandments have a close parallel in the admonition that David gives to his son and successor Solomon immediately before his death in 1 Kgs 2:3–4 (see also 9:6; 11:34). The phraseology of this text, which is usually designated as Deuteronomistic,[9] clearly stands in the background of 1 Kgs 6:11–13, as shown by the following parallels.

1 Kgs 2:3–4

ושמרת את משמרת יהוה אלהיך ללכת בדרכיו לשמר חקתיו מצותיו ומשפטיו ועדותיו ...
למען יקים יהוה את דברו אשר דבר עלי לאמר אם ישמרו בניך את דרכם ללכת לפני באמת ...

³ And you shall keep the charge of Yhwh your God, by walking in his ways and keeping his statutes, his commandments, his ordinances, and his testimonies … ⁴ that Yhwh will establish his word that he spoke concerning me: "If your sons take heed to their way, to walk before me in faithfulness … "

1 Kgs 6:12

אם תלך בחקתי ואת משפטי תעשה ושמרת את כל מצותי ללכת בהם והקמתי את דברי אתך אשר דברתי אל דוד אביך.

---

7. E.g., Burney, *Notes*, 69; Würthwein, *1. Kön. 1–16*, 65.

8. Noth, *Könige*, 118.

9. E.g., Timo Veijola, *Die ewige Dynastie: David und die Entstehung seiner Dynastie nach der deuteronomistischen Darstellung* (AASF B.193; Helsinki: Academia Scientiarum Fennica, 1975), 27–29.

If you will walk in my statutes, obey my ordinances, and keep all my commandments by walking in them, then I will establish my word with you, which I spoke to David your father.

However, 1 Kgs 6:11–13 may also be influenced by priestly phraseology. Although the phrase אם תלך בחקתי ואת משפטי תעשה ("If you will walk in my statutes and obey my ordinances") uses Deuteronomistic terminology, it is at the same time very similar to the opening of the great admonition at the end of the so-called Holiness Code in Lev 26 (v. 3: אם בחקתי תלכו ואת מצותי תשמרו ועשיתם אתם, "If you walk in my statutes and keep my commandments and obey them"). Furthermore, the promise ושכנתי בתוך בני ישראל ("I will dwell among the Israelites"; 1 Kgs 6:13) is quoted verbatim from Exod 29:45 (cf. Exod 25:8; Num 5:3; 35:34).[10]

Consequently, the author of 1 Kgs 6:11–13 used traditional Deuteronomistic and priestly language in striking density,[11] which may attest to the relatively late stage of this kind of editorial activity.[12] On the basis of the parallels with several passages, it would also seem that the author of vv. 11–14 was familiar not only with the book of Kings but also with a Pentateuch that already included at least parts of the priestly texts in Exodus and Leviticus.

8.5. Conclusions and Methodological Consequences

The comparison between the oldest text of the LXX and the MT in 1 Kgs 6 provides empirical evidence of late editorial activity. It can reasonably be assumed that the plus of 1 Kgs 6:11–14 MT was inserted into the proto-MT only after the Hebrew *Vorlage* of the LXX diverged from this textual tradition. Even during such a late stage of the literary development, an editor was able to create a new passage from traditional Deuteronomis-

---

10. Cogan, *1 Kings*, 241.

11. For a comprehensive analysis of the phraseology of 1 Kgs 6:11–13, see Burney, *Notes*, 68–69.

12. Hence the theory of a mere Deuteronomistic origin of the passage, as proposed by some commentators (e.g., Burke O. Long, *1 Kings: With an Introduction to Historical Literature* [FOTL 9; Grand Rapids: Eerdmans, 1984], 85; Simon J. DeVries, *1 Kings* [WBC 12; Waco, Tex.: Word, 1985], 93; Fritz, *Erste Buch der Könige*, 71; Marvin A. Sweeney, *I and II Kings: A Commentary* [OTL; Louisville, Ky.: Westminster John Knox, 2007], 109), is improbable.

tic and priestly formulations. The addition was later adopted in nearly all other witnesses, including many Greek manuscripts.

This example shows that the classic methodology of literary or redaction criticism can provide reliable results. The fact that the oracle of vv. 11–13 was secondarily inserted could easily be discerned by virtue of the repetition of v. 9 in v. 14 even without a glance at the empirical evidence that is extant in this case. The digressive context of vv. 11–13 would further corroborate the assumption that we are dealing with an addition. The shorter version of the original LXX confirms an assumption that would probably be made by literary or redaction critics, even if this evidence were not available. The classic criteria of a narrative being interrupted by a digressive theme and resumptive repetition would turn out to be viable in 1 Kgs 6:11–14.

9
From Small Additions to Rewriting in the Story about the Burning of Jerusalem

9.1. Introduction

The burning of Jerusalem is portrayed in five different biblical passages: 2 Kgs 25:8–12; Jer 52:12–16; Jer 39:8–10; 2 Chr 36:19–20; and 1 Esd 1:52–54. Three of the passages contain both the Hebrew and Greek versions, whereas Jer 39:4–13 is transmitted only in Hebrew and 1 Esd 1:52–54 only in Greek.[1] Despite some significant differences among the accounts, the word-for-word parallels imply, beyond any question, that all of the passages are literarily dependent. Moreover, there are no features or details in any of the passages that necessitate an external source. The differences are very probably due to literary changes, because the motive for most of the changes can be deduced from the general conceptions of the authors. For example, the Chronicler's theological conceptions have shaped the new account in relation to the donor text. There are also many technical reasons that reveal how and why the text was changed. It is very likely that 2 Kgs 25:8–12 and Jer 52:12–16 preserve the oldest account of the events, whereas Jer 39:8–10 and 2 Chr 36:19–20 are later developments of one or both of these two passages.[2]

---

1. Although other translations and versions could shed more light on the editorial processes of the Hebrew Bible, it lies beyond this investigation to take them into account here. The Greek versions are significant because they contain some readings that are probably older than the Hebrew text.

2. Clearly, this does not mean that 2 Kgs 25:8–12 and Jer 52:12–16 should be an authentic eyewitness account of the events concerning the burning of Jerusalem. It is probable that these texts also have a literary prehistory, but its development is not preserved in the witnesses.

Because of the high number of different accounts of the same event, a comparison of the passages is especially fruitful for understanding the literary development of texts in various different textual and literary traditions. They provide significant documented evidence for various editorial processes in the formative period of these texts. In the following, the most illustrative intentional editorial changes will be discussed, whereas smaller and unintentional changes will be left out of this investigation.³

9.2. The Addition of the Tearing Down of the Walls in 2 Kings 25:8–12

The Hebrew and Greek texts of 2 Kgs 25:8–12 contain a significant difference that is the result of an intentional change. With the exception of the expression ὁ ἀρχιμάγειρος ("captain of the guard"), Codex Vaticanus lacks a parallel to v. 10. The MT contains a large plus that describes the tearing down of Jerusalem's walls. Most other Greek manuscripts⁴ generally follow the MT in this verse, but it is probable that they have been harmonized after the Masoretic reading.⁵

2 Kgs 25:8–11 MT

בא נבוזראדן רב־טבחים עבד מלך־בבל ירושלם
וישרף את־בית־יהוה ואת־בית המלך ואת כל־בתי ירושלם ואת־כל־בית
גדול שרף באש
ואת־חומת ירושלם סביב נתצו כל־חיל כשדים אשר רב־טבחים
ואת יתר העם הנשארים בעיר ואת־הנפלים אשר נפלו על־המלך בבל ואת
יתר ההמון הגלה נבוזראדן רב־טבחים

---

3. For example, Jer 52:15 is missing in the Greek version. Although some scholars have suggested that the Greek preserves the more original text, it is more probable that we are dealing with an accidental omission in the Greek version caused by haplography (compare vv. 15 and 16: ומדלות, "from the poorest"). Both views have been represented; see William McKane, *Commentary on Jeremiah 1–25* (vol. 1 of *A Critical and Exegetical Commentary on Jeremiah*; ICC; Edinburgh: T&T Clark, 1986), 1368–69, for a review.

4. Including the Lucianic group boc₂e₂.

5. Note that in v. 10 the English passive is used although the Hebrew uses the active *qal*. This passive is used in the translation in order to better reflect the word order of the Hebrew and especially the order between the addition and the original text of the verse.

THE BURNING OF JERUSALEM   111

⁸ Nebuzaradan the captain of the guard, a servant of the king of Babylon, came to Jerusalem. ⁹ He burned the temple of Yhwh, and the king's house, and all the houses of Jerusalem; every ~~great~~ house he burned with fire. ¹⁰ The walls of Jerusalem were torn down by all the army of the Chaldeans who were with the captain of the guard. ¹¹ And Nebuzaradan the captain of the guard exiled the rest of the people who were left in the city, and the deserters who had defected to the king of Babylon, and the rest of the multitude.

2 Kgs 25:8–11 Codex Vaticanus

⁸ ἦλθεν Ναβουζαρδαν ὁ ἀρχιμάγειρος ἑστὼς ἐνώπιον βασιλέως Βαβυλῶνος εἰς Ιερουσαλημ. ⁹ καὶ ἐνέπρησε τὸν οἶκον κυρίου καὶ τὸν οἶκον τοῦ βασιλέως καὶ πάντας τοὺς οἴκους Ιερουσαλημ, καὶ πᾶν οἶκον ἐνέπρησεν ¹⁰ ὁ ἀρχιμάγειρος. ¹¹ καὶ τὸ περισσὸν τοῦ λαοῦ τὸ καταλειφθὲν ἐν τῇ πόλει καὶ τοὺς ἐμπεπτωκότας, οἳ ἐνέπεσον πρὸς βασιλέα Βαβυλῶνος, καὶ τὸ λοιπὸν τοῦ στηρίγματος μετῆρεν Ναβουζαρδαν ὁ ἀρχιμάγειρος.

⁸ Nebuzaradan the captain of the guard, a servant of the king of Babylon, came to Jerusalem. ⁹ He burned the temple of the Lord, and the king's house, and all the houses of Jerusalem; every house (was) burned down ¹⁰ (by) the captain of the guard. ¹¹ And Nebuzaradan the captain of the guard exiled the rest of the people who were left in the city, and the deserters who had defected to the king of Babylon, and the rest of the multitude.

The parallel passages in Jer 39:8–10 and 52:12–16, however, include a parallel to the MT of 2 Kgs 25:10. Although an accidental omission in Codex Vaticanus or in its *Vorlage* cannot be completely excluded, it is more probable that it preserves the more original text and that v. 10 of the MT text is a secondary addition. This is suggested by the following considerations.

1. There are no apparent technical reasons in the Hebrew text, such as homoioteleuton, that would have provided a basis for an accidental omission.

2. The syntax of the sentence in v. 10 is awkward with the expression אשר רב טבחים ("who were with the captain of the guard"). It is probable that the peculiar use of אשר is an attempt to integrate the expansion with the older text.

3. The part missing in the Greek version forms a separate event with a separate subject. An accidental omission often confuses the text, but here one would have to assume that the accidental omission cut precisely a sep-

arate unit, the tearing down of the walls, out of the text. Although this is always possible, it is not very likely.

4. It is difficult to see any reason for its intentional omission in the Greek version. Since the Babylonians are already described as destroying all houses, the temple, and the royal palace, it would be illogical that a later editor would have wanted to omit the destruction of the walls.

5. The main actor against the Judeans in vv. 9 and 11 is Nebuzaradan, captain of the guard, but in v. 10 it is the Babylonian army. According to v. 9, Nebuzaradan burned the temple, naturally meaning that he ordered it to be done. This verse does not make it explicit that he had someone do it for him, although it is implied. The same applies to v. 11, where he is said to have taken away the Jerusalemites to exile. The author of these verses referred only to the main official who was responsible for the actions and did not find it necessary to mention who executed his orders. In contrast, v. 10 makes it explicit that the actual executors of the measures were the Babylonian soldiers. The author of v. 10 seems to have had a slightly different perspective than the author of vv. 9 and 11, which suggests that v. 10 is a later addition.

6. Connected to the previous point, the verbs in vv. 9 and 11 are in the singular, while in v. 10 the plural is used. The use of the plural in v. 10 contrasts with Nebuzaradan, mentioned at the end of the verse. The conflicting number implies later editorial activity.

Because the reading in Codex Vaticanus is supported by so many considerations rising out of the content and grammar, it probably preserves the more original text. This would mean that the MT and the other textual witnesses following it contain a later addition. The addition was then later adopted by the other witnesses that used 2 Kgs 25 as a source, including the parallel texts and other Greek versions of 2 Kgs 25:10.[6]

---

6. One should further note that in Codex Vaticanus 2 Kgs 25:8–12 does not form a very fluent text. However, this is not an argument to assume that this Greek version is younger than the Hebrew version, since the Hebrew version is also not a fluent text. For example, the verb "burning" is repeated in a disturbing way. These problems are probably caused by earlier editing, which is not reflected in the witnesses. The final part of the burning (ואת־כל־בית [גדול] שרף באש רב־טבחים, "and the captain of the guard burned every [great] house with fire") may have been added later. In addition to the superfluous repetition of the verb, the subject is unnecessarily repeated as well. Moreover, after it has been said that all the houses of Jerusalem were burned, it is needless to add that all the large houses were burned. The earlier editing explains

This example shows how details or even an entire event, although a short text in this case, may have been added to a passage. While the older text does not refer to the destruction of the walls at all, the addition had considerable impact on the final text and on our later understanding of what happened to Jerusalem in 586 BCE. The text shows a typical development of biblical texts. Through later additions, a catastrophic event was made more and more severe. As the older text described the destruction of the royal palace, the temple, and all the houses, the destruction of the walls would be a logical next step to increase the destruction even further. A later editor may also have wanted to stress the complete nature of the destruction and to show that Jerusalem had become uninhabitable and indefensible. This would be in line with other texts that emphasize that Jerusalem became uninhabited, or that even form a theological motif that Jerusalem should remain empty.[7] Besides possible theological reasons, the editor who added v. 10 may have seen or otherwise known that the walls of Jerusalem were in ruins and, on account of v. 9, he deduced that the destruction must have been caused by the Babylonians. He may also have deduced it from the older text. In any case, there is no reason to assume that the destruction of the walls is based on an external literary source. If there had been a further source, one would expect it to have preserved other information as well, not merely the destruction of the walls. It is more probable that a later editor increased the destruction of Jerusalem for theological and other reasons.

Based on the Hebrew version, which now seems to be secondary in 2 Kgs 25:10, many scholars have assumed that the destruction of the walls by the Babylonian army is a historical event,[8] and the view is also reflected

---

the awkward text in both Greek and Hebrew. If one would assume that the Greek is secondary, one would still have to explain the awkwardness in both versions.

7. Jer 25:8–14 in particular develops the idea that because of the sins of the Israelites the country will become desolate and empty for seventy years, during which time they will have to serve the king of Babylon. This idea is further developed in 2 Chr 36:20–21, which refers to the resting of the land for seventy years until it has made up for its Sabbaths.

8. Many scholars (e.g., Gwilym H. Jones, *1 and 2 Kings* [2 vols.; NCBC; Grand Rapids: Eerdmans, 1984], 2:643–44) have sought to validate the historicity of the passage by seeking archaeological and other evidence for it. In his recent commentary, Marvin A. Sweeney (*I and II Kings* [OTL; Louisville: Westminster John Knox, 2007], 468) implies that the events described in 2 Kgs 25:8–12, including the destruction of the walls, are historical. According to Ernst Würthwein (*Die Bücher der Könige:*

in many histories of Israel.⁹ It is also noteworthy that quite a number of commentaries make no reference to the missing v. 10 in Codex Vaticanus.¹⁰ If the verse is recognized as a later addition, the historicity of the event becomes considerably less likely,¹¹ and our picture of the destruction of Jerusalem will be different. This case demonstrates the significance of recognizing additions if we intend to use the biblical text to reconstruct ancient history.

9.3. The Addition of the Year of King Nebuchadnezzar in Jeremiah 52:12 MT

According to the MT in Jer 52:12, Nebuzaradan came to Jerusalem in the nineteenth year of King Nebuchadnezzar, but the reference to the year of his coming is missing in the original Greek version.¹²

Jer 52:12 MT

ובחדש החמישי בעשור לחדש
היא שנת תשע־עשרה שנה למלך נבוכדראצר מלך־בבל
בא נבוזראדן רב־טבחים עמד לפני מלך־בבל בירושלם

---

1. Kön. 17–2. Kön. 25 [ATD 11.2; Göttingen: Vandenhoeck & Ruprecht, 1984], 476–78), 2 Kgs 25:10 is part of the original text that derives from the annals, which also implies that the event is historical. They all fail to recognize that the verse is missing in most Greek manuscripts.

9. See, e.g., J. Alberto Soggin, *An Introduction to the History of Israel and Judah* (3d ed.; London: SCM Press, 1999), 280–81; and J. Maxwell Miller and John H. Hayes, *A History of Ancient Israel and Judah* (2d ed.; Louisville, Ky.: Westminster John Knox, 2006), 478.

10. Thus, among many others, John Gray, *I and II Kings* (OTL; Philadelphia: Westminster John Knox, 1963), 698–99; Jones, *1 and 2 Kings*, 643–44; Sweeney, *I and II Kings*, 468. However, Immanuel Benzinger, *Die Bücher der Könige* (KHC 9; Freiburg i. B.: Mohr Siebeck, 1899), 199, notes that the verse is missing in Codex Vaticanus, but instead of assuming that it represents the original text, he reconstructs the verse after Jer 52.

11. Although one cannot exclude the possibility that some later additions contain historical information, in this case theological and other reasons for the addition are more probable.

12. Some Greek manuscripts follow the MT (e.g., Codex Sinaiticus and the Lucianic manuscripts), but this is very probably a later development influenced by the MT or the parallel in 2 Kgs 25:8.

> And in the fifth month, on the tenth day of the month—it was the nineteenth year of King Nebuchadnezzar, king of Babylon—Nebuzaradan the captain of the guard, who served the king of Babylon, came to Jerusalem.

Jer 52:12 LXX

> Καὶ ἐν μηνὶ πέμπτῳ δεκάτῃ τοῦ μηνὸς ἦλθεν Ναβουζαρδαν ὁ ἀρχιμάγειρος ὁ ἑστηκὼς κατὰ πρόσωπον τοῦ βασιλέως Βαβυλῶνος εἰς Ιερουσαλημ.

> And in the fifth month, on the tenth day of the month, Nebuzaradan the captain of the guard, who served the king of Babylon, came to Jerusalem.

The plus is also found in both Greek and Hebrew versions of 2 Kgs 25:8. It is probable that the Greek of Jer 52:12 represents the oldest reading and that the reference to the year is a later addition in the other witnesses. This is suggested by the following considerations. The plus is grammatically awkward, because it breaks the main sentence and the connection between the months and the verb/subject: ובחדש החמישי ... בא נבוזראדן ("And in the fifth month ... Nebuzaradan came"). It would seem to function like a parenthesis to the main sentence. The use of the word היא also corroborates the suspicion that we are dealing with a later interruption to the original text. Accordingly, many scholars have assumed that the reference to the year is secondary.[13] The addition may have been influenced by 2 Kgs 24:12, which refers to the year when Jehoiachin was imprisoned, or by Jer 32:1, which refers to the eighteenth year of the king, when the Babylonian army began to besiege Jerusalem.[14] A later editor may have wanted to correlate the events to the same chronology and therefore added a reference to the year when Jerusalem was conquered.[15] Such expansions that add chronological details or connect a passage with a chronological development of a wider composition are common in the Hebrew Bible.[16]

---

13. Thus already Bernhard Duhm, *Das Buch Jeremia* (KHC 11; Tübingen: J. C. B. Mohr, 1901), 378, and many following him (e.g., McKane, *Jeremiah 1–25*, 1366).

14. Thus McKane, *Jeremiah 1–25*, 1366.

15. Thus many; e.g., Duhm, *Jeremia*, 378. Jehoiachin was imprisoned in the eighth year of Nebuchadnezzar's reign (2 Kgs 24:12). Zedekiah ruled eleven years after Jehoiachin (2 Kgs 24:18), which would mean that his rule ended in the nineteenth year of the Babylonian king.

16. For example, in Ezra-Nehemiah originally independent stories or passages

For the reconstruction of Israel's history, it is important to recognize such additions, because the chronological framework of a composition may primarily serve compositional purposes and obscure historical developments. In this example, one should not rely on the dating of the destruction of Jerusalem on the basis of 2 Kgs 25:8 and Jer 52:12 but instead argue for dating on the basis of other considerations.[17]

9.4. New Rendering of the Burning of Jerusalem in Jeremiah 39:8–9

Jeremiah 39:8–10 differs considerably from 2 Kgs 25:8–11 and Jer 52:12–15. The relationship between Jer 39 and Jer 52/2 Kgs 25 is complicated and debated, and it is not possible to provide a comprehensive solution here. Nevertheless, most scholars assume that Jer 39:8–9 is dependent on 2 Kgs 25:8–11 and Jer 52:12–15,[18] a view that seems probable. The passage is therefore illustrative of the formation of new passages that were extracted from older texts. Jeremiah 39:8–9 contains a new account describing the conquest of Jerusalem but was composed primarily to provide a wider historical setting for Jeremiah's release. It should further be noted that Jer 39:4–12/13, which is completely missing in the LXX, is probably a later addition to Jer 39.[19] Our interest lies in vv. 8–9 and especially in the illustrative changes made in these verses in relation to the source text(s) in 2 Kgs 25:8–11 and/or Jer 52:12–15.

---

were knitted together by placing them within the same chronologically developing story. Many of the references to dates in Ezra-Nehemiah are later additions.

17. Unfortunately the Babylonian Chronicle breaks off after the eleventh year; see A. K. Grayson, *Assyrian and Babylonian Chronicles* (Winona Lake, Ind.: Eisenbrauns, 2000), 99–102.

18. As noted by McKane, *Jeremiah 1–25*, 982–83: "There is general agreement (Giesebrecht, Duhm, Cornill, Streane, Peake, H. Schmidt, Rudolph, Weiser, Hyatt, Bright, Nicholson) that vv. 1–2 and 4–10 [of Jer 39] have been extracted from Jer 52/2 Kgs 25."

19. See, e.g., ibid., 983. Some scholars (e.g., Robert P. Carroll, *Jeremiah: A Commentary* [OTL; Philadelphia: Westminster, 1986], 691) assume that these verses are missing in the Greek version because of a homoioteleuton, but the accidental omission of such a large section would be unlikely.

2 Kgs 25:8–11 (//Jer 52:12–15)

ובחדש החמישי בשבעה לחדש ... בא נבוזראדן רב־טבחים עבד מלך־בבל
ירושלם
וישרף את־בית־יהוה ואת־בית המלך ואת כל־בתי ירושלם ואת־כל־בית
גדול שרף באש
ואת־חומת ירושלם סביב נתצו כל־חיל כשדים אשר רב־טבחים
ואת יתר העם הנשארים בעיר ואת־הנפלים אשר נפלו על־המלך בבל ואת
יתר ההמון
הגלה נבוזראדן רב־טבחים

⁸ And in the fifth month, on the seventh day of the month ... Nebuzaradan the captain of the guard, a servant of the king of Babylon, came to Jerusalem. ⁹ He burned the temple of Yhwh, and the king's house, and all the houses of Jerusalem; every great house he burned with fire. ¹⁰ All the army of the Chaldeans who were with the captain of the guard tore down the walls of Jerusalem.¹¹ And Nebuzaradan the captain of the guard exiled the rest of the people who were left in the city, and the deserters who had defected to the king of Babylon, and the rest of the multitude.

Jer 39:8–9 MT

ואת־בית המלך ואת־בית העם שרפו הכשדים באש ואת־חמות ירושלם
נתצו ואת יתר העם הנשארים בעיר ואת־הנפלים אשר נפלו עליו
ואת יתר העם הנשארים הגלה נבוזר־אדן רב־טבחים בבל

⁸ The king's house and the houses of the people the Chaldeans burned with fire and tore down the walls of Jerusalem. ⁹ And Nebuzaradan the captain of the guard exiled the rest of the people who were left in the city, and the deserters who had defected to him, and the rest of the people who were left to Babylon.

The reference to the coming of Nebuzaradan to Jerusalem in 2 Kgs 25:8 and Jer 52:12 does not find a parallel in Jer 39, although Nebuzaradan is otherwise mentioned in Jer 39 (in vv. 9, 10, 11, and 13). The omission is probably intentional as the information is not necessary for the passage and could even be seen to distract from the main event, the destruction of Jerusalem. Nebuzaradan is properly introduced as the captain of the guard in the first verse where he is mentioned, in Jer 39:9, and the resulting text does not need any further introduction or reference to his coming to Jerusalem; it is evident from the context that he was there.[20] The date mentioned in 2 Kgs 25:8 is also less important in Jer 39 than in the parallel passages because the temple has been omitted in Jer 39 (see below). The date of the destruction of the temple would be of interest to many authors and editors during the Second Temple period, whereas the destruction of the palace would probably be less important.[21] These two examples show that in extracting the text from 2 Kgs 24–25 and Jer 52, the author of Jer 39 left out much information that was unnecessary for his compositional purposes.

According to 2 Kgs 25:9 and Jer 52:13, the Babylonians burned the temple of Yhwh, the palace of the king, and the houses of the people. Apart from changes to the structure and word order of the sentence, the most prominent change in Jer 39:8 is the omission of a reference to the burning of Yhwh's temple. Jeremiah 39 reports only the burning of the king's palace and the houses of the people (changed from כל־בתי ירושלם ואת־כל־בית גדול, "all the houses of Jerusalem and every great house," to ואת־בית העם, "and the houses of the people"). The minus in Jer 39:8 may be part of a systematic omission of all references to the temple and things related to it in this chapter and its immediate context. For example, there is no reference to the cult vessels or other items that, according to 2 Kgs 25:13–17 and Jer 52:17–23, were taken from the temple. Although one should not completely rule out the possibility that all references to the temple in the parallel passages are later additions,[22] it is more probable that the author of Jer

---

20. Note that עליו of v. 9 would now appear to refer to Nebuzaradan before he is introduced later in the sentence. However, the source text in 2 Kgs 25 and Jer 52 shows that the reference was originally to the king of Babylon. The confusion arose when ואת־הנפלים אשר נפלו על־המלך בבל was changed to ואת־הנפלים אשר נפלו עליו in Jer 39:9.

21. For example, Josephus (*Ant.* 10.8.5) writes on the destruction of the temple: "Now the temple was burnt four hundred and seventy years, six months, and ten days after it was built. It was then one thousand and sixty-two years, six months, and ten days from the departure out of Egypt; and from the deluge to the destruction of the temple, the whole interval was one thousand nine hundred and fifty-seven years, six months, and ten days; but from the generation of Adam, until this befell the temple, there were three thousand five hundred and thirteen years, six months, and ten days; so great was the number of years hereto belonging" (trans. William Whiston, *The Works of Flavius Jospehus* [London: Baynes & Son, 1825], 411).

22. 2 Kgs 25:13–17 may be a later addition in any case—note the continuity from v. 12 to v. 18. The burning of the temple may be the only reference to the temple in the

39 intentionally left out all references to the destruction of Yhwh's temple. The motive for the omission is, however, not entirely clear. One possibility is that the author merely assumed everyone knew that the temple had been destroyed with the destruction of Jerusalem and therefore a brief reference to the destruction of the city sufficed. The author's compositional aims also may not have been focused on the temple, so that it could have been left out. Some scholars have suggested that the reference to the temple may have been accidentally omitted in Jer 39:8 (homoiarchon; see אֶת־בֵּית־יְהוָה וְאֶת־בֵּית הַמֶּלֶךְ, "the house of Yhwh and the house of the king"),[23] but the other abridgements suggest that Jer 39 more likely provides a deliberately shortened version of the events.[24] This accords with the other changes discussed above. In addition, Jer 39 lacks any reference to the robbing of the temple, while 2 Kgs 25:13–17 and Jer 52:17–23 describe it relatively extensively.

Jeremiah 39:8 shows a case where an editor or author omitted a reference to an important event because it may not have fitted into his wider compositional and narrative plan. A reference to the destruction of the temple would have necessitated a more comprehensive explanation of the event, which the author of the chapter may have been unwilling to do because it would have digressed from the main focus of his story. Although we may never fully understand the exact motives of the author, Jer 39:8 is an example where a source text was used selectively to form a new passage. Behind the changes are probably compositional and theological considerations as well as the motive to shorten the text.

9.5. Extensive Rewriting in 2 Chronicles 36:18–20

The Chronicler's version of the burning of Jerusalem differs considerably from all other versions, but the extensive parallels suggest that 2 Kgs 25:9–11 was the main source of the Chronicler. Theological conceptions can be seen behind the changes.

---

entire passage. Whether this could be a later addition as well would have to be investigated separately, but in a different context.

23. Thus, e.g., Wilhelm Rudolph, *Jeremia* (3d ed.; HAT 12; Tübingen: Mohr Siebeck, 1968), 208–9.

24. Thus many; e.g., already Duhm, *Jeremia*, 311.

2 Kgs 25:9–11

וישרף את־בית־יהוה ואת־בית המלך ואת כל־בתי ירושלם ואת־כל־בית
גדול שרף באש
ואת־חומת ירושלם סביב נתצו כל־חיל כשדים אשר רב־טבחים
ואת יתר העם הנשארים בעיר ואת־הנפלים אשר נפלו על־המלך בבל
ואת יתר ההמון הגלה נבוזראדן רב־טבחים

[9] ~~He~~ burned the temple of Yhwh, ~~and the king's house, and all the houses of Jerusalem~~; every great house he burned with fire. [10] ~~All the army of the Chaldeans who were with the captain of the guard~~ tore down the walls of Jerusalem. [11] And Nebuzaradan the captain of the guard exiled the rest of the people who were left in the city, and the deserters who had defected to the king of Babylon, and the rest of the multitude.

2 Chr 36:18–20

וכל כלי בית האלהים הגדלים והקטנים ואצרות בית יהוה ואצרות המלך
ושריו הכל הביא בבל
וישרפו את־בית האלהים וינתצו את חומת ירושלם וכל־ארמנותיה שרפו
באש וכל־כלי מחמדיה להשחית
ויגל השארית מן־החרב אל־בבל
ויהיו־לו ולבניו לעבדים עד־מלך מלכות פרס

[18] All the vessels of the temple of God, large and small, and the treasures of the house of Yhwh, and the treasures of the king and of his officials, all these he brought to Babylon. [19] They burned the temple of God and tore down the walls of Jerusalem, and all its palaces they burned with fire, and they destroyed all its precious vessels. [20] He took into exile in Babylon those who had escaped from the sword, and they became servants to him and to his sons until the establishment of the kingdom of Persia.

Whereas the author of Jer 39:8–10 omitted all references to the temple, the Chronicler concentrated his attention on the temple, as shown by the plusses in his version. In this respect, the passages are, in part, developed in two opposite directions. In the Chronicler's account, the burning of the temple is mentioned separately, followed by the destruction of the walls. There is no reference to the burning of all the houses of Jerusalem, while the burning of the royal palace and the great houses, now relocated after the destruction of the walls, is rendered with a general reference to the burning of all the palaces (כל־ארמנותיה). This is probably a free rendering of

בית המלך ("the king's house") and בית גדול ("[every] great house"), which are mentioned in the source text. These changes are well in line with the Chronicler's focused attention on the temple throughout his work. Before v. 19, where the burnings are reported, the Chronicler also added a reference to the robbing of the temple vessels (v. 18), which in the source text is located after the deportation of the people, in 2 Kgs 25:13–17. The Chronicler's story is more logical, because the temple would evidently have to be robbed before it was burned.[25] These changes highlight the Chronicler's interest in the temple and suggest that he revised the story to be more consistent, especially in matters relating to the temple. What happened to the temple had high priority, whereas most other issues were less important and could be omitted or shortened accordingly. The Chronicler also added a reference to the precious items of the palaces that were destroyed, but this information may be an analogy to the items of the temple and thus be the Chronicler's own invention.

The Chronicler used 2 Kgs 25 as the source text but took considerable liberties in relocating words, sentences, and passages to fit his own compositional and ideological aims. He could also omit parts of the older text and add new details if ideological and other considerations so required. Theological conceptions in particular can be seen as the main motive behind most of the changes, and similar liberties on the micro-level may be observed throughout the Chronicler's text in relation to his sources. Although the nature of the Chronicler's account may be different from the parallel accounts in 2 Kgs 25 and Jer 52, the comparison of the new text with its source reveals how a donor text could develop and how much it could be changed when used in a new composition.

Some scholars have tried to explain the differences between Chronicles and its sources by assuming that it was created as a kind of theological commentary or interpretation of 1–2 Kings.[26] Although space does

---

25. The inconsistency in 2 Kgs 25 and Jer 52 in this respect may imply that the robbing of the temple vessels in 2 Kgs 25:13–17 is a later addition. Nevertheless, among others, Würthwein, *1. Kön. 17–2. Kön. 25*, 477–78, assumes that at least 2 Kgs 25:13–14 is part of the pre-Deuteronomistic text from the annals.

26. Thus many, perhaps most prominently Thomas Willi, *Die Chronik als Auslegung: Untersuchung zur literarischen Gestaltung der historischen Überlieferung Israels* (Göttingen: Vandenhoeck & Ruprecht, 1972), *passim*, esp. 49–52. See also Julius Wellhausen, *Prolegomena zur Geschichte Israels* (3d ed.; Berlin: Georg Reimer, 1895), 228; Edward L. Curtis, *A Critical and Exegetical Commentary on the Books of Chronicles*

not allow an extensive discussion of this issue here,[27] the weakness of this theory becomes apparent especially in passages where an account in the source text has been effectively replaced by an entirely new account of the events (e.g., 2 Chr 24 in relation to 2 Kgs 12). In such passages the Chronicler has made no apparent attempt to explain the details of the source text but has largely rewritten those sections he did not agree with. If Chronicles had been meant as an interpretation or midrash of the source, one would expect much more reverence toward the source text and attempts to explain some of its problems. In contrast, the Chronicler has taken the liberty of dropping out sections of the source when its conceptions clearly conflict with his own. It is therefore likely that Chronicles was written in order to replace 1–2 Kings as the theologically correct and updated account of Israel's history during the monarchy.[28]

In many ways the Chronicler's account represents a new redaction of 1–2 Kings, although the changes may be more radical than what is usually assumed of redactions. The fact that we also possess the source text has marginalized 1–2 Chronicles, but did we not possess the sources, much of scholarship since the nineteenth century would probably have tried to reconstruct the prehistory of Chronicles. Here we are at the core of literary- or redaction-critical investigations, and therefore observations made by comparing Chronicles with its sources are directly relevant for the discussion about how the texts were edited. An alleged different genre of Chronicles, such as midrash or interpretation, is not a pretext for ignoring Chronicles as a significant witness for editorial development. In view of the massive changes that the Chronicler has made in some passages—

(ICC; Edinburgh; T&T Clark; New York: Scribner's, 1910), 9; Martin Noth, *Überlieferungsgeschichtliche Studien* (Tübingen: Niemayer, 1957), 171; Georg Steins, *Die Bücher der Chronik: Einleitung in das Alte Testament* (ed. Erich Zenger et al.; 5th ed.; Kohlhammer: Stuttgart, 2004), 249–62, here 258.

27. The discussion about the position of the Chronicler toward his source has been debated since early research; see, e.g., Wilhelm Martin Leberecht de Wette, *Lehrbuch der historisch-kritischen Einleitung in die Bibel Alten und Neuen Testaments* (7th ed.; Berlin: Georg Reimer, 1852), 237–57; and Wellhausen, *Prolegomena zur Geschichte Israels*, 169–228.

28. The so-called *Verdrängungstheorie*, or replacement theory, has been represented by many scholars since early research; see, e.g., Carl Steuernagel, *Lehrbuch der Einleitung in das Alte Testament* (Tübingen: J. C. B. Mohr, 1912), 389; Isaac Kalimi, *An Ancient Israelite Historian: Studies in the Chronicler, His Time, Place and Writing* (SSN 46; Leiden: Brill, 2005), 39.

for example, in 2 Chr 36:19-20—the attempts to reconstruct the process of editing would have been difficult indeed. In many cases, we can see how the text was changed only by comparing the Chronicler's text with the donor text.

9.6. Conclusions and Methodological Consequences

The parallel versions of the burning of Jerusalem in 2 Kgs 25:8-12 and Jer 52:12-16 contain some differences. Especially the Greek versions have preserved important variants that probably represent the oldest reading in comparison with the other witnesses. The MT versions contain additions similar to ones often assumed in literary criticism. The cases discussed here show how entire sentences may have been added to the passage and indicate how the text gradually grew. Even without access to the earlier version of the text, many of these sentences could provide reasons to suspect that they were added. This is particularly evident in the case of 2 Kgs 25:10*.

Jeremiah 39:8-9 represents a freer rendering of the same passage. The author used either 2 Kgs 25:8-12, Jer 52:12-16, or both passages as sources but could omit, rearrange, rewrite, and expand the source text to accord with his own conceptions and to accommodate it to his wider compositional aims in the book of Jeremiah. The radical changes, omissions, and rewritings highlight the liberties that the author took in relation to his source text(s). It is evident that it would be difficult to reconstruct the literary prehistory of Jer 39:8-9 without access to 2 Kgs 25:8-12 or Jer 52:12-16. The resulting text in Jer 39:8-9 is, in part, more fluent than its sources (especially 2 Kgs 25:8-12 with the addition of v. 10), which would complicate the reconstruction.

The author of Jer 39:8 used as a source a passage that already contained the reference to the destruction of the walls, which is probably a later addition. At the same time, he omitted the more original destruction of the temple. This shows that in the transmission of texts a section of the text could be added at some point, while an older reading could be omitted. This is significant, because it means that in a long transmission of texts such processes can lead to a situation where a resulting late text may theoretically have omitted all of the oldest text and consist of only what were later additions.[29] Here we have only one example of a short addition-

---

29. For example, the development of the Gilgamesh epic has shown that the

omission sequence, but it can be imagined how such changes accumulate after successive redactions.

The Chronicler's version of the passage is even more radical than Jer 39:8–10. Whereas the author of Jer 39 generally followed the source text and made some changes, in 2 Chr 36:19–20 the Chronicler has given a more comprehensive revision of the source to accommodate the story to his own compositional and theological conceptions. He elevated the motifs and themes that he considered important and omitted those that were less important to him. As for reconstructing the literary prehistory of 2 Chr 36:19–20 without its preserved sources, the same that is said of Jer 39:8–9 is probably true. The resulting text is concise, more logical, and less repetitive than the source, so that critical scholars would perhaps not even suspect that its older literary stage had been so fundamentally different. It is unlikely that critical scholars could successfully penetrate 2 Chr 36:19–20 to reach its older history unless they had the possibility to compare it with 2 Kgs 25:8–12.

Later developments of the account can be found in 1 Esd 1:52–53 and Josephus, *Ant.* 10.8.5. Whereas 1 Esd 1:52–53 follows 2 Chr 36:19–20 almost slavishly, Josephus adopted the temple-centered approach of Chronicles but went beyond it and also extracted information from 2 Kgs 25, and possibly from other sources as well. He made several further changes and additions in his rendering of the events.

Comparing literarily dependent texts that describe the same event—the burning of Jerusalem—we can see that the text could be reproduced slavishly in an early (2 Kgs 25:8–12 and Jer 52:12–16) and late (1 Esd 1:52–53) stage in its transmission. A freer attitude toward the source can be found relatively early (Jer 39), but it is also met later (2 Chr 36:19–20) or even in the Common Era, as Josephus's text would indicate. The texts show several kinds of editorial changes, but it is noteworthy that, contrary to what one would expect, a late use of the text, 2 Chr 36:19–20,[30] repre-

---

oldest and the youngest witness differ to such extent that it is difficult to find parallel texts. Because we know also the middle development, we may see that they are part of the same tradition. For discussion about the development, see Jeffrey H. Tigay, *The Evolution of the Gilgamesh Epic* (Philadelphia: University of Pennsylvania Press, 1982), 10–13, 241–42, 251; and Andrew R. George, *The Babylonian Gilgamesh Epic* (Oxford: Oxford University Press, 2003), 3–70.

30. Thus also in Josephus, *Ant.* 10.8.5. While Josephus clearly represents a different genre from the other witnesses, it still shows how an older text could be used

sents the most radical and changed rendering of the text. The often-taken assumption that the later scribes or authors were increasingly reluctant to make changes to the source text cannot be taken for granted. The development of the texts may have been less linear in this respect.

---

rather freely as a source. A detailed discussion of Josephus lies beyond the scope of this volume.

10
Evidence for the Literary Growth of Gedaliah's Murder in 2 Kings 25:25, Jeremiah 41:1–3 MT, and Jeremiah 48:1–3 LXX

After the destruction of Judah in 587 BCE, the Babylonians appointed Gedaliah as governor over the remaining population. According to the Hebrew Bible, Gedaliah was soon murdered by Ishmael, one of the army commanders who had come to Mizpah. Two passages in the Hebrew Bible describe the murder: 2 Kgs 25:25 and Jer 41:1–3 (≈ Jer 48:1–3 LXX). While the Hebrew and Greek texts of 2 Kgs 25:25 contain only minor differences, the Greek and Hebrew of Jer 41:1–3 (≈ Jer 48:1–3 LXX) differ considerably from each other as well as from 2 Kgs 25:25. It is apparent that the different versions of the passage preserve different stages in the literary development of the text. It is necessary to discuss each difference separately with no predetermined presupposition as to which witness is more original, and a reason for each plus has to be understood. Nevertheless, the assumption that the plusses are the result of expansions provides the most probable explanation in most cases.[1] Thus, we can assume that 2 Kgs

---

1. Nevertheless, some scholars (e.g., Bernhard Duhm, *Das Buch Jeremia* [KHC 11; Tübingen: J. C. B. Mohr, 1901], 316; Walter Dietrich, *Prophetie und Geschichte: Eine redaktionsgeschichtliche Untersuchung zum deuteronomistischen Geschichtswerk* [FRLANT 108; Göttingen: Vandenhoeck & Ruprecht, 1972], 143; Gwilym H. Jones, *1 and 2 Kings* [NCBC; Grand Rapids: Eerdmans,1984], 647) have assumed that 2 Kgs 25:25 may be a shortened and thus younger version of the Jeremiah passage, but this is unlikely. Most of the differences between the passages can be shown to be secondary additions that accord with very typical editorial changes that have been made to the texts of the Hebrew Bible. Reasons or motives for the changes also become apparent, while it would be difficult to explain the opposite direction of textual development. Some of the most substantial differences relate to ideological issues. To assume that they had been omitted in 2 Kgs 25:25 would necessitate a more comprehensive expla-

25:25, which is the shortest version, probably also represents the oldest literary stage. The Greek text in Jer 48:1–3 LXX contains several plusses in relation to 2 Kgs 25:25, while the Hebrew of Jer 41:1–3 contains further plusses in relation to both other versions. Jeremiah 41:1–3 MT most likely represents the youngest literary stage. The comparison of the variant versions thus reveals significant information about the editorial techniques and processes of the Hebrew Bible. Many techniques assumed in redaction criticism have been applied in the transmission of this text.[2]

10.1. The Hebrew and Greek Texts of 2 Kings 25:25

The Hebrew and Greek texts of 2 Kgs 25:25 differ only in minor details.

2 Kgs 25:25 MT

ויהי בחדש השביעי בא ישמעאל בן־נתניה בן־אלישמע מזרע המלוכה
ועשרה אנשים אתו ויכו את־גדליהו וימת ואת־היהודים ואת־הכשדים
אשר־היו אתו במצפה

In the seventh month, Ishmael son of Nethaniah son of Elishama, of royal seed, came with ~~ten~~ men, and they struck down Gedaliah, so that he died, along with the Judeans and the Chaldeans who were with him at Mizpah.

2 Kgs 25:25 LXX

καὶ ἐγενήθη ἐν τῷ ἑβδόμῳ μηνὶ ἦλθεν Ισμαηλ υἱὸς Ναθανιου υἱοῦ Ελισαμα ἐκ τοῦ σπέρματος τῶν βασιλέων καὶ (δέκα) ἄνδρες μετ' αὐτοῦ. καὶ ἐπάταξεν/ αν τὸν Γοδολιαν, καὶ ἀπέθανεν, καὶ τοὺς Ιουδαίους καὶ τοὺς Χαλδαίους, οἳ ἦσαν μετ' αὐτοῦ εἰς/ἐν Μασσηφαθ.

---

nation than merely the requirement to shorten, as assumed by scholars who regard 2 Kgs 25:25 as younger. See the discussion below concerning each difference between the versions.

2. These same texts were discussed in Juha Pakkala, "Gedaliah's Murder in 2 Kgs 25:25 and Jer 41:1–3," in *Scripture in Transition: Essays on Septuagint, Hebrew Bible, and Dead Sea Scrolls in Honour of Raija Sollamo* (ed. A. Voitila and J. Jokiranta; Brill: Leiden, 2008), 401–11. The perspective here is somewhat different, the text has been completely revised, and many new arguments for the literary changes have been added.

In the seventh month, Ismael son of Nathanias son of Helisama, of the seed of the kings [≈ of royal seed], came with (ten) men, and they/he struck down Godolias, so that he died, along with the Judeans and the Chaldeans who were with him at Massephath.

There are some differences between the Greek manuscripts, but most of them are inconsequential for the current investigation.³ Over against the MT and the parallel versions in Jer 41:1–3 MT and Jer 48:1–3 LXX, the differences have little bearing. However, one difference should be noted. Against other Greek manuscripts (and the MT) of 2 Kgs 25:25, Codex Vaticanus lacks the word δέκα ("ten"). This minus could represent the original reading, because the secondary addition of detail, also seen in many of the plusses discussed below, is common. There is no technical reason why the word should have been accidentally omitted, and there is also no apparent reason for an intentional omission. The problem with the originality of this minus is that it is found only in one Greek manuscript, and therefore we may suggest only tentatively that it represents the original reading. Apart from the word "ten," the *Vorlage* of the LXX translator may have been identical with the MT.

10.2. Three Parallel Versions That Represent Three Literary Stages

More significant are the differences between 2 Kgs 25:25 and both versions in Jeremiah. A reconstructed Hebrew *Vorlage* of the Greek text in

---

3. Most Greek manuscripts read Ισμαηλ, but Vaticanus has Μαναηλ instead. The Antiochene text reads τῆς βασιλείας instead of τῶν βασιλέων found in other Greek witnesses. The Antiochene reading may be a harmonization toward the MT. Against most Greek witnesses, which read ἀπέθανεν ("he died"), the Antiochene text has ἐθανάτωσαν αὐτόν ("they killed him"). This corresponds, in part, to the MT of Jer 41:2: וימת אתו ("they killed him"). The addition of the object is probably a later development and a misunderstanding of וימת for וָיָּמָת, as in Jer 41:2 (see below). The Antiochene reading follows the plural of the MT and is possibly original. Another plus is found at the end of the verse, where the Antiochene text adds ἀπέκτεινεν Ισμαηλ ("Ismael killed"). This refers to the killing of the Judeans and Chaldeans. It is probably a clarifying addition influenced by Jer 41:3 (הכה ישמעאל); see below. Instead of מזרע המלוכה ("of royal seed"), the Greek reads ἐκ τοῦ σπέρματος τῶν βασιλέων ("of the seed of the kings"), which literally corresponds to מזרע המלכים. Instead of the result of a different *Vorlage*, the difference was probably created in the translation process, as the meaning is largely retained.

Jer 48:1–3 LXX (or a Hebrew retroversion of the LXX) will be provided, as this will facilitate the comparison. Since Jer 48:1–3 LXX can be compared with two Hebrew versions, we can be relatively certain about its *Vorlage*, although one of its minuses is debatable (see below).[4] It is evident that the differences between the versions are numerous and substantial. Each difference will be discussed separately below.[5]

2 Kgs 25:25 MT/LXX

ויהי בחדש השביעי בא ישמעאל בן־נתניה בן־אלישמע מזרע המלוכה
ועשרה אנשים אתו
ויכו את־גדליהו [וימת] ואת־היהודים ואת־הכשדים אשר־היו אתו במצפה

In the seventh month, Ishmael son of Nethaniah son of Elishama, of royal seed, came with (ten) men, and they struck down Gedaliah, so that he *died*, along with the Judeans and the Chaldeans who were with him at Mizpah.

Reconstructed Hebrew *Vorlage* of Jer 48:1–3 LXX

ויהי בחדש השביעי בא ישמעאל בן־נתניה בן־אלישמע מזרע המלך
ועשרה אנשים אתו אל־גדליהו המצפתה ויאכלו שם לחם יחדו
ויקם ישמעאל ועשרה אנשים אשר־היו אתו ויכו את־גדליהו אשר־הפקיד
מלך־בבל בארץ
ואת כל־היהודים אשר־היו אתו במצפה ואת־הכשדים אשר נמצאו־שם

---

4. The LXX* (according to Joseph Ziegler, ed., *Jeremias, Baruch, Threni, Epistula Jeremiae* [vol. 15 of *Septuaginta: Vetus Testamentum Graecum*; Göttingen: Vandenhoeck & Ruprecht, 2006]) reads: ¹ Καὶ ἐγένετο τῷ μηνὶ τῷ ἑβδόμῳ ἦλθεν Ισμαηλ υἱὸς Ναθανιου υἱοῦ Ελασα ἀπὸ γένους τοῦ βασιλέως καὶ δέκα ἄνδρες μετ' αὐτοῦ πρὸς Γοδολιαν εἰς Μασσηφα, καὶ ἔφαγον ἐκεῖ ἄρτον ἅμα. ² καὶ ἀνέστη Ισμαηλ καὶ οἱ δέκα ἄνδρες, οἳ ἦσαν μετ' αὐτοῦ, καὶ ἐπάταξαν τὸν Γοδολιαν, ὃν κατέστησε βασιλεὺς Βαβυλῶνος ἐπὶ τῆς γῆς, ³ καὶ πάντας τοὺς Ιουδαίους τοὺς ὄντας μετ' αὐτοῦ ἐν Μασσηφα καὶ πάντας τοὺς Χαλδαίους τοὺς εὑρεθέντας ἐκεῖ.

5. The plusses in the Jeremiah passages in relation to 2 Kgs 25:25 are underlined. The plusses in the MT of Jer 41:1–3 in relation to Jer 48:1–3 LXX are displayed in double underline. The relocated words are displayed in a gray font. In Jer 48:1 most Greek manuscripts of Jer 48:1 read ἀπὸ γένους τοῦ βασιλέως ("of the family of the king") for מזרע המלך. The difference more probably came about in the translation process rather than from a reading different from what can be found in the parallel passages, since the meaning is largely preserved.

¹ In the seventh month, Ishmael son of Nethaniah son of Elishama, of royal seed, came with ten men <u>to Gedaliah to Mizpah, and they ate bread there together.</u> ² <u>And Ishmael and the ten men that were with him rose up</u>, and they struck down Gedaliah, <u>whom the king of Babylon had appointed governor over the land,</u> ³ and <u>all</u> the Judeans who were with him at Mizpah and the Chaldeans <u>who were found there.</u>

Jer 41:1–3 MT

ויהי בחדש השביעי בא ישמעאל בן־נתניה בן־אלישמע מזרע המלוכה <u>ורבי המלך</u> ועשרה אנשים אתו
אל־גדליהו בן־אחיקם המצפתה ויאכלו שם לחם יחדו <u>במצפה</u>
ויקם ישמעאל <u>בן־נתניה</u> ועשרה אנשים אשר־היו אתו ויכו את־גדליהו <u>בן־אחיקם בן־שפן בחרב</u>
<u>וימת אתו אשר־הפקיד מלך־בבל בארץ</u>
ואת <u>כל</u>־היהודים אשר־היו אתו <u>את־גדליהו</u> במצפה ואת־הכשדים
אשר נמצאו־שם <u>את אנשי המלחמה הכה ישמעאל</u>

¹ In the seventh month, Ishmael son of Nethaniah son of Elishama, of royal seed, <u>one of the chief officers of the king</u>, came with ten men to <u>Gedaliah</u> son of Ahikam <u>to Mizpah, and they ate bread there together, at Mizpah.</u> ² <u>And Ishmael</u> <u>son of Nethaniah</u> <u>and the ten men that were with him rose up</u>, and they struck down Gedaliah <u>son of Ahikam son of Shaphan with the sword, and he killed him</u>, <u>whom the king of Babylon had appointed governor over the land,</u> ³ and <u>all</u> the Judeans who were with him, <u>with Gedaliah</u>, at Mizpah and the Chaldeans <u>who were found there; Ishmael killed the soldiers.</u>

10.3. Additions to Jeremiah 41:1–3 MT and Jeremiah 48:1–3 LXX Missing in 2 Kings 25:25

Both versions of Jeremiah contain a large plus that refers to a joint meal attended by Gedaliah and Ishmael. According to the plus, the murder took place after the meal. The following considerations suggest that the plus is a later addition. There is no apparent reason why this motif should have been omitted in 2 Kgs 25:25. Its intentional omission would mean that the editor had sought to diminish the treachery of Ishmael (see below), but this is unlikely. One can also see a resumptive repetition (*Wiederaufnahme*) here. The last words before the addition are repeated at the end of the addition: ועשרה אנשים אתו ... ועשרה אנשים אשר־היו אתו ("and ten men were with him ... and the ten men that were with him"). This is a common technique of later editors who sought to return to the older text so that the transition would be as smooth as possible. A motive for the plus can also be identified. The editor tried to increase the treachery of Ishmael's actions. A common meal followed by an immediate murder gives the impression that Ishmael is a particularly dishonorable person. Not only did Ishmael misuse Gedaliah's hospitality and trust, but he also ate with the host before murdering him. The same tendency to increase the negative standing of Ishmael can be seen in other passages of Jer 41 as well. In Jer 41:4–9 Ishmael murders mourning pilgrims who were on their way to bring sacrifices to the temple. He fakes that he is mourning as well and invites the pilgrims to Gedaliah's home, but when they reach the center of Mizpah, he murders them. In the following passage, Ishmael imprisons the remaining Judeans, including the king's daughters, and tries to take them to Ammon. When the other army commanders try to catch him, he flees to Ammon in a cowardly manner (Jer 41:10–15). It is apparent that Jer 41 portrays Ishmael as a disgraceful murderer who is careless about the remaining Judean population. His portrayal here is much more negative than the portrayal in 2 Kgs 25:25. The large plus that contains the motif of the meal should be seen as part of the broader tendency that can be observed throughout Jer 41.

The Jeremiah passages further add אשר־הפקיד מלך־בבל בארץ ("whom the king of Babylon had appointed governor over the land"). This plus is probably influenced by Jer 40:7 MT, which refers to Gedaliah's appointment to office by the Babylonian king.[6] This addition is similar in nature to the addition of titles and genealogical details, which was common in the transmission of the Hebrew Bible.[7] It is unlikely that the original author would have needed to repeat the reference to the appointment, and therefore it is probable that 2 Kgs 25:25 represents the original text, the plus thus being a secondary addition.

---

6. Jer 40:7 is a more probable source of influence than 2 Kgs 25:22–23. This is suggested by the closer language parallel (Jer 40:7: כי־הפקיד מלך־בבל את־גדליהו בארץ; 2 Kgs 25:22: כי־הפקיד מלך־בבל את־; 2 Kgs 25:23: מלך בבל ויפקד עליהם את־גדליהו). Like Jer 41:2, Jer 40:7 refers to Gedaliah being governor in the land (בארץ), while this word is missing in 2 Kgs 25:22. Cf. Jer 41:2: אשר־הפקיד מלך־בבל בארץ.

7. This is particularly evident in the book of Jeremiah. William McKane, *Commentary on Jeremiah 1–25* (vol. 1 of *A Critical and Exegetical Commentary on Jeremiah*; ICC; Edinburgh: T&T Clark, 1986), 1013, notes: "The filling-out of genealogical information, which has already been explained as a secondary operation in MT, is a prominent feature of the longer Hebrew text of chapter 41."

The word כל ("all") is included in Jer 41:3 MT and Jer 48:3 LXX, but it is missing in 2 Kgs 25:25. This is also probably a secondary addition, because there is no reason to assume an omission in 2 Kgs 25:25. Moreover, the word seems to have been added rather frequently in the transmission of Jeremiah, as a comparison of the MT and LXX shows.[8]

Jeremiah 41:3 MT and Jer 48:3 LXX specify that Ishmael killed only those Chaldeans who were found at Mizpah, אשר נמצאו־שם, while 2 Kgs 25:25 lacks this reference. The plus is probably a secondary addition caused by the displacement of ואת־הכשדים ("and the Chaldeans"). The motive for these changes may be the attempt to avoid the impression that Babylonians had been with Gedaliah, or had been invited by Gedaliah. In 2 Kgs 25:25 both the Judeans and the Chaldeans are said to be with Gedaliah, while in Jeremiah only the Judeans are with him. The Babylonians that were killed are those that were found in Mizpah. The change is subtle, but it changes the setting, for one receives the impression from Jeremiah that there had been some Babylonians who were perhaps accidentally in Mizpah but who were not necessarily connected with Gedaliah. This change is in line with the tendency in Jeremiah to increase the positive standing of Gedaliah and portray Ishmael more negatively. Second Kings 25 is more neutral in this respect, and one does not receive the impression that Ishmael's act was necessarily negative: Ishmael, who is of royal blood, kills someone who had been instated as a puppet by the Babylonians and who spoke for them (v. 24). One should also note that due to the displacement of the phrase ואת־הכשדים ("and the Chaldeans") after the reference to Mizpah, it was necessary to specify the location again, the word שם obviously referring to Mizpah. Without this addition, Ishmael would have been said to have murdered all Babylonians (cf. "and he killed him ... the Judeans who were with him ... at Mizpah and the Chaldeans").

10.4. Additions to Jeremiah 41:1–3 MT

The MT of Jer 41:1–3 contains several additions that are not found in the other two versions. The development of the proto-Masoretic version seems to have continued after Jer 48:1–3 LXX. The MT of Jer 41:1 contains

---

8. For example, the word was added in the MT of Jer 25:1, 4, 17, 19, and 29. The LXX, which is lacking the word in this chapter, is probably more original. In some cases, however, the LXX is more expansive, while the MT lacks the word (e.g., Jer 41:8–9 LXX vs. Jer 34:8–9).

the plus רבי המלך ("[one of] the chief officers of the king"). This is probably a secondary addition.[9] Dominique Barthélemy has suggested that רבי המלך was accidentally omitted in the other versions due to a homoiarchon: הַמֶּלֶךְ מִזֶּרַע הַמְּלוּכָה וְרַבֵּי.[10] Although an accidental omission cannot be ruled out, a secondary addition is more likely. Especially the generally expansive nature of Jer 41:1-3 MT in relation to the other versions suggests that we are dealing with an addition here as well. Some scholars have suggested that רבי המלך was added as a result of an accidental or corrupted dittography,[11] but this theory assumes that a copyist read מזרע as ורבי, which is not very likely. It is more probable that the addition is intentional and that the editor drew the information from 2 Kgs 25:23 or Jer 40:8. According to these passages Ishmael had been שר החילים ("an army commander"). The addition would thus exemplify a typical textual development. A further title was added on the basis of information gained from another passage. The editor may also have attempted to highlight the drama of Gedaliah's murder. Even former members of the military or former administrators of the king were against the new order instated by the Babylonians.[12]

The MT of Jer 41:1-2 contains references to Nethaniah and Ahikam, the fathers of Gedaliah and Ishmael, respectively. The names are missing in the parallel verses in Jer 48:1-2 LXX, and it is probable that the MT is secondary here. Added genealogical detail is very common in the Hebrew

---

9. Thus, many; e.g., Friedrich Giesebrecht, *Das Buch Jeremia* (HKAT 3.2.1; Göttingen: Vandenhoeck & Ruprecht, 1907), 214; Arnold B. Ehrlich, *Jesaia, Jeremia* (vol. 4 of *Randglossen zur hebräischen Bibel*; Leipzig: Hinrichs, 1912), 345; McKane, *Jeremiah 1-25*, 1014.

10. Dominique Barthélemy, *Critique textuelle de l'Ancien Testament* (4 vols.; OBO 50; Fribourg: Éditions Universitaires; Göttingen: Vandenhoeck & Ruprecht, 1982-2005), 2:741-43. He also speculates about the possibility that the רבי המלך is Ishmael's grandfather, but this is not convincing and is also irrelevant for the discussion on which text, the MT or LXX, is to be given priority. See the discussion and the reflection on Barthélemy's theory in McKane, *Jeremiah 1-25*, 1014.

11. Thus, e.g., Duhm, *Jeremia*, 316; Wilhelm Rudolph, *Jeremia* (HAT 12; Tübingen: Mohr Siebeck, 1947), 214; and Robert P. Carroll, *Jeremiah: A Commentary* (OTL; Philadelphia: Westminster, 1986), 706.

12. On the other hand, Jer 41:4-15 portrays Ishmael in a very negative light—he murders pilgrims and subsequently flees to Ammon—which could indicate that the later editor wanted to increase the perception of Ishmael's treachery toward the new order.

Bible,[13] and Jer 41:1–2 MT provides further documented evidence for this. The same tendency in the MT of Jer 41 to add ancestors continues later in v. 2, for it refers to Gedaliah's grandfather by adding בן־אחיקם בן־שפן ("son of Ahikam son of Shaphan"). It is also peculiar that Gedaliah's grandfather is only now introduced, while the preceding verse already refers to Gedaliah's father. On the basis of Jer 41:1–2 MT, later editors seem to have been particularly prone to repeat ancestral detail. It is reasonable to assume that an original author would have mentioned the fathers' names only once, usually when a person is mentioned for the first time, and there would be no need to repeat such ancestral details later. In 2 Kgs 25, for example, this works well. Gedaliah's father and grandfather are mentioned only in v. 22, while further references to Gedaliah leave out this information.[14] Jeremiah 41:1–2 is particularly repetitive in this respect, and thus the unnecessary references to the fathers and grandfathers are probably secondary. This assumption is confirmed by the fact that they are also missing in Jer 48:1–2 LXX.

The location of the meal was further specified in Jer 41:1 MT, but the secondary nature of this plus is evident. It repeats the reference to the location in a disturbing way: בְּמִצְפָּה וַיֹּאכְלוּ שָׁם לֶחֶם יַחְדָּו ("and they ate bread there together, at Mizpah"). One should also note that the preceding sentence already refers to Mizpah as the location where the event takes place. Thus, this addition seems quite unnecessary, and it may be a gloss that failed to notice the almost immediately preceding reference to the same location. One cannot exclude an accidental repetition of the word. In any case, the word is likely to be a later addition to Jer 41:1 MT, as implied by the parallel versions.[15] The addition shows that later editorial activity often caused a redundancy in the resulting text. It is apparent that on the basis of the disturbing repetition a modern critic would also probably be able to

---

13. E.g., in Ezra 7:1–5; see Juha Pakkala, *Ezra the Scribe* (BZAW 347; Berlin: de Gruyter, 2004), 23–26, for discussion.

14. Note, however, that there is an unnecessary reference to Ishmael's father and grandfather in 2 Kgs 25:25, for he was introduced for the first time in v. 23, where his father is also mentioned. It is possible that vv. 23 and 25 derived from different authors, but the complexities of this passage cannot be analyzed here. Because the prehistory of 2 Kgs 25 is not preserved in variant editions of the text, an analysis would necessitate a literary- and redaction-critical approach.

15. Thus already Duhm, *Jeremia*, 316.

identify this addition even without knowledge of the earlier stages of the text, Jer 48:1 LXX and 2 Kgs 25:25.

Jeremiah 41:2 MT contains a plus according to which Gedaliah was killed בחרב ("with the sword"). It is very likely that the plus is another secondary addition and that Jer 48:2 LXX and 2 Kgs 25:25 are more original here.[16] Expansions that add detail are common in the transmission of the Hebrew Bible. The editor was perhaps led by his imagination to think about the way Gedaliah was killed and thus added the sword. On the other hand, the idea of killing with the sword is frequently met in other parts of the book of Jeremiah, so it is possible that the addition was influenced by the other uses of the expression נכה בחרב ("kill with the sword").[17] The addition may also have been intended to increase the dramatic nature of the event. In any case, this addition is an example illustrative of added detail.

The MT of Jer 41:3 adds Gedaliah as the one the Judeans were with: את־גדליהו. This is certainly a secondary addition, as suggested by the unnecessary repetition of Gedaliah, for the suffix in אתו already refers to him.[18] The suffix of the preposition את can logically refer only to Gedaliah, although theoretically it could also refer to the king of Babylon. Since the reference to the king was also added later, this theoretical confusion could arise in the expanded text. This is probably the main reason for the addition; the editor wanted to be explicitly clear that Gedaliah was meant.[19] The result was an awkward repetition that can hardly derive from the original author of the passage. This conclusion is confirmed by the fact that את־גדליהו is missing in the other two versions. The addition suggests that unnecessary repetitions should be suspected of being later additions.

---

16. Nevertheless, some scholars, such as Giesebrecht, *Jeremia*, 214, have assumed that the MT is more original, but they provide no evidence for their assumption.

17. E.g., Jer 26:23; 27:13; 34:4; 38:2; 41:2; 42:17, 22. According to Jeremiah's prophecy all who remain in Jerusalem will be killed by the sword (Jer 38:2). Although Gedaliah was not in Jerusalem, perhaps the addition in Jer 41:2 was influenced by this idea.

18. Thus, many; e.g., Duhm, *Jeremia*, 316; Giesebrecht, *Jeremia*, 214; Ehrlich, *Jesaia, Jeremia*, 345; Carroll, *Jeremiah*, 706; and McKane, *Jeremiah 1–25*, 1014–15.

19. Ehrlich, *Jesaia, Jeremia*, 345, suggests that the suffix could refer to Ishmael, but this would necessitate a very different understanding of the whole passage. McKane, *Jeremiah 1–25*, 1015, notes with regard to this theory that it "places unacceptable strains on the grammar of the sentence."

At the end of Jer 41:3, the MT contains the plus את אנשי המלחמה
הכה ישמעאל ("Ishmael killed the soldiers"). The killing of the soldiers is
mentioned separately from the other killings. The sentence hangs loosely
at the end of the verse and is poorly integrated with the preceding text.
The sentence repeats the subject, Ishmael, as well as the verb נכה. One
should also note that the verb is conspicuously placed after the object. It
is hardly probable that the original author would have separated the killing of the soldiers in this way. The fact that the sentence is missing in the
other witnesses confirms the suspicion that it is a secondary addition.[20]
The additional information may have been deduced from the older text. It
could be reasoned that there must have been some soldiers with Gedaliah,
since he was the governor.[21] The example suggests that poorly integrated
loose sentences are often later additions. Even without the other witnesses,
an able literary critic would have suspected that the sentence might have
been added later to Jer 41:3 MT.

As a consequence, all plusses in the MT of Jer 41:1–3 can be regarded
as later additions. Most of them have disturbed the context or created
other tensions within the text, as we have seen. This text thus corroborates
the assumption that tensions and confusion within a text are often the
result of editorial activity.

10.5. A Possible Original Reading in Jeremiah 48:2 LXX

The MT of Jer 41:2 reads וימת אתו ("and he killed him"). This reading is
partly shared by 2 Kgs 25:25, which omits only the object marker and the
suffix, while Jer 48:2 LXX also omits the verb. This is the only place where
2 Kgs 25:25 contains a plus in comparison with one of the parallels. A
further complication here is the diverging verb form implied by the Masoretic vocalization of the Hebrew: וִיָּמָת (hiphil, "and he killed") in Jer 41:2

---

20. Thus, many; e.g., Duhm, *Jeremia*, 316; Barthélemy, *Critique textuelle*, 2:743–
44; McKane, *Jeremiah 1–25*, 1017–18, 1022.

21. Nonetheless, the text does not reveal whether the soldiers were Babylonian
or Gedaliah's Judean guard. The missing conjunction in the object marker את may
indicate that the author of the sentence meant it to specify who the Chaldeans were.
This would mean that the Babylonian soldiers are a more probable candidate. In any
case, is unlikely that the other army commanders mentioned in Jer 40 MT and 2 Kgs
25:23 were meant, for Johanan and the other commanders later seek to kill Ishmael
(Jer 41:11–15 MT).

and וימת (*qal*, "and he died") in 2 Kgs 25:25. The subject in Jer 41:2 is thus Ishmael, while in 2 Kgs 25:25 it is Gedaliah. Although not fully evident, the most probable solution is that the shortest reading, represented by Jer 48:2 LXX, is also the most original one. Second Kings 25:25 probably represents the second stage, while Jer 41:2 MT, as the most expansive, is the youngest reading.

One could make a case for an intentional stylistic shortening by the translator of Jer 48:2 LXX. The translator would have rendered the two partly synonymous words ויכו ("and they struck down") and וימת ("and he killed") with ἐπάταξαν, for the Greek root πατάσσω may refer to striking and killing.[22] The Hebrew *Vorlage* of Jer 48:2 LXX would then have contained וימת ("and he died/killed") like the other versions. However, this alternative is unlikely for the following reasons. The difference between the MT of Jer 41:2 and 2 Kgs 25:25 implies a more complicated development. An object, as in Jer 41:2 MT, is needed if the verb וימת is interpreted as a *hiphil* ("he killed"). This would be required if two Hebrew verbs were rendered with one Greek verb, ἐπάταξαν. Without an object, וימת would have to be read as *qal*, making Gedaliah the subject ("he died"), but this would not correspond to the translation. The only possibility would then be that ἐπάταξαν τὸν Γοδολιαν corresponds to ויכו את־גדליהו וימת אתו, but this already goes beyond the limits of likelihood, because the translator is often rather literal. More probable is that the *Vorlage* of the translator in Jer 48:2 lacked וימת אתו or וימת altogether. This assumption is substantiated by the disturbing position of וימת in 2 Kgs 25:25, for it breaks the connection between the members in the list whom Ishmael and his men killed: ויכו את־גדליהו [וימת] ואת־היהודים ואת־הכשדים ("they struck down Gedaliah, [so that he died,] along with the Judeans and the Chaldeans"). In the present text of 2 Kgs 25:25 the object marker before היהודים ("the Judeans") is puzzling since the preceding verb in the *qal* cannot receive an object. The object markers of the list can be governed only by the verb ויכו ("and they struck down"), but וימת ("and he died") breaks the connection, and therefore וימת ("and he died") is probably a later addition. The assumption that וימת is secondary also explains the incongruence between the plural ויכו and the singular וימת of Jer 41:2 MT. Consequently, it seems

---

22. For example, מות is translated with the verb πατάσσω in Jer 48:4 LXX: *hiphil* המית is translated as πατάξαντος.

more probable that Jer 48:2 LXX is original in omitting וימת and that it here represents an earlier stage of the text than the other witnesses.

The addition of וימת ("and he died") disturbed the original text, causing a further addition. וימת was probably originally meant to be read as a *qal*, with Gedaliah as the subject, but because it confused the text, later editors and interpreters would have sought to read it as a *hiphil*, with Ishmael as the subject, which suits the grammatical context much better. To be clear, this reading would have necessitated an additional object marker, which is now found in Jer 41:2 MT. When Ishmael became the subject of the verb, the suffix of the object marker would refer to Gedaliah. This editorial change removed the confusion, but the plus can hardly be original, confirmed by the lack of the word in the other two versions. This example illustrates how an earlier addition eventually occasioned a further addition by another editor: First וימת was added, with Gedaliah as subject, but because of the confusion, a later editor sought to improve the sentence by a further addition, אתו.

10.6. Conclusions and Methodological Consequences

Although only a very short passage, Gedaliah's murder is a very productive text for investigating editorial processes in the Hebrew Bible. It provides documented evidence for editorial techniques and additions, many of which are commonly assumed in literary- and redaction-critical investigations. The gradual addition of detail is evident. The text grew by means of successive small additions. Some of the additions are unrelated to each other, but some are part of a broader ideological editing of the text. The latter is especially apparent in the changes made in Jer 41 MT and 48 LXX that portray Ishmael in a more negative light than in 2 Kgs 25.

In many cases, the additions have caused thematic tensions or grammatical problems in the expanded text. We have seen several examples where these problems would have given the literary critic reason to suspect later editing even without access to the older versions of the text. Some of the expansions in the Jeremiah passages could have been identified without 2 Kgs 25:25. This is probable in the case of added ancestral information that repeats what is already said in the preceding text (e.g., "son of Nethaniah" or "son of Ahikam" in Jer 41 MT). The repetition of "the ten men [that were] with him" could also give reason to investigate whether the text between the repeated sentence was added, and here the critic would probably suspect resumptive repetition. Because the clause אשר־הפקיד

מלך־בבל בארץ ("whom the king of Babylon had appointed governor over the land") is unnecessary after Jer 40:7 and 12 MT, a critic could be able to detect that it was added as well. A repetition of what has already been said twice would not be necessary in Jer 41:3. Perhaps the clearest expansion is found at the end of Jer 41:3 MT: את אנשי המלחמה הכה ישמעאל ("Ishmael killed the soldiers"). Because the sentence is poorly connected to the preceding text, as discussed above, it is probable that most literary critics would have been able to identify it as a later addition.

Nonetheless, not all additions would give the critic reason to suspect that they were inserted by a later editor. It would be very difficult to identify some of the small additions, especially כל ("all") or בחרב ("with the sword"). The addition of one word that does not substantially change the meaning of the text or confuse its grammar would probably be left unnoticed in most cases. Even if one suspected that a word is an addition, it is difficult to find arguments for the secondary nature of a single word. It is perhaps also unlikely that one would be able to notice that ורבי המלך ("[one of] the chief officers of the king") had been added later, although the whole sentence has become somewhat congested after its addition. Despite these exceptions, the passage is an encouraging example of the possibilities of literary criticism. The classic methodology could detect many additions. Here it should be added that in this example text, with the exception of the relocation of ואת־הכשדים ("and the Chaldeans"), all editorial changes have been additions, which accords with the conventional assumption in the literary-critical method.

This passage has also shown how substantially some texts have been inflated by later editors. The oldest literary stage, 2 Kgs 25:25, is less than half the size in comparison with the youngest text, Jer 41:1–3 MT.[23] The additions in the youngest text contain more words than the whole oldest text. The intermediary stage, Jer 48:1–3 LXX,[24] shows that the growth of the text was gradual. It corresponds to the idea of a snowball or rolling corpus where successive hands are behind the additions. It is unlikely that the additions in the present text example were all written by two editors only. Three stages of the development have been preserved in these witnesses, but they are only glimpses of some arbitrary points in the development of

---

23. 2 Kgs 25:25 consists of 22 words, or 124 characters; Jer 48:1–3 LXX consists of 39 words, or 225 characters; and Jer 41:1–3 MT consists of 54 words, or 308 characters.

24. With the exception of וימת, in which case Jer 48:1–3 LXX probably preserves the original reading in omitting it.

the text. On the basis of the discussed documented evidence, one could assume that the text now preserved in Jer 41:1–3 MT is the result of at least five to seven different editors,[25] which corresponds to some of the most radical redaction-critical models. Even if we do not distinguish between the potentially different editors and concentrate only on the three literary stages, our resulting reconstruction would seem rather radical. If we take the youngest edition of the text, with the different redactions marked, the resulting text would not essentially differ from the reconstructions of redaction critics, except that here we have documented evidence for it.[26]

Jer 41:1–3 MT[27]

ויהי בחדש השביעי בא ישמעאל בן־נתניה בן־אלישמע מזרע המלוכה ו‏רבי המלך ועשרה אנשים אתו אל־גדליהו בן־אחיקם המצפתה ויאכלו שם לחם יחדו במצפה ויקם ישמעאל בן־נתניה ועשרה אנשים אשר־היו אתו ויכו את־גדליהו בן־אחיקם בן־שפן בחרב (וימת) אתו אשר־הפקיד מלך־בבל בארץ ואת כל־היהודים ואת־הכשדים אשר־היו אתו את־גדליהו במצפה ואת־הכשדים אשר נמצאו־שם את אנשי המלחמה הכה ישמעאל

In the seventh month, Ishmael son of Nethaniah son of Elishama, of royal seed, <u>one of the chief officers of the king</u>, came with (ten) men <u>to Gedaliah</u> son of Ahikam <u>to Mizpah, and they ate bread there together, at Mizpah</u>. And Ishmael <u>son of Nethaniah</u> and the ten men who were with him rose up, and they struck down Gedaliah <u>son of Ahikam son of Shaphan with the sword,</u> (so that he died > and he killed <u>him</u>,) whom the king of Babylon had appointed governor over the land, and <u>all</u> the Judeans and the Chaldeans who were with him, <u>with Gedaliah</u>, at Mizpah and the Chaldeans <u>who were found there; Ishmael killed the soldiers.</u>

---

25. For example, the word "sword" may not have been added by the same editor who added "one of the chief officers of the king."

26. It should further be added that this text shows only those literary stages that were preserved in the documented evidence. It is quite possible that the oldest documented literary stage, 2 Kgs 25:25, is also the result of earlier editing that is not witnessed by documented evidence.

27. The first stage of expansions is underlined, and the second stage is double underlined.

11
TECHNIQUES OF REWRITING PROPHECY:
JEREMIAH 48 COMPARED WITH ISAIAH 15–16

The oracle concerning Moab in Jer 48 contains sections that have close parallels with the prophetic lament on Moab in Isa 15–16. Scholars commonly agree that in all likelihood one of these texts is directly dependent on the other.[1] Most commentators regard Isa 15–16 as the literary source of parts of Jer 48.[2] There are good reasons to assume that the core of Jer 48 was secondarily supplemented with material from Isa 15–16.

---

1. Exceptions are Helmer Ringgren, "Oral and Written Transmission in the O.T.," *ST* 3 (1949), 34–59, esp. 50–52, who assumes that the author of Jer 48 knew his sources, which included Isa 15–16, from oral transmission; and John Bright, *Jeremiah* (AB 21; Garden City, N.Y.: Doubleday, 1965), 322, who explains the parallels with "anonymous sayings which were treasured among the followers both of Isaiah and Jeremiah, and which thus found their way, albeit in different forms, into the books of both prophets."

2. Cf., e.g., Wilhelm Rudolph, *Jeremia* (HAT 12; Tübingen: Mohr Siebeck, 1947), 243; Hans Wildberger, *Jesaja 13–27* (vol. 2 of *Jesaja*; BKAT 10.2; Neukirchen-Vluyn: Neukirchener Verlag, 1978), 605–6; Otto Kaiser, *Der Prophet Jesaja: Kapitel 13–39* (3d ed.; ATD 18; Göttingen: Vandenhoeck & Ruprecht, 1983), 51; Robert P. Carroll, *Jeremiah: A Commentary* (OTL; Philadelphia: Westminster, 1986), 792; Gerald L. Keown, Pamela J. Scalise, and Thomas G. Smothers, *Jeremiah 26–52* (WBC 27; Nashville: Thomas Nelson, 1995), 310; William McKane, *Commentary on Jeremiah 26–52* (vol. 2 of *A Critical and Exegetical Commentary on Jeremiah*; ICC; Edinburgh: T&T Clark, 1996), 1188; William L. Holladay, *Jeremiah* (2 vols.; Hermeneia; Minneapolis: Fortress, 1986–89), 2:347–48; Jack R. Lundbom, *Jeremiah 37–52: A New Translation with Introduction and Commentary* (AB 21C; New York: Doubleday, 2004), 287; Georg Fischer, *Jeremia 26–52* (HTKAT; Freiburg im Breisgau: Herder, 2005), 517; Willem A. M. Beuken, *Jesaja 13–27* (HTKAT; Freiburg im Breisgau: Herder, 2007), 128. The priority of Jer 48 was advocated by Hans Bardtke, "Jeremia der Fremdvölkerprophet," *ZAW* 54 (1936), 240–62, esp. 247–48.

In the following, we will have a closer look at the parallel passages. The comparison gives striking insight into how editors worked with older material that was used as a source. Jeremiah 48 provides empirical evidence of a technique of rewriting that leaves virtually no traces in the new text. The example bears witness to a case where, without knowledge of the source text itself, it would be very difficult to discern what kind of editorial changes had taken place.

11.1. A Rewritten Oracle: Jeremiah 48:29–33 Compared with Isaiah 16:6–10

The part of Jer 48 where most parallels with Isa 15–16 occur begins in v. 29.³ In this verse, a group of people, presumably the Israelite community, speaks about the arrogance of Moab.⁴

Jer 48:29

שמענו גאון מואב גאה מאד גאונו וגאותו ורם לבו

We have heard of the pride of Moab—he is very proud—of his pride and his arrogance and the highness of his heart.

In v. 30, Yhwh answers this statement with a similar critique of Moab's pride.

Jer 48:30

אני ידעתי נאם יהוה עברתו ולא כן בדיו לא כן עשו

I myself—oracle of Yhwh⁵—know his insolence, and not right are his boastings, not right is what they did.

---

3. Apart from the parallel sections of Isa 15:2–7; 16:6–12; and Jer 48:29–38, another parallel can be found in Jer 48:5, which is similar to Isa 15:5b (see below, 11.2).

4. The MT adds וגבהו ("his loftiness and") before גאונו וגאותו, while it is missing in the LXX, probably also in its Hebrew *Vorlage*. It is easy to assume that the *lectio brevior* is original and was secondarily expanded by inserting a third term describing Moab's arrogance.

5. The formula נאם יהוה ("oracle of Yhwh") is missing in the LXX, which might be the original *lectio brevior* (thus, e.g., Holladay, *Jeremiah*, 2:343). However, the case is difficult to decide, since the LXX also reads the first-person singular instead of the

Verses 29–30 have a close parallel with Isa 16:6, although no dialogue can be found in this verse; it contains only a statement of the community.

Isa 16:6

שָׁמַעְנוּ גְאוֹן־מוֹאָב גֵּא מְאֹד גַּאֲוָתוֹ וּגְאוֹנוֹ וְעֶבְרָתוֹ לֹא־כֵן בַּדָּיו׃

We have heard of the pride of Moab—he is very proud—of his arrogance and his pride and his insolence; not right are his boastings.

Jer 48:29–30

שָׁמַעְנוּ גְאוֹן־מוֹאָב גֵּאֶה מְאֹד גָּבְהוֹ וּגְאוֹנוֹ וְגַאֲוָתוֹ וְרֻם לִבּוֹ
אֲנִי יָדַעְתִּי נְאֻם־יְהוָה עֶבְרָתוֹ וְלֹא־כֵן בַּדָּיו לֹא־כֵן עָשׂוּ

²⁹ We have heard⁶ of the pride of Moab—he is very proud—⁷ of his pride and his arrogance and the highness of his heart. ³⁰ I myself—oracle of Yhwh—know his insolence, and not right are his boastings, not right is what they did.

It becomes clear at first glance that these texts cannot be independent from each other. Both versions closely overlap. Basically, there are three options to explain the relationship: (1) The author of Jer 48:29–30 has used Isa 16:6. (2) The author of Isa 16:6 has used Jer 48:29–30. (3) Both texts are dependent on a third source that is now lost.

The third option is theoretically possible, but this is not a necessary assumption, since nothing indicates that such a source existed.⁸ Since the relationship can be explained on the basis of the two preserved sources, the theory of a third source should be rejected (Occam's razor).

In order to decide between the first and the second option, the character of the plusses in Jeremiah has to be taken into consideration. Since all

---

plural, thus assimilating v. 29 with v. 30 and creating the notion of a continuous prophetic speech. Thus, it is also possible that the נאם יהוה formula was secondarily omitted in the LXX in order to create a text with a coherent speech of the prophet.

6. The LXX reads the first-person singular, thus simplifying the transition between v. 29 and v. 30. Since the formula נאם יהוה in v. 30 has no equivalent in the LXX, it is easy to assume that the LXX presents vv. 29–30 as a coherent speech of the prophet.

7. Cf. n. 4.

8. Wildberger, *Jesaja 13–27*, 605–6.

these plusses can be characterized as interpretive additions, it is reasonable to assume that the longer version of Jeremiah was created on the basis of the Isaiah text. Otherwise, one would have to assume that the plusses were intentionally omitted in Isaiah, but it is difficult to find a reason or motive for such omissions, since the plusses are not stylistically or theologically problematic. In contrast, a clear reason for the expansion of the source material can be found. It is easy to imagine that the communal statement of Isa 16:6 was changed into a short dialogue between the community and Yhwh, who both agree on Moab's pride and arrogance. The opening of the newly created divine oracle in Jer 48:30, אני ידעתי ("I myself know"), could have been influenced by Jer 29:11, where a speech of Yhwh includes the phrase אנכי ידעתי.

A striking technical aspect is that virtually all words and phrases of Isa 16:6 are reused in Jer 48:29–30. The statement of the community in Jer 48:29 is formulated almost identically to the formulation in Isa 16:6. One phrase is added (ורם לבו, "and the highness of his heart"[9]), and two similar words occur in inverted order (גאותו, "his arrogance," and גאונו, "his pride"). The tendency of expanding the text can also be observed in the MT, where, compared to the shorter LXX, a third term is added (גבהו, "his loftiness"). The remainder of Isa 16:6 is reused in the divine oracle of v. 30 (עברתו, "his insolence," and לא כן בדיו, "not right are his boastings"), and a new phrase is added (לא כן עשו, "not right is what they did"). In sum, the short dialogue between the community and Yhwh in Jer 48:29–30 can be explained as a slightly expanded, rewritten version of Isa 16:6. Verbatim quotations of the source text are mixed with some new terms and ideas.

The next verse of the Jeremiah text, Jer 48:31, provides another close parallel to the Moab oracle in Isaiah (Isa 16:7). Again, the versions overlap, but there are also some differences.

Isa 16:7

לכן ייליל מואב למואב כלה ייליל לאשישי קיר חרשת תהגו אך נכאים

Therefore Moab will wail over Moab, all of him will wail; for the raisin cakes of Kir-hareseth you will moan; surely they are stricken.

---

9. Cf. Ezra 31:10.

Jer 48:31

עַל כֵּן עַל מוֹאָב אֲיֵלִיל וּלְמוֹאָב כֻּלֹּה אֶזְעָק אֶל אַנְשֵׁי קִיר־חֶרֶשׂ יֶהְגֶּה

On this account over Moab I will wail, and for all of Moab I will cry out; toward the men of Kir-ḥeres one will moan.

In contrast to the preceding text, Jer 48:31 is not simply an expanded version of Isa 16:7. Several modifications of grammar and meaning can be observed. In Jer 48:31, the subject of wailing is set in the first-person singular, which probably implies that the speaker is still Yhwh, as in the preceding verse (Jer 48:30; see also v. 33: השבתי, "I made to cease").[10] By virtue of this change, the material is assimilated to the context of the divine oracle in Jer 48:30–31. In addition, the strange expression of Isa 16:7, לאשישי קיר חרשת ("for the raisin cakes of Kir-hareseth") is replaced in Jer 48:31 with the easily readable אל אנשי קיר חרש ("toward the men of Kir-ḥeres"). Another facilitation of meaning is the replacement of the second person in Isa 16:7 ("you will moan") with the third person in Jer 48:31 ("one will moan"), since, in the respective contexts, the third person is used for Moab.[11] These clarifications are an additional argument for the priority of the Isaiah material; the opposite direction of influence would mean that the text was intentionally made less clear.

It is more difficult to explain why the phrase אך נכאים ("surely they are stricken") is missing in Jer 48:31. Given the probable priority of the Isaiah version, there are two possible explanations for this. Either the phrase was secondarily omitted in Jer 48:31, or it was secondarily added to the Isaiah text, perhaps in the form of a marginal gloss. The reasons for the former alternative could be poetological since Jer 48:31 seems to be composed as a tricolon,[12] while Isa 16:6 shows a different structure.

Jeremiah 48:32 has a parallel in Isa 16:8–9:

Isa 16:8–9

כִּי שַׁדְמוֹת חֶשְׁבּוֹן אֻמְלָל גֶּפֶן שִׂבְמָה בַּעֲלֵי גוֹיִם הָלְמוּ שְׂרוּקֶיהָ עַד־יַעְזֵר נָגָעוּ תָּעוּ מִדְבָּר שְׁלֻחוֹתֶיהָ נִטְּשׁוּ עָבְרוּ יָם

---

10. Lundbom, *Jeremiah 37–52*, 289.
11. E.g., Wildberger, *Jesaja 13–27*, 594.
12. E.g., Lundbom, *Jeremiah 37–52*, 287.

עַל כֵּן אֶבְכֶּה בִּבְכִי יַעְזֵר גֶּפֶן שִׂבְמָה אֲרַיָּוֶךְ דִּמְעָתִי חֶשְׁבּוֹן וְאֶלְעָלֵה כִּי עַל קֵיצֵךְ וְעַל קְצִירֵךְ הֵידָד נָפָל

⁸ For the fields of Heshbon languish; the vine of Sibmah, the lords of the nations have broken down her choice vines; as far as Jazer they reached; they strayed through the desert; her branches were stretched out; they crossed the sea. ⁹ᵃ Therefore I weep with the weeping of Jazer for the vine of Sibmah; I drench you with my tears, O Heshbon and Elealeh, ⁹ᵇ for upon your summer fruit and upon your harvest a shout has fallen.

Jer 48:32

מִבְּכִי יַעְזֵר אֶבְכֶּה לָּךְ הַגֶּפֶן שִׂבְמָה נְטִישֹׁתַיִךְ עָבְרוּ יָם עַד יַעְזֵר נָגָעוּ עַל קֵיצֵךְ וְעַל בְּצִירֵךְ שֹׁדֵד נָפָל

More than the weeping of Jazer I weep for you, O vine, Sibmah; your branches crossed the sea; as far as[13] Jazer they reached. Upon your summer fruit and upon your vintage a devastator has fallen.

It is conspicuous that here the text of Jeremiah is much shorter than that of Isaiah. At first glance, this seems to indicate the priority of the Jeremiah text, which would contrast with the observations made on the preceding verses. Yet, another explanation can be given for the different length of the texts. It is possible that the author of Jer 48:32 did not use all of Isa 16:8–9 for poetological reasons and/or because of considerations about content and context. Alternatively, the author of Jer 48:32 used a version of Isa 16 that was somewhat shorter than the MT version.

There are several details that corroborate the priority of Isa 16:8–9. Difficult and peculiar expressions have been replaced in the Jeremiah text. Instead of the *hapax legomenon* שלחות ("branches")[14] that is found in Isa 16:8, Jer 48:32 has the more common word for branches נטישת,[15] and instead of the strange sentence הידד נפל ("a shout has fallen"), as in Isa

---

13. The translation according to the shorter text of the LXX. MT adds ים before יעזר.

14. Wilhelm Gesenius, *Hebräisches und Aramäisches Handwörterbuch über das Alte Testament* (ed. Herbert Donner; 18th ed.; Heidelberg: Springer, 2010), 6:1363; David J. A. Clines, ed., *The Dictionary of Classical Hebrew* (8 vols; Sheffield: Sheffield Phoenix, 1993– 2011), 8:365.

15. Cf. Jer 5:10.

16:9, Jer 48:32 has the more comprehensible שדד נפל ("a devastator has fallen"). This change is also a harmonization with the broader context of Jer 48:32, since the word שדד ("devastator") already occurs in Jer 48:8 and 18. Another facilitation of meaning is the change of קצירך ("your harvest") into בצירך ("your vintage"), because the latter fits better with the preceding קיץ ("your summer fruit"). The word קציר usually refers to grain harvest that was done earlier in the year, whereas summer fruit and grapes were harvested around the same time. This modification was made by the change of only one consonant (בציר/קציר).

The different order of the shared material is notable. The beginning and end of Jer 48:32 find parallels in Isa 16:9, while parts of the middle section of Jer 48:32 correspond to Isa 16:8. If we assume that the Jeremiah text is dependent on Isa 16:8–9, we have to conclude that its author rearranged the source material with considerable freedom. Sentences were relocated and restructured. In effect, the source text has been rewritten.

The parallels with Isa 16 continue in Jer 48:33. This verse corresponds to Isa 16:10.

Isa 16:10

וְנֶאֱסַף שִׂמְחָה וָגִיל מִן הַכַּרְמֶל וּבַכְּרָמִים לֹא יְרֻנָּן לֹא יְרֹעָע יַיִן בַּיְקָבִים לֹא יִדְרֹךְ הַדֹּרֵךְ הֵידָד הִשְׁבַּתִּי

And joy and rejoicing are taken away from the orchard, and in the vineyards no songs are sung, no shouts are raised, no treader treads out wine in the presses; I have made the shout to cease.

Jer 48:33

וְנֶאֶסְפָה שִׂמְחָה וָגִיל מֵאֶרֶץ מוֹאָב וְיַיִן מִיקָבִים הִשְׁבַּתִּי לֹא יִדְרֹךְ הֵידָד הֵידָד לֹא הֵידָד

And joy and rejoicing are taken away[16] from the land of Moab, and I have made wine to cease from the presses; none treads with shouting; the shouting is no shouting.

---

16. Here the shorter text of the LXX is probably to be preferred (e.g., Holladay, *Jeremiah*, 2:343). The MT adds ומכרמל ("from the orchard and"), which could be a secondary assimilation to Isa 16:10.

These verses also contain some differences that indicate the priority of the Isaiah version. Some of the material is assimilated to the context of Jer 48 (מארץ מואב, "from the land of Moab," instead of מן הכרמל, "from the orchard," seems to be borrowed from Jer 48:24), and some is amplified (Jer 48:33 adds the peculiar sentence[17] הידד לא הידד, "the shouting is no shouting," which modifies the motif of the ceased shouting by explaining that a shout of horror has replaced the joyful shouting[18]). The Isaiah version also contains a major plus: ובכרמים לא ירנן לא ירעע ("and in the vineyards no songs are sung, no shouts are raised"). This passage was either deliberately omitted by the author of Jer 48, or it was secondarily added to Isa 16. The first option is more probable than the second since the passage adds virtually nothing beyond the rest of the text, and the author of Jer 48 could have regarded it as superfluous in the context of his new composition.

In sum, the cumulative evidence from all the verses strongly speaks for the secondary nature of Jer 48:29–33 in relation to Isa 16. Some passages of the Isaiah material have been expanded, and several modifications of terms and phrases can be explained as attempts to express an idea in a clearer way, for example, by using more common words than in the source text. Especially important are those changes that seem to be influenced by both the immediate context of Jer 48 and the wider context of the entire book of Jeremiah. The author of Jer 48 obviously sought to harmonize the text adopted from Isa 16 with its new context in the book of Jeremiah. From a technical perspective, Jer 48:29–33 can be characterized as a rewritten version of Isa 16:6–10.

The author of this rewritten prophecy used the material from Isaiah in striking density. He did not add much of his own, but it also seems that he was not bound to use all material of his source. To be sure, it is possible that some of the plusses of the Isaiah version were added later. Nevertheless, it would be rather difficult to explain all of the plusses in Isa 16:6–10 as later expansions, since many of them are indispensable parts of the syntactic and poetic structure. One has to assume that in rendering the new text the author of Jer 48:29–33 deliberately skipped some sections of the source text.

Although Jer 48:29–33 turns out to be a text in which most parts of Isa 16:6–10 have been recycled, it is at the same time a completely new com-

---

17. The MT is often regarded as corrupt; thus, e.g., Rudolph, *Jeremia*, 242; Holladay, *Jeremiah*, 2:344.

18. Thus already Rashi; see Lundbom, *Jeremiah 37–52*, 294.

position. Without the source, one would not be able to recognize that Jer 48:29–33 is a rewritten version of an older text. It is remarkable that this prophecy, despite being a rewritten text, is composed as poetry, as indicated by the cola structure and the parallelisms.[19] The late editor behind Jer 48:29–33 was thus able to emulate older poetical texts and/or create new texts of corresponding structure.

11.2. A Prose Supplement: Jeremiah 48:34

The following verse, Jer 48:34, differs from the preceding composition, because it has no poetical structure.

Jer 48:34

מזעקת חשבון עד אלעלה עד יהץ נתנו קולם מצער עד חרנים עגלת שלשיה
כי גם מי נמרים למשמות יהיו

> From the cry of Heshbon as far as Elealeh, as far as Jahaz they raised their voice, from Zoar as far as Horonayim, Eglath-Shelishiyah; indeed, even the waters of Nimrim are a desolation.

This verse appears to be a prose supplement to the preceding poem of Jer 48:29–33. One could conclude from this observation that v. 34 was added by another hand.[20] This assumption is also suggested by the fact that the verse corresponds to an entirely different part of the Isaiah oracle than does Jer 48:29–33. Jeremiah 48:34 uses words and phrases that are found in Isa 15:4–6.

Isa 15:4–6

ותזעק חֶשְׁבּוֹן וְאֶלְעָלֵה עַד יַהַץ נשמע קוֹלָם עַל כן חלצי מואב יריעו נפשו ירעה לו
לבי למואב יזעק בריחה עד צֹעַר עֶגְלַת שְׁלִשִׁיָּה כי מעלה הלוחית בבכי יעלה
בו כי דרך חוֹרֹנַיִם זעקת שבר יעערו
כִּי מֵי נִמְרִים מְשַׁמּוֹת יִהְיוּ כי יבש חציר כלה דשא ירק לא היה

---

19. *Pace BHS*, this probably also includes vv. 30–31 (Carroll, *Jeremiah*, 789; Holladay, *Jeremiah*, 2:343; Lundbom, *Jeremiah 37–52*, 286–87).
20. Lundbom, *Jeremiah 37–52*, 294.

⁴ And Heshbon cried out and Elealeh; as far as Jahaz their voice is heard; therefore the armed men of Moab shout; his soul has trembled within him. ⁵ My heart cries out for Moab; his fugitives flee to Zoar, Eglath-Shelishiyah. Indeed, on the ascent of Luhith they climb up upon it with weeping. Indeed, on the way of Horonayim they raise a cry of destruction. ⁶ Indeed, the waters of Nimrim are a desolation; indeed, the grass is withered, the new growth fails, there is no green thing.

Jer 48:34

מִזַּעֲקַת חֶשְׁבּוֹן עַד אֶלְעָלֵה עַד יַהַץ נָתְנוּ קוֹלָם מִצֹּעַר עַד חֹרֹנַיִם עֶגְלַת שְׁלִשִׁיָּה
כִּי גַם מֵי נִמְרִים לִמְשַׁמּוֹת יִהְיוּ

From the cry of Heshbon as far as Elealeh, as far as Jahaz they raised their voice, from Zoar as far as Horonayim, Eglath Shelishiyah; indeed, even the waters of Nimrim are a desolation.

It is peculiar that a part of this source text already has another parallel in Jer 48, namely in the opening verses of the chapter.

Isa 15:5

לִבִּי לְמוֹאָב יִזְעָק בְּרִיחֶהָ עַד צֹעַר עֶגְלַת שְׁלִשִׁיָּה
כִּי מַעֲלֵה הַלּוּחִית בִּבְכִי יַעֲלֶה בּוֹ
כִּי דֶּרֶךְ חוֹרֹנַיִם זַעֲקַת שֶׁבֶר יְעֹעֵרוּ

My heart cries out for Moab; his fugitives flee to Zoar, Eglath-Shelishiyah. Indeed, on the ascent of Luhith they climb up upon it with weeping. Indeed, on the way of Horonayim they raise a cry of destruction.

Jer 48:5

כִּי מַעֲלֵה הַלֻּחוֹת
בִּבְכִי יַעֲלֶה בֶּכִי
כִּי בְּמוֹרַד חוֹרֹנַיִם
צַעֲקַת שֶׁבֶר שָׁמֵעוּ

Indeed, on the ascent of Luhith,²¹ they climb up with weeping, with

---

21. With Qere.

weeping. Indeed, on the descent of Horonayim,²² they have heard a cry of destruction.

These parallels are difficult to explain since they are found within a completely different section of Jer 48. William Holladay assumes that the two cola of Jer 48:5 originally belonged to v. 34, but after a scribal mistake they were "written in the margin" and later "erroneously incorporated into the previous column."²³ Clearly, without documented evidence this is rather speculative and not the only possible explanation: Jer 48:5 could also be a quotation of Isa 15:5 that is independent of the secondary v. 34. The author of v. 34 could have been inspired by the fact that Jer 48:5, which was part of an older version of the chapter, already drew on Isa 15:5. Another possibility is that Jer 48:5 was secondarily added to its current location, inspired by the parallels to Isa 15–16 in the last verses of Jer 48. All three options are conceivable, but without further documented evidence it remains difficult to determine which is correct.

11.3. Another Oracle Composed of Isaianic Phrases: Jeremiah 48:35–38a

The parallels with Isa 15–16 continue in Jer 48:35–38a. In contrast to the preceding verses (Jer 48:29–33, 34), the parallels of this passage are found not in a single part of the Isaiah text (as in Jer 48:29–33 // Isa 16:6–10 and Jer 48:34 // Isa 15:5) but in three different parts of Isa 15–16 (Isa 16:11–12; 15:2–3; 15:7). Given the priority of the Isaiah material, this indicates a change of the editorial method. The author or authors of Jer 48:35–38 composed this text by collecting material from different passages in Isa 15–16.

Isa 16:11-12; 15:2-3, 7

16:12 וְהָיָה כִי נִרְאָה כִּי נִלְאָה מוֹאָב עַל הַבָּמָה
וּבָא אֶל מִקְדָּשׁוֹ לְהִתְפַּלֵּל וְלֹא יוּכָל
16:11 עַל כֵּן מֵעַי לְמוֹאָב כַּכִּנּוֹר יֶהֱמוּ
וְקִרְבִּי לְקִיר חָרֶשׂ

---

22. With LXX; MT adds צרי ("the adversaries of"), which probably goes back to a marginal gloss.

23. Holladay, *Jeremiah*, 2:340 (see also 346).

15:7 עַל בֵּן יִתְרָה עָשָׂה וּפְקֻדָּתָם
על נחל הערבים ישאום
15:2 ... בְּכָל רָאשָׁיו קָרְחָה בָּל זָקָן גְּרוּעָה
15:3 בחוצתיו חגרו שָׂק
עַל גַּגּוֹתֶיהָ וּבִרְחֹבֹתֶיהָ כֻּלֹּה יְיֵלִיל יֹרֵד בַּבֶּכִי

16:12 And when he appears, when Moab wearies himself on the high place and comes to his sanctuary to pray, he will not be able.
16:11 Therefore my bowels moan for Moab like a harp, and my inward parts for Kir-heres.
15:7 Therefore the riches he has made and their provisions, they carry over the wadi of the poplars.
15:2 ... On all his heads is baldness; every beard is cut off.
15:3 On his streets they are girded with sackcloth; on her roofs and in her squares all of him wails, going down with weeping.

Jer 48:35–38

והשבתי למואב נאם יהוה מעלה [עַל הַ]בָּמָה ומקטיר לאלהיו
עַל כֵּן לִבִּי לְמוֹאָב כַּחֲלִלִים יֶהֱמֶה וְלִבִּי אֶל אַנְשֵׁי קִיר חֶרֶשׂ כַּחֲלִילִים יֶהֱמֶה
עַל בֵּן יִתְרַת עָשָׂה אָבָדוּ
כִּי כָל רֹאשׁ קָרְחָה וְכָל זָקָן גְּרֻעָה עַל כָּל יָדַיִם גְּדֻדֹת וְעַל מָתְנַיִם שָׂק
עַל כָּל גַּגּוֹת מוֹאָב וּבִרְחֹבֹתֶיהָ כֻּלֹּה מִסְפֵּד כִּי שָׁבַרְתִּי אֶת מוֹאָב כִּכְלִי אֵין חֵפֶץ בּוֹ נְאֻם יהוה

35 And I will bring to an end in Moab—oracle of Yhwh—who offers [on the]²⁴ high place and burns to his god. 36 Therefore my heart moans for Moab like flutes, and my heart toward the men of Kir-heres moans like flutes; therefore the riches he has made have perished. 37 Indeed, every head is baldness, and every beard is cut off; on all hands are gashes, and on the loins is sackcloth. 38 On all the roofs of Moab and in her squares, all of him is lamentation. For I have broken Moab like a jar in which no one takes delight—oracle of Yhwh.

In contrast with the Isaiah version, the composition of Jer 48:35–38 is introduced in v. 35 as an oracle of Yhwh. Although this verse contains only a short parallel with the Isaiah text (עַל הבמה, "on the high place"), it can be regarded as an interpretation of this text. While according to Isa 16:12 Moab will not be able to pray, Jer 48:35 adds that Yhwh himself brings

---

24. With LXX. The MT (מעלה במה) seems to be the result of haplography.

an end to the worship of Moab's god (השבתי, "I will bring to an end," is resumed from the preceding v. 33). The participles מעלה ("who offers") and מקטיר ("who burns") could have been borrowed from another passage of the book of Jeremiah (Jer 33:18).

The next verse (Jer 48:36) combines material from two different parts of Isa 15–16 (Isa 16:11 and 15:7). Isaiah 16:11 is considerably modified in Jer 48:36a: מעי ("my bowels") is replaced with לבי ("my heart"), כנור ("harp") with חללים ("flutes"),[25] and the city name "Kir-heres" is expanded with the phrase אל אנשי ("toward the men of"), which is resumed from v. 31. However, Jer 48:36b seems to be rather mechanically copied from Isa 15:7a: על כן ("Therefore") fits the context in Isa 15 but not in Jer 48:36b, because what is mentioned here is not the consequence of the moaning but its reason.[26] The addition of the verb אבדו ("they have perished"), which probably refers to the collective noun יתרת ("abundance, riches"),[27] can be regarded as an interpretation of the source text since Isa 15:7 describes how the rest of Moab's wealth is carried away. The word אבד ("to be lost") is already used in another part of Jer 48, namely, in v. 8, which belongs to the older core of the chapter.

Jeremiah 48:37–38a is composed of motifs and phrases from Isa 15:2 and 3 that describe signs and rites of mourning. In this case, only minor changes can be observed that do not affect the meaning substantially: חגרו שק ("they are girded with sackcloth") is replaced with על מתנים שק ("on the loins is sackcloth"), and instead of כלה ייליל ירד בבכי ("all of him wails, going down with weeping"), the Jeremiah text has the short and simple nominal clause כלה מספד ("all of him is lamentation"). The Jeremiah text adds על כל ידים גדדת ("on all hands are gashes")—the motif of gashes is mentioned repeatedly in the book of Jeremiah in the context of mourning rites.[28]

The rewriting of phrases from Isa 15–16 suddenly stops after Jer 48:38a. Verse 38b adds another oracle that has no parallel in the Isaiah material: "For I have broken Moab like a jar in which no one takes delight—oracle of Yhwh." This is clearly influenced by Jer 22:28, where the phrase כלי אין חפץ בו ("a jar in which no one takes delight") occurs.

---

25. Flutes seem to be more closely related to the ritual of mourning; see Rudolph, *Jeremia*, 244, who refers to Matt 9:23 and Josephus, *J.W.* 3.9.5.

26. McKane, *Jeremiah 26–52*, 1189.

27. Rudolph, *Jeremia*, 242.

28. Cf. Jer 16:6; 41:5; 47:5; and the conjecture in 49:3.

11.4. Results and Methodological Consequences

The parallels between Isa 15–16 and Jer 48 give exemplary insight into the production of literary prophecy. Many details indicate that the author(s) of Jer 48:29–38 used Isa 15–16 as a quarry of words, phrases, and motifs to create a new text. Some of the material taken from the source was left unaltered, some was slightly modified, and some was rearranged or more substantially changed, and some new formulations were added. The material in Jer 48:29–38 that finds no parallel in Isa 15–16 was mostly inspired by or taken from the older core of Jer 48, or from other parts of the book. These additions served to adapt the material taken from Isaiah to its new context.

This process of creating new Jeremianic prophecies continued at the end of Jer 48, which utilizes material from other parts of the Hebrew Bible. Quotations of the so-called Isaiah apocalypse (Isa 24:17–18 // Jer 48:43–44) are combined with material about Moab taken from the book of Numbers (Num 21:28 // Jer 48:45; Num 24:17 // Jer 48:45–46). In part, these expansions seem to have been made after the Hebrew *Vorlage* of the LXX diverged from the shared textual tradition with the MT since the MT contains several sentences that are not yet included in the LXX. In particular, the quotations from Numbers are still missing in the LXX, which implies that they were added to the proto-MT at a very late stage.

The authors of these literary prophecies at the end of Jer 48 (beginning with the use of Isa 16:6–10 in Jer 48:29–33) were writing in the name of Jeremiah, since they contributed to the large scroll that bears the title דברי ירמיהו ("The words of Jeremiah"; Jer 1:1 MT). It is probable that they identified their scribal activity, or wanted it to be identified, with the authority of this great prophet. At the same time, they made extensive use of another prophetic book. They did not create a completely new text but reused words and phrases that already existed somewhere else in the prophetic literature. This editorial attitude may derive from the assumption that all prophets were inspired by the same divine spirit and thus were using similar words and phrases. Clearly, the authors behind Jer 48:29–33 regarded the texts used as sources as having considerable authority, for otherwise they would hardly have used them in the first place. At the same time, however, these authors had no problems in making considerable changes to these texts.

The passage where the parallels with Isa 15–16 occur can be divided into three parts: vv. 29–33, v. 34, and vv. 35–38a. These parts show basically the same technique of rearranging the Isaiah material, but there are also some differences. In the first and second parts, coherent sections of the Isaiah text are used, whereas the author(s) of the third part collected material from three different parts of Isa 15–16. The style of the rearranged material also varies. While vv. 29–33 have a poetical structure, v. 34 is written in prose, and vv. 35–38a display a prosaic style with some poetic elements that could be described as rhythmic prose.[29] It is possible that these differences of scribal technique indicate the activity of three different editors who subsequently adapted material from Isa 15–16 to the context of Jer 48.

The comparison between Jer 48 and Isa 15–16 shows how limited the means of reconstructing the literary prehistory of a transmitted text can be in some cases. This seems to be especially true for poetic texts. Without knowledge of Isa 15–16, it would be next to impossible to reconstruct the original form of the source text, and, indeed, it could even be asked if one would be able to discern that this passage consists of recycled material from an older source. In relation to Isa 15–16, the author(s) of Jer 48:29–38 used a method that can be characterized as rewriting. Due to this method, the text does not betray that it was written on the basis of an older source text. Consequently, the analysis of Jer 48 provides a firm methodological warning against trusting too much in the potential for reconstructing the textual sources of a given text, especially in poetic compositions. The possibility that such rewriting took place in the history of a text has to be taken into account.

---

29. Lundbom, *Jeremiah 37–52*, 296.

12

Evidence of Psalm Composition: Psalm 108 as a Secondary Compilation of Other Psalm Texts

Psalm exegesis often does not pay much attention to the intricate problems of literary history. Psalms are interpreted as given literary units, irrespective of whether they were in fact initially created as such units or bear marks of editorial work. There is evidence, however, that gives strikingly clear insight into the editorial processes that took place in the literary history of single psalms and of the entire Psalter. Clear documented evidence for these processes is found at Qumran, in particular in the great Psalms scroll 11QPs^a and in the manuscript 4Q236, both of which show considerable differences from the versions of the MT and the LXX.[1] Yet, some empirical evidence for editorial activity can also be found within the canonical Psalter, for some psalms are found in two different versions in different parts of the Psalter—for example, Ps 14 and Ps 53, or Ps 40:14–18 and Ps 70. This chapter focuses on one such case, Ps 108 and its parallels in Pss 57 and 60. The example shows how some psalm texts were rearranged and altered by editors. The textual evidence is based mainly on the MT, but the LXX version will also be considered.

---

1. On 11QPs^a, see, e.g., Ulrich Dahmen, *Psalmen- und Psalterrezeption im Frühjudentum: Rekonstruktion, Textbestand, Struktur und Pragmatik der Psalmenrolle 11QPsa aus Qumran* (STDJ 49; Leiden: Brill, 2003); Martin Leuenberger, *Konzeptionen des Königtums Gottes im Psalter: Untersuchungen zu Komposition und Redaktion der theokratischen Bücher IV–V im Psalter* (ATANT; Zürich: Theologischer Verlag, 2004), 11–16. On 4Q236, see Peter W. Flint, "A Form of Psalm 89 (4Q236 = 4QPs89)," in *Pseudepigraphic and Non-Masoretic Psalms and Prayers* (Vol. 4A of *The Dead Sea Scrolls: Hebrew, Aramaic, and Greek Texts with English Translations*; ed. James H. Charlesworth; Tübingen: Mohr Siebeck; Louisville: Westminster John Knox, 1997), 40–45.

12.1. The Phenomenon: Psalm 108 and Its Parallels in Psalms 57 and 60

Apart from the superscription שיר מזמור לדוד ("A song, a psalm of David"; v. 1),[2] Ps 108 has a close parallel in two other psalms. The first part (vv. 2–6) is almost identical to Ps 57:8–12, while the second part (vv. 7–14) corresponds with Ps 60:7–14.[3]

Ps 108:2–6	Ps 57:8–12
נכון לבי אלהים	נכון לבי אלהים
	נכון לבי
אשירה ואזמרה	אשירה ואזמרה
אַף כבודי	עוּרָה כבודי
עורה הנבל וכנור	עורה הנבל וכנור
אעירה שחר	אעירה שחר
אודך בעמים יְהוָה	אודך בעמים אֲדֹנָי
וַאזמרך בל אמים	אזמרך בל אמים
כי גדול מֵעַל שמים חסדך	כי גדל עַד שמים חסדך
ועד שחקים אמתך	ועד שחקים אמתך
רומה על שמים אלהים	רומה על שמים אלהים
וְעל כל הארץ כבודך	על כל הארץ כבודך

Ps 108:2–6

[2] My heart is steadfast, O God; I will sing and make melody, even with my glory!
[3] Awake, O harp and lyre; I will awake the dawn!
[4] I will give thanks to you among the peoples, O Yhwh, and I will sing praises to you among the nations.
[5] For your steadfast love is higher than the heavens, and your faithfulness extends to the clouds.

---

2. Verse numbers for all English translations refer to the MT numbering.
3. In this chapter, the plusses in one version are underlined, while other differences are displayed in dashed underline. Dotted underline marks parallels.

PSALM 108

⁶ Be exalted above the heavens, O God, and let your glory be over all the earth!

Ps 57:8–12

⁸ My heart is steadfast, O God, my heart is steadfast; I will sing and make melody!
⁹ Awake, my glory, awake, O harp and lyre; I will awake the dawn!
¹⁰ I will give thanks to you among the peoples, O Lord; I will sing praises to you among the nations.
¹¹ For your steadfast love is as high as the heavens, and your faithfulness extends to the clouds.
¹² Be exalted above the heavens, O God; let your glory be over all the earth!

Ps 108:7–14	Ps 60:7–14
למען יחלצון ידידיך	למען יחלצון ידידיך
הושיעה ימינך וענֵנִי	הושיעה ימינך וענֵנוּ
אלהים דבר בקדשו	אלהים דבר בקדשו
אעלזה אחלקה שכם	אעלזה אחלקה שכם
ועמק סכות אמדד	ועמק סכות אמדד
לי גלעד לי מנשה	לי גלעד וְלי מנשה
ואפרים מעוז ראשי	ואפרים מעוז ראשי
יהודה מחקקי	יהודה מחקקי
מואב סיר רחצי	מואב סיר רחצי
על אדום אשליך נעלי	על אדום אשליך נעלי
עלי פלשת אֶתְרוֹעָע	עלֵי פלשת הִתְרוֹעָעִי
מי יבלני עיר מַבְצָר	מי יבלני עיר מָצוֹר
מי נחני עד אדום	מי נחני עד אדום
הלא אלהים זנחתנו	הלא אַתָּה אלהים זנחתנו
ולא תצא אלהים בצבאותינו	ולא תצא אלהים בצבאותינו
הבה לנו עזרת מצר	הבה לנו עזרת מצר
ושוא תשועת אדם	ושוא תשועת אדם
באלהים נעשה חיל	באלהים נעשה חיל
והוא יבוס צרינו	והוא יבוס צרינו

Ps 108:7–14

⁷ That those whom you love may be rescued, save with your right hand, and answer me.
⁸ God has spoken in his sanctuary: "With exultation I will divide up Shechem and portion out the Vale of Succoth.
⁹ Gilead is mine, Manasseh is mine, and Ephraim is the defense of my head; Judah is my scepter.
¹⁰ Moab is my washbasin; on Edom I hurl my shoe; over Philistia I shout (in triumph)."
¹¹ Who will bring me to the fortified city? Who will lead me to Edom?
¹² Is it not, O God, that you rejected us? And you do not go out, O God, with our armies!
¹³ O grant us help against the foe, for human help is worthless.
¹⁴ With God we shall do valiantly; it is he who will tread down our foes.

Ps 60:7–14

⁷ That those whom you love may be rescued, save with your right hand and answer us.
⁸ God has spoken in his sanctuary: "With exultation I will divide up Shechem and portion out the Vale of Succoth.
⁹ Gilead is mine, and Manasseh is mine, and Ephraim is the defense of my head; Judah is my scepter.
¹⁰ Moab is my washbasin; on Edom I hurl my shoe; over me, O Philistia, shout!"
¹¹ Who will bring me to the fortress city? Who will lead me to Edom?
¹² Is it not, O God, that you rejected us? And you do not go out, O God, with our armies!
¹³ O grant us help against the foe, for human help is worthless.
¹⁴ With God we shall do valiantly; it is he who will tread down our foes.

These parallels can be explained in two ways:[4] Ps 108 could have been composed by quotations from Ps 57 and 60, or both Ps 57 and 60 could

---

4. A third option is proposed by Mitchell Dahood, *Psalms III: 101–150* (AB 17A; Garden City, N.Y.: Doubleday, 1970), 93; he assumes that in all three psalms the same "ancient religious poems" are used. This assumption, however, is not necessary, for it does not bring any heuristic advantage (Occam's razor). It is also possible that the source texts of Ps 108 are simply identical with Ps 57 and Ps 60, which would make the assumption of an unknown source irrelevant. The elohistic shape of Ps 108, which cannot be explained by Dahood's theory (see below, 12.2), further suggests that an

quote parts of Ps 108. However, the comparison between the parallel texts supports only the first possibility.[5]

12.2. General Arguments for the Priority of Psalm 57 and Psalm 60

A good starting point to reconstruct the relationship between the three psalms is the observation that both parts of Ps 108 differ in form and content. These differences are related to those parts of Ps 57 and Ps 60 that have no parallel in Ps 108.[6]

The first part of Ps 108 (vv. 2–6) is a praise of Yhwh spoken by an individual. The parallel section in Ps 57:8–12 forms the closing part of the prayer of an individual and is thus its intrinsic part. The praise of Ps 57:8–12 is also linked to this prayer in the first half of Ps 57 by shared vocabulary (שמים, "heavens"; חסד, "steadfast love"; אמת, "faithfulness" in vv. 4, 11 and the root כון in vv. 7, 8). In addition, an entire verse of the first part of the psalm is repeated in the second part (vv. 6 and 12). By virtue of these links, both parts of Ps 57 closely correspond to each other.

Ps 57:2–12

חנני אלהים חנני כי בך חסיה נפשי ובצל כנפיך אחסה עד יעבר הוות
אקרא לאלהים עליון לאל גמר עלי
ישלח מִשָּׁמַיִם וְיוֹשִׁיעֵנִי חֵרֵף שֹׁאֲפִי סֶלָה יִשְׁלַח אֱלֹהִים חַסְדּוֹ וַאֲמִתּוֹ
נפשי בתוך לבאם אשכבה להטים בני אדם וחצים ושנם חרב חדה
רוּמָה עַל הַשָּׁמַיִם אֱלֹהִים עַל כָּל הָאָרֶץ כְּבוֹדֶךָ
רשת הֵכִינוּ לִפְעָמַי כָּפַף נפשי כרו לפני שיחה נפלו בתוכה סלה
נָכוֹן לִבִּי אֱלֹהִים נָכוֹן לִבִּי אָשִׁירָה וַאֲזַמֵּרָה
עורה כבודי עורה הנבל וכנור אעירה שחר
אודך בעמים אדני אזמרך בל אמים
כִּי גָדֹל עַד שָׁמַיִם חַסְדֶּךָ וְעַד שְׁחָקִים אֲמִתֶּךָ
רוּמָה עַל שָׁמַיִם אֱלֹהִים עַל כָּל הָאָרֶץ כְּבוֹדֶךָ

---

unknown source is improbable. In addition, the detailed comparison reveals nothing that indicates that such independent poems existed, as the following observations show (see below, 12.3).

5. Raymond Jacques Tournay, "Psaumes 57, 60 et 108: Analyse et interprétation," *RB* 96 (1989): 5–26, esp. 23–26.

6. Leslie C. Allen, *Psalms 101–150* (WBC 21; Waco, Tex.: Word, 1983), 67.

² Be merciful to me, O God, be merciful to me, for in you my soul takes refuge; in the shadow of your wings I will take refuge, until the destroying storms pass by.
³ I cry to God Most High, to God who fulfills his purpose for me.
⁴ He will send from heaven and save me; he will put to shame those who trample on me. Selah. God will send forth his steadfast love and his faithfulness.
⁵ I lie down among lions—set on fire are human beings—their teeth are spears and arrows, their tongues sharp swords.
⁶ Be exalted above the heavens, O God; let your glory be over all the earth!
⁷ They set a net for my steps; my soul was bowed down. They dug a pit in my path, but they have fallen into it themselves. Selah.
⁸ My heart is steadfast,[7] O God, my heart is steadfast; I will sing and make melody!
⁹ Awake, my glory, awake, O harp and lyre; I will awake the dawn!
¹⁰ I will give thanks to you among the peoples, O Lord; I will sing praises to you among the nations.
¹¹ For your steadfast love is as high as the heavens, and your faithfulness extends to the clouds.
¹² Be exalted above the heavens, O God; let your glory be over all the earth!

The second part of Ps 108 (vv. 7–14) includes a plea for help (v. 7), a divine oracle (vv. 8–10), questions of an individual speaker (v. 11), and concluding prayers and confessions of the community (vv. 12–13, 14). The parallels to these verses are found in Ps 60:7–14, and they are closely linked with the first part of the psalm, Ps 60:1–6. For example, the plea for help (Ps 60:7) is the continuation of the preceding lamentations of the community in vv. 3–6, as indicated by לְמַעַן ("That") in v. 7. The closing prayers and confessions of the community in Ps 60:12–13, 14 are related to the opening lamentations in vv. 3–5, and v. 12 is also similar to v. 3.

Ps 60:3–14

אֱלֹהִים זְנַחְתָּנוּ פְרַצְתָּנוּ אָנַפְתָּ תְּשׁוֹבֵב לָנוּ
הִרְעַשְׁתָּה אֶרֶץ פְּצַמְתָּהּ רְפָה שְׁבָרֶיהָ כִי מָטָה

---

7. Verses 7 and 8 are linked by the root כון; thus, e.g., John Goldingay, *Psalms 42–89* (vol. 2 of *Psalms*; Baker Commentary on the Old Testament Wisdom and Psalms; Grand Rapids: Baker Academic, 2007), 198.

PSALM 108

הִרְאִיתָה עַמְּךָ קָשָׁה הִשְׁקִיתָנוּ יַיִן תַּרְעֵלָה
נָתַתָּה לִּירֵאֶיךָ נֵּס לְהִתְנוֹסֵס מִפְּנֵי קֹשֶׁט סֶלָה
לְמַעַן יֵחָלְצוּן יְדִידֶיךָ הוֹשִׁיעָה יְמִינְךָ וַעֲנֵנוּ
אֱלֹהִים דִּבֶּר בְּקָדְשׁוֹ אֶעְלֹזָה אֲחַלְּקָה שְׁכֶם וְעֵמֶק סֻכּוֹת אֲמַדֵּד
לִי גִלְעָד וְלִי מְנַשֶּׁה וְאֶפְרַיִם מָעוֹז רֹאשִׁי יְהוּדָה מְחֹקְקִי
מוֹאָב סִיר רַחְצִי עַל אֱדוֹם אַשְׁלִיךְ נַעֲלִי עָלַי פְּלֶשֶׁת הִתְרוֹעָעִי
מִי יֹבִלֵנִי עִיר מָצוֹר מִי נָחַנִי עַד אֱדוֹם
הֲלֹא אַתָּה אֱלֹהִים זְנַחְתָּנוּ וְלֹא תֵצֵא אֱלֹהִים בְּצִבְאוֹתֵינוּ
הָבָה לָּנוּ עֶזְרָת מִצָּר וְשָׁוְא תְּשׁוּעַת אָדָם
בֵּאלֹהִים נַעֲשֶׂה חָיִל וְהוּא יָבוּס צָרֵינוּ

³ O God, you have rejected us, broken our defenses; you have been angry; now restore us!

⁴ You have caused the land to quake; you have torn it open; repair the cracks in it, for it is tottering.

⁵ You have made your people suffer hard things; you have given us wine to drink that made us reel.

⁶ You have set up a banner for those who fear you, to rally to it out of bowshot. Selah.

⁷ That those whom you love may be rescued, save with your right hand and answer us.

⁸ God has spoken in his sanctuary: "With exultation I will divide up Shechem and portion out the Vale of Succoth.

⁹ Gilead is mine, and Manasseh is mine, and Ephraim is the defense of my head; Judah is my scepter.

¹⁰ Moab is my washbasin; on Edom I hurl my shoe; over me, O Philistia, shout!"

¹¹ Who will bring me to the fortified city? Who will lead me to Edom?

¹² Is it not, O God, that you rejected us? And you do not go out, O God, with our armies!

¹³ O grant us help against the foe, for human help is worthless.

¹⁴ With God we shall do valiantly; it is he who will tread down our foes.

In other words, both Ps 57:8–12 and Ps 60:7–14 cannot be separated from their respective contexts without seriously disturbing the entire structure of those psalms. In contrast, Ps 108:1–6 and 7–14, the parallels to Ps 57:8–12 and Ps 60:7–14, are largely unrelated to each other. Apart from the word אלהים ("God") and most common vocabulary, like ו ("and") or על ("over"), the vocabulary of the two sections is unrelated. In addition, after the speaking of the individual in the opening of the psalm, it is surprising that the psalm closes with statements of the community (vv.

12–14).⁸ Even if we did not possess the parallel texts of Ps 108 in Pss 57 and 60, the internal tension in Ps 108 is evident and would easily lead to the assumption that the psalm does not form an integral unity and that it indeed consists of two originally different parts.

Another important argument for the secondary character of Ps 108 is related to the so-called elohistic psalter in Pss 42–83. Both Ps 57 and Ps 60 belong to this psalm group, in which the appellative אלהים ("God") occurs frequently while the divine name יהוה ("Yhwh") is used rarely. Like most psalms of Pss 42–83, Ps 108 uses אלהים ("God") throughout the text (vv. 2, 6, 8, 12, 14; v. 4 is an exception because יהוה replaces אדני from Ps 57:10⁹). This conspicuous phenomenon suggests that Ps 108 could be dependent on the elohistic psalms 57 and 60. This is corroborated by the fact that in the psalms that surround Ps 108, the use of אלהים ("God") is restricted to Ps 108. In the entire fifth book of the Psalter (Pss 107–150), the word אלהים ("God") is used in the singular only in Pss 108 and 144:9.

12.3. Minor Textual Changes in Psalm 108 Provide Additional Evidence for Its Secondary Character

These general considerations are supported by a close comparison between the parallel passages. Compared with Ps 57 and Ps 60, the text of Ps 108 differs in several details.¹⁰ Most of the differences can be explained as deliberate modifications of the source texts related to the composition of the new psalm.¹¹

---

8. On the first-person singular in v. 7 (עננִי), see below (12.3, no. 4).

9. On this difference see below (12.3, no. 2).

10. Some minor differences that need not be discussed at length are related to the use of the copula ו ("and"). It forms a small plus in Ps 108:4, 6 compared with Ps 57:10, 12, and it occurs in Ps 60:9 while it is missing in the parallel passage of Ps 108:9; in all these cases the LXX has assimilated the text of both psalms by the constant use of καί. It is possible that the use of the copula in Ps 108:4, 6 is a syntactical facilitation compared to the asyndetical bicola of the source text, while, in the case of Pss 108:9 // 60:9, the MT of Ps 108:9 could attest to a more original text. However, one should not place too much weight on this, because such small variations can always be due to scribal mistakes.

11. Ernst Axel Knauf, "Psalm lx und Psalm cviii," *VT* 50 (2000): 55–65, 63 with n. 39; Erich Zenger, in Frank-Lothar Hossfeld and Erich Zenger, *Psalmen 101–150* (Freiburg: Herder, 2008), 163–65.

1. The second colon of Ps 57:8 (נכון לבי, "my heart is steadfast") is missing in Ps 108:2. It is unlikely that this colon was secondarily added to Ps 57:8,[12] since in Ps 57:8-9 it is closely integrated into the poetic structure. These verses are composed as elaborate tricola with repetitive and climactic parallelisms.[13]

Ps 57:8-9

נכון לבי אלהים
נכון לבי
אשירה ואזמרה
עורה כבודי
עורה הנבל וכנור
אעירה שחר

[8] My heart is steadfast, O God, my heart is steadfast; I will sing and make melody!
[9] Awake, my glory, awake, O harp and lyre; I will awake the dawn!

This structure cannot be found in Ps 108:2, because the second colon, נכון לבי ("my heart is steadfast"), is not repeated.

Ps 108:2	Ps 57:8
נכון לבי אלהים	נכון לבי אלהים
	<u>נכון לבי</u>
אשירה ואזמרה	אשירה ואזמרה

Ps 108:2: My heart is steadfast, O God; I will sing and make melody.

Ps 57:8: My heart is steadfast, O God, <u>my heart is steadfast</u>; I will sing and make melody!

The missing colon is attested in the LXX version of Ps 108:2.[14] It is therefore theoretically possible that the Greek text represents here the original

---

12. *Pace*, e.g., Charles Augustus Briggs and Emily Grace Briggs, *The Book of Psalms* (2 vols.; ICC; Edinburgh: T&T Clark, 1909), 2:41.

13. Beat Weber, "'Fest ist mein Herz, o Gott!' Zu Ps 57,8-9," *ZAW* 107 (1995): 294-95.

14. Here and following, numbers for LXX psalms refer to the MT numbering.

Hebrew text, which was secondarily shortened in the proto-MT either by mistake or by intention.

Ps 108:2 MT	Ps 108:2 LXX
נכון לבי אלהים	Ἑτοίμη ἡ καρδία μου, ὁ θεός,
	ἑτοίμη ἡ καρδία μου,
אשירה ואזמרה	ᾄσομαι καὶ ψαλῶ
אף כבודי	ἐν τῇ δόξῃ μου.

Ps 108:2 MT: My heart is steadfast, O God; I will sing and make melody, even with my glory!

Ps 108:2 LXX: My heart is steadfast, O God, my heart is steadfast; I will sing and make melody in my glory!

However, it is more probable that the shortening in Ps 108 MT is related to a deliberate poetic change of the source text and that the reading in the LXX is a later harmonization of Ps 108:2 with Ps 57:8. This is indicated by another difference between Ps 108:2 MT and Ps 57:8–9 MT. The first colon of Ps 57:9 (עורה כבודי, "Awake, my glory") is modified in Ps 108:2 so that it has a different syntactical position within a tricolon.

Ps 108:2–3	Ps 57:8–9
נכון לבי אלהים	נכון לבי אלהים
	<u>נכון לבי</u>
אשירה ואזמרה	אשירה ואזמרה
אַף כבודי	<u>עוּרָה</u> כבודי
עורה הנבל וכנור	עורה הנבל וכנור
אעירה שחר	אעירה שחר

Ps 108:2–3: My heart is steadfast, O God; I will sing and make melody, <u>even with</u> my glory!
Awake, O harp and lyre; I will awake the dawn!

Ps 57:8–9: My heart is steadfast, O God, <u>my heart is steadfast</u>; I will sing and make melody!
<u>Awake</u>, my glory, awake, O harp and lyre; I will awake the dawn!

Instead of עורה כבודי ("Awake, my glory"), Ps 108:2 reads אף כבודי ("even with my glory").[15] By this change, the colon is set apart from the continuation עורה הנבל וכנור אעירה שחר ("Awake, O harp and lyre; I will awake the dawn!"). Introduced by the emphatic particle אף ("even"), כבודי ("my glory") becomes an adverbial accusative.[16] This adverbial accusative continues the preceding אשירה ואזמרה ("I will sing and make melody"). The creation of this structure is the probable poetological reason for the omission of נכון לבי ("my heart is steadfast"), since now the opening of Ps 108 (v. 2) forms a new tricolon, which culminates in the words אף כבודי ("even with my glory").

The LXX renders אף by the preposition ἐν ("in") and thus creates the phrase ἐν τῇ δόξῃ μου ("in my glory"). This reading is probably a simplifying interpretation of the unusual expression אף כבודי ("even with my glory"). Because of this change, the LXX, which adds a second colon, according to Ps 57:8 (ἑτοίμη ἡ καρδία μου, "my heart is steadfast"), as we have seen above, is able to open Ps 108 with a tricolon similar to Ps 57:8. Thus, the Greek text merges both versions of the verse. Psalm 108:2 LXX seems to have been created in order to assimilate the opening of Ps 108 with Ps 57:8.[17]

---

15. Thus KJV; cf. William G. Braude, ed., *The Midrash on Psalms* (2 vols.; Yale Judaica Series 13; New Haven: Yale University, 1959), 2:200.

16. Corresponding to GKC §118m.

17. Allen, *Psalms 101-150*, 66. This tendency of assimilation can be observed in other cases as well; see below 4, 5, and 7. It is difficult to decide if this tendency goes back to the Greek translation or to its Hebrew *Vorlage*. Related to this question is the phenomenon that two peculiar translations of the Hebrew text occur in both Ps 60:9-10 and Ps 108:9-10, which indicates that one translation influenced the other, or that both were done by the same translator (יהודה מחקקי, "Judah is my scepter," is translated with Ιουδας βασιλεύς μου, "Judas is my king," and מואב סיר רחצי, "Moab is my washbasin," with Μωαβ λέβης τῆς ἐλπίδος μου, "Moab is the cauldron of my hope"; these translations could give an important clue for the dating of the LXX Psalter; cf. Joachim Schaper, "Der Septuaginta-Psalter: Interpretation, Aktualisierung und liturgische Verwendung der biblischen Psalmen im hellenistischen Judentum," in *Der Psalter in Judentum und Christentum*, [ed. Erich Zenger; Herder's Biblical Studies 18; Freiburg: Herder, 1998], 168-72). However, it has to be noted that there are also three instances where the LXX translates the parallel passages differently even though the MT does not differ (Ps 108:8: Ὑψωθήσομαι, "I will be exalted" // Ps 60:8: Ἀγαλλιάσομαι, "I will rejoice"; Ps 108:9: ἀντίλημψις, "help" // Ps 60:9: κραταίωσις, "strength"; Ps 108:14: τοὺς ἐχθροὺς ἡμῶν, "our enemies" // Ps 60:14 τοὺς θλίβοντας ἡμᾶς, "those who oppress

2. Psalm 108:4 uses the word יהוה ("Yhwh") instead of אדני ("Lord"), which is used in Ps 57:10.

Ps 108:4   Ps 57:10

אודך בעמים יְהוָה   אודך בעמים אֲדֹנָי

Ps 108:4: I will give thanks to you among the peoples, O Yhwh.

Ps 57:10: I will give thanks to you among the peoples, O Lord.

Erich Zenger has proposed two possible explanations for this alteration, both related to the context of Ps 108 in the Psalter.[18] First, the phrase אודך בעמים יהוה ("I will give thanks to you among the peoples, O Yhwh") could refer to the preceding Ps 107, where the expression "giving thanks [ידה hiphil] to Yhwh" is recurrently used (vv. 1, 8, 15, etc.). This would explain why אדני ("Lord") was replaced by יהוה ("Yhwh"). Second, this change could also be related to the context of the small Davidic composition of Pss 108–110. In Ps 110:1 the word אדון ("lord") is distinctly referring to the messianic king, not to Yhwh (נאם יהוה לאדני, "The oracle of Yhwh to my lord"). The replacement of אדני ("Lord") by יהוה ("Yhwh") in Ps 108:4 would avert the possible misunderstanding that Ps 108 could address the messianic king.[19] Both reasons are well imaginable, and it is possible that either caused the replacement of אדני ("Lord") with יהוה ("Yhwh").

3. A strong argument for the secondary and composite nature of Ps 108 is found in v. 5, which attests to a theologically motivated change.

Ps 108:5   Ps 57:11

כי גדל מֵעַל שמים חסדך   כי גדל עַד שמים חסדך

ועד שחקים אמתך   ועד שחקים אמתך

Ps 108:5: For your steadfast love is higher than the heavens, and your faithfulness extends to the clouds.

---

us"). These different translations are much more difficult to explain; perhaps they are related to certain theological lines of the LXX Psalter.

18. Hossfeld and Zenger, *Psalmen 101–150*, 164.

19. It is not a counterargument that Ps 109:21 refers to יהוה אדני ("Yhwh, my Lord"), since here a misunderstanding of אדני is not possible, as the word is combined with the divine name.

Ps 57:11: For your steadfast love is as high as the heavens, and your faithfulness extends to the clouds.

The prepositional phrase מעל ("higher than") expands the dimension of the divine חסד ("steadfast love") beyond the heavens. While Ps 57 praises God's חסד as comparable with the heavens, Ps 108 stresses that it is even larger than this cosmic entity. This can be explained as a tendentious or dogmatic change, since Ps 108:5 tries to avoid the notion that the divine חסד is limited by the heavens. The altered text is also attested by the LXX and is likely to have been contained in its Hebrew *Vorlage*.

4. A very small but possibly important difference can be found between Pss 60:7 and 108:7. Psalm 60:7 contains the Kethib ענונ ("answer *us*"; Qere: עננ, "answer *me*"), while Ps 108:7 reads עננ ("answer *me*"). To be sure, one could argue that the reading of Ps 108:7 simply goes back to a scribal mistake, since the letters ו and י were often confounded in the process of copying. However, it is also possible to explain the small variation as an intentional change related to the context in Ps 108. The singular suffix עננ ("answer *me*") links the plea closely to the preceding prayer (108:2–6), which has a speaker in the first-person singular, while in Ps 60:7 the first-person plural is closely related to the first part of the psalm.

Ps 108:2, 7	Ps 60:3, 7
נכון לבי אלהים	אלהים זנחתנו פרצתנו
...	...
למען יחלצון ידידיך	למען יחלצון ידידיך
הושיעה ימינך וענני	הושיעה ימינך וענננו

Ps 108:2, 7: *My* heart is steadfast, O God, ...
That those whom you love may be rescued, save with your right hand and answer *me*.

Ps 60:3, 7: O God, you have rejected *us*, broken *our* defenses; ...
That those whom you love may be rescued, save with your right hand and answer *us*.

The LXX reads καὶ ἐπάκουσόν μου ("and hear *me*") in both Ps 60:7 and Ps 108:7. This reading corresponds to the Masoretic Qere of Ps 60:7 (עננ, "answer *me*") and the MT of Ps 108:7. It can be assumed that both the LXX reading and the Qere of Ps 60:7 have been influenced by the proto-MT of

Ps 108:7, thus further attesting to the harmonization between the parallel sections of Ps 108 in Pss 57 and 60.

5. A theologically important difference can be observed in Ps 108:10 and Ps 60:10. Whereas in Ps 60:10 Philistia is called by God to shout joyfully over him, in Ps 108:10 God himself is shouting over Philistia.

Ps 108:10	Ps 60:10
מואב סיר רחצי	מואב סיר רחצי
על אדום אשליך נעלי	על אדום אשליך נעלי
עלי פלשת אֶתְרוֹעָע	עָלַי פְּלֶשֶׁת הִתְרוֹעָעִי

Ps 108:10: Moab is my washbasin; on Edom I hurl my shoe; over Philistia I shout (in triumph).

Ps 60:10: Moab is my washbasin; on Edom I hurl my shoe; over me, O Philistia, shout!

In Ps 60, Philistia takes part in the worldwide joy because of Yhwh's triumph,[20] but in Ps 108, a hostile attitude toward Philistia comes to the fore. Theoretically, either version could be original, but it is more probable that the hostile attitude is a contextual facilitation. This is suggested by the fact that the verse relates to Judah's neighbors in the east, Moab and Edom, in a clearly hostile manner.[21] In other words, Ps 108:10 assimilates the attitude toward Philistia and the attitude toward Moab and Edom. In addition, compared with the parallel passage in Ps 60:10, the version of Ps 108:10 is easier to read because both verbs occur in the first-person singular (אשליך, "I hurl"; אתרועע, "I shout"), and the third colon forms a synonymous parallelism with the second. Compared to this version, Ps 60:10 is syntactically and poetically more difficult, since the imperative in the colon that addresses Philistia is not set up by the preceding text. Thus, it can be assumed that the verbal form was modified in Ps 108 in order to create a smoother and more coherent version of the verse.

In comparison, the LXX renders both passages identically: ἐμοὶ ἀλλόφυλοι ὑπετάγησαν ("to me foreign tribes were subjugated"). This seems to be an interpretation of Ps 60:10 MT that was transferred into Ps

---

20. Cf. רוע *hitpolel* in Ps 65:14, which refers back to v. 9.
21. Goldingay, *Psalms 42–89*, 231.

108:10 LXX in order to assimilate both texts. This further corroborates the assumption that the passages have been harmonized in the textual tradition of the LXX, which undermines the textual value of the LXX as far the differences between these parallel psalms are concerned.

6. Instead of the rare expression "fortified city" עיר מצור in Ps 60:11,[22] Ps 108:11 has the more common expression "fortress city" עיר מבצר.[23] The reading in Ps 108:11 can be regarded as a semantic facilitation of an uncommon expression.[24]

7. A different case is found in Ps 108:12 compared with Ps 60:12. The pronoun אתה ("you"), part of a rhetorical question in Ps 60:12, is missing in Ps 108:12.

Ps 108:12	Ps 60:12
הלא אלהים זנחתנו	הלא אתה אלהים זנחתנו
ולא תצא אלהים בצבאותינו	ולא תצא אלהים בצבאותינו

Ps 108:12: Is it not, O God, that you rejected us? And you do not go out, O God, with our armies!

Ps 60:12: Is it not, O God, that *you* rejected us? And you do not go out, O God, with our armies!

To be sure, it is possible to explain this small difference as a scribal mistake (perhaps by homoiarchon: אַתָּה אֱלֹהִים). However, this is not the only possible explanation.[25] Without the pronoun אתה ("you") the sentence is

---

22. Cf. Ps 31:22; 2 Chr 8:5; 11:5.

23. Cf. Num 32:36; Josh 19:29, 35; 1 Sam 6:18; 2 Kgs 3:19; 10:2; 17:9; 18:8; Jer 1:18; 5:17; 34:7; Dan 11:15.

24. Some scholars assume that עיר מצור in Ps 60:11 refers to the Edomite capital Bozrah (Knauf, "Psalm lx und Psalm cviii," 60–61; Zenger, in Hossfeld and Zenger, *Psalmen 101–150*, 165), which was destroyed in 552 BCE by Nabonidus. The oracle against Bozrah could have been deliberately generalized after its destruction; cf. the use of מבצר in the context of the Edom oracle of Isa 34 (v. 13). However, this historical explanation cannot be regarded as cogent, since both expressions could also refer to other Edomite cities in later times.

25. Zenger (Hossfeld and Zenger, *Psalmen 101–150*, 165) proposes that the lament of Ps 60:12 was changed by an intentional omission of אתה ("you") in Ps 108:12 into a retrospective view on Israel's doom in the past. However, it is difficult to see how such a small change would create such a substantially different meaning. In addition,

more difficult to read, since the pronoun emphasizes that God is addressed here in the second person. This could indicate that אתה ("you") was secondarily added during the textual history of Ps 60:12, since with this word it is easier to comprehend the syntax and the meaning of this verse. Therefore, Ps 108:12 may attest to the original wording of Ps 60:12. The word אתה could only have been added to Ps 60:12 after the author of Ps 108 used Ps 60 as a source.

The LXX renders both passages identically: οὐχὶ σύ, ὁ θεός, ὁ ἀπωσάμενος ἡμᾶς; ("Is it not you, O God, who rejected us?"). This seems to be a relatively literal translation of the longer text: הלא אתה אלהים זנחתנו ("Is it not, O God, that *you* rejected us?"). That the LXX version of Ps 108:12 also includes the word σύ, perhaps going back to the Hebrew pronoun אתה in the *Vorlage*, implies that the two psalms have been harmonized in the tradition of the LXX.

12.4. The Context of the Composite Psalm 108 in the Psalter

Psalm 108 has the short title שיר מזמור לדוד ("A song, a psalm of David"; v. 1). Apart from לדוד, this title has nothing in common with the long titles of Ps 57 (v. 1) and Ps 60 (vv. 1–2).[26] The combination of שיר and מזמור could have been inspired by the phrase אשירה ואזמרה ("I will sing and make melody") in the opening of the psalm itself (Ps 108:2).

The title could reveal a redactional purpose that is related to the immediate context of the psalm. This perspective could clarify why Ps 108 was composed at all. Together with the titles of Ps 109 and Ps 110, the title of Ps 108 opens a small collection of Davidic psalms. After Ps 108, the collection is continued by a prayer against foes in Ps 109, and it culminates in the famous royal Ps 110.

Psalm 108 is thematically related to Ps 110 in one crucial aspect. The oracle of Ps 110:1, by which Yhwh addresses the (probably messianic) king, is set up by the oracle of Ps 108:8–10. In Ps 108 God proclaims that he is

---

Zenger does not take into account the possibility that Ps 108 attests to a more original version here.

26. See Ps 57:1: "To the leader: Do Not Destroy; of David; a *miktam*; when he fled from Saul, in the cave"; and Ps 60:1–2: "To the leader: according to the Lily of the Covenant; a *miktam* of David; for instruction; when he struggled with Aram-naharaim and with Aram-zobah, and when Joab on his return killed twelve thousand Edomites in the Valley of Salt."

ruling over Israel by the leadership of Judah (v. 9: יהודה מחקקי, "Judah is my scepter") and that he is victorious over Judah's hostile neighbors. The questions of Israel's military leader in Ps 108:11 imply that this divine announcement begins to be fulfilled. The military leader who is probably presupposed as the speaker of the whole psalm can be identified either with David or with the Messiah (as the new David). These thematic lines are resumed in the second oracle of the small collection (Ps 110:1): Yhwh enthrones the king and promises that he will subjugate his enemies. The obvious connection between both oracles could explain why Ps 108 combines the prayers for God's help and God's triumphant oracle, both taken from Ps 60, with the likewise triumphant praise of God from the second part of Ps 57.[27]

12.5. Results and Methodological Consequences

The three psalms, 57, 60, and 108, provide clear evidence of editorial activity that took place during the literary prehistory of the Psalter. A comparison between the parallel texts gives insight into the composite nature of Ps 108. The cumulative evidence presented above makes the case quite clear that Ps 108 is a secondary composition. It would be difficult, if not impossible, to see how Ps 108 could have been the source text for the composi-

---

27. Ernst Axel Knauf ("Psalm lx und Psalm cviii," 62–64) proposes that the small Davidic composition of Pss 108–110 had a distinct historical background in the late second century. He assumes that Ps 108 was composed under John Hyrkan, who, according to Josephus (*Ant.* 13.9.1; 13.10.2), conquered all the territories that are mentioned in the oracle of vv. 8–10 between 129 and 108 BCE; in contrast with Ps 60, Ps 108 would imply that this oracle is now fulfilled. Accordingly, *David redivivus*, the speaker of the psalm, would stand implicitly for Hyrkan himself. Ps 108 would be one of the latest psalms in the canonical Psalter. To be sure, it remains a matter of debate whether this idea can be the correct explanation. Zenger (Hossfeld and Zenger, *Psalmen 101–150*, 167) gives three counterarguments: (1) The three psalms show no perspective of fulfillment. (2) They present Yhwh as the main actor, which does not fit in with the self-understanding of the Hasmoneans. (3) Such a late dating of the three psalms does not coincide with Zenger's own theory about the last redaction of the Psalter between 200 and 150 BCE. It has to be noted, however, that all three arguments are not compelling: (1) The fulfillment could be regarded as just beginning; prayers for divine help are never superfluous. (2) We do not know enough about the self-understanding of the Hasmoneans to exclude this possibility. (3) The argument about dating is circular. Thus, Knauf's theory remains possible, although it is also clear that it represents only one historical possibility.

tion of both Ps 57 and Ps 60. Such a theory would face considerable problems. For example, one could hardly explain why Ps 108 almost exclusively uses אלהים ("God"), while the surrounding psalms do not use this word at all. The fact that both Ps 57:8–12 and Ps 60:7–14 are closely connected with the respective first parts of these psalms would also find no convincing explanation. In addition, most of the minor differences between both psalms clearly corroborate the priority of Ps 57 and Ps 60.

Methodologically, three aspects about editorial techniques in the Psalter and the possibility of reconstructing them can be observed. First, there existed a technique of psalm composition that was just the opposite of free poetical invention. The entire Ps 108 is composed by using parts of other psalms. These psalms were probably already contained in some psalm collection, such as the elohistic psalter, in which Ps 57 and Ps 60 are placed close to each other.[28] The same compositional technique is, in part, also attested in 1 Chr 16:8–36, where a long passage of Ps 105 and the whole of Ps 96 are used. Psalm 96 itself is composed with a similar technique. This psalm is a kind of *florilegium* of different psalm passages, especially from Pss 29, 93, 97, and 98. It is fair to assume that such techniques were used in other cases as well, although we have no documented evidence for that.

Second, even if Ps 57 and Ps 60 had not been included in the Psalter, the composite nature of Ps 108 could be deduced from inner-textual arguments. Perhaps it would be hypothesized that the oracle of vv. 8–10 and the communal prayer and confession of vv. 12–14 did not originally belong to the preceding prayer of an individual that forms the first part of the psalm. This would lead the critic in the right direction. Although this is a hypothetical case, the example of Ps 108 could teach us that observations on textual incoherence are not misleading, even in a poetical corpus like the Psalter. There should always be a reason for incoherence and tensions, and often the reasons are related to the composition history of the text.

It is doubtful, however, that without knowledge of Ps 57 and Ps 60 a reconstruction would lead exactly to the theory that Ps 108 consists of two passages that were copied from two older psalms. With regard to the join between the two parts of the composition, it can also be doubted that the exact position of this join could be detected. The change of עננו ("answer us") in Ps 60:7 into עניני ("answer me") in Ps 108:7, which connects the two

---

28. This collection could have consisted of at least Pss 42–83, as the elohistic shape of Ps 108 indicates; perhaps this collection was still independent from the psalm collection for which Ps 108 was composed.

texts closely,[29] would easily deceive the scholar in reconstruction, leading perhaps to the false assumption that v. 7 originally belonged to the preceding prayer of an individual. Thus, the example of Ps 108 warns against being too precise in the attempt to reconstruct the exact texts that were earlier literary forms of a psalm.

Third, the editor who created Ps 108 as the opening of the small Davidic composition of Pss 108–110 (see above, 12.4) seems to have deliberately changed the source texts slightly. These changes include replacements of single words, minor changes of grammatical forms, and short omissions. Without knowledge of Ps 57 and Ps 60, these changes would be impossible to detect, since they left no discernible traces within their context. Accordingly, similar changes should also be taken into account in other texts where parallel passages for comparison are lacking.

---

29. Erhard S. Gerstenberger, *Psalms, Part 2, and Lamentations* (FOTL 15; Grand Rapids: Eerdmans, 2001), 254.

13
REVISION OF EZRA-NEHEMIAH IN 1 ESDRAS: EXPANSIONS, OMISSIONS, AND REWRITINGS

13.1. INTRODUCTION

The Masoretic version of Ezra-Nehemiah and the Greek 1 Esdras contain several differences.[1] It has become increasingly probable that 1 Esdras generally represents a later literary stage than the MT.[2] In some cases, however, 1 Esdras may preserve older readings than the MT, so that each case has to be investigated separately to determine the more original reading and the exact development of the text. The two versions reward comparison, because they provide many examples of diverse changes made to the older text. Although 1 Esdras contains many substantial changes as well,[3] in this chapter we will draw attention mainly to examples of small expansions and rewritings. It should be further noted that many, or per-

---

1. The second Greek version, the so-called 2 Esdras, follows the MT closely in most passages. Differences between 2 Esdras and the MT will be noted separately in cases where they are significant for the examples discussed here.

2. See discussion and articles in Lisbeth S. Fried, *Was 1 Esdras First?* (SBLAIL 7; Atlanta: Society of Biblical Literature, 2011). The priority of 1 Esdras has been defended most prominently by Dieter Böhler, *Die Heilige Stadt in Esdras α und Esra-Nehemia: Zwei Konzeptionen zur Wiederherstellung Israels* (OBO 158; Fribourg: Universitätsverlag; Göttingen: Vandenhoeck & Ruprecht, 1997).

3. For example, 1 Esdras shows that some passages could be relocated. The passage describing the opposition to the building of the temple was split into two parts, and the first part was relocated to a different position in the text (Ezra 4:1–6 and 7–24 parallels 1 Esd 2:16–20 and 5:66–73). In this process the list of returnees (Ezra 2:1–70 // 1 Esd 5:7–46) was placed after the first opposition to the building of the temple and the large expansion in 1 Esd 3:1–5:6. Moreover, 1 Esdras contains large plusses, namely, 1:1–58 and 3:1–5:6. The scene in the Persian court in 1 Esd 3:1–4:63 may have been taken from an external source, but, being a well-integrated part of the

haps most, of the differences between the MT and 1 Esdras were already present in the Hebrew *Vorlage* of 1 Esdras.[4]

13.2. The Addition of the Sabbath Offerings in 1 Esdras 5:51

Ezra 3:5 contains a list of offerings that the exiles began to offer after they had returned to Jerusalem and set up the altar in its old place (Ezra 3:2–3). The MT lists continual burnt offerings, offerings of the new moon, offerings of the feasts, and the freewill offerings. First Esdras 5:51 follows this list closely but contains one additional offering, namely, that of the Sabbaths.

Ezra 3:5

ואחריכן עלת תמיד ולחדשים ולכל־מועדי יהוה המקדשים ולכל מתנדב נדבה ליהוה

After that the regular offerings, the offerings at new moons and at all the sacred feasts <u>of Yhwh</u>, and the offerings of all who made a vow to Yhwh.

1 Esd 5:51–52

⁵¹ καὶ μετὰ ταῦτα προσφορὰς ἐνδελεχισμοῦ <u>καὶ θυσίας σαββάτων</u> καὶ νουμηνιῶν καὶ ἑορτῶν πασῶν ἡγιασμένων. ⁵² καὶ ὅσοι εὔξαντο εὐχὴν τῷ θεῷ ...

---

present composition, it must have been altered to accommodate the present context in 1 Esdras.

4. This is assumed by many; see, e.g., Zipora Talshir, *I Esdras: From Origin to Translation* (SBLSCS 47; Atlanta: Scholars Press, 1999), 113–79. Nonetheless, some scholars have assumed that all or most of the editorial changes in 1 Esdras were made by the translator; thus, e.g., W. J. Moulton, "Über die Überlieferung und den Textkritischen Werth des dritten Esrabuchs," *ZAW* 19 (1899): 209–58. Some scholars have assumed that all or nearly all of the changes were made before the translation in the Hebrew/Aramaic *Vorlage* of 1 Esdras. The latter view is represented, among others, by Wilhelm Rudolph, *Esra und Nehemia samt 3. Esra* (HAT 20; Tübingen: J.C.B. Mohr, 1949). It is probable that the truth lies somewhere between these positions, so that each case would have to be discussed separately. For the purposes of the present volume, this is not a crucial question.

After that the regular offerings <u>and sacrifices on the Sabbaths</u> and offerings at new moons and at all the consecrated feasts, and who had made any vow to God ...

It is probable that the plus in 1 Esdras is a later addition, because its omission—accidental[5] or intentional—in the MT (and 2 Esdras LXX) would be difficult to explain.[6] Moreover, the Sabbath is known to have been inserted into several passages in the Hebrew Bible where it was originally missing. The most famous of such additions is the commandment to observe the Sabbath in the Decalogue (Exod 20:9–10; Deut 5:13–14).[7]

The addition of the Sabbath offerings is very typical of scribal changes in the Hebrew Bible. The older list of the Masoretic tradition reflects earlier conceptions of the most important offerings that had to be observed, but a later editor updated the list to be in agreement with contemporary conceptions. It is apparent that the Sabbath and thereby the Sabbath offerings had also become so important that they had to be included in this list. The impetus for the expansion may have been the fact that the original list consisted of offerings from the most-frequent offerings (regular, thus daily) to the least-frequent ones (feast), followed finally by the voluntary offerings that could be made at any time. A later editor noticed that the weekly Sabbath offerings should logically be mentioned between the daily offerings and the monthly offerings (חֳדָשִׁים), where he then also added them.

Because the older phase of the text was preserved in the MT, we can be certain that the Sabbath offerings were added to 1 Esdras by a later editor. If we possessed only 1 Esdras, it would be next to impossible to identify καὶ θυσίας σαββάτων ("and sacrifices on the Sabbaths") as an addition. Addi-

---

5. There is no technical reason (homoioteleuton or homoiarchon) that would explain its accidental omission.

6. However, Antonius H. J. Gunneweg, *Esra* (KAT 19.1; Gütersloh: Mohn, 1985), 70; and Joseph Blenkinsopp, *Ezra-Nehemiah* (OTL; Philadelphia: Westminster, 1988), 98, have suggested that the Sabbath offerings may have dropped out here. Both note that the Sabbath offerings and the new moon are often met together (Num 28:9–15; 2 Chr 2:3; 8:13). On the other hand, exactly because these are otherwise met together, the addition of the Sabbath offerings in our passage is probable. If they are met together in many other passages, it would have been an incentive for a later editor to add the Sabbath offerings here.

7. See, e.g., Timo Veijola, *Das fünfte Buch Mose: Deuteronomium; Kapitel 1,1–16,17* (ATD 8.1; Göttingen: Vandenhoeck & Ruprecht, 2004), 160–63.

tions to lists whose components are separated with a conjunction are particularly difficult to identify by technical considerations (e.g., by observing grammatical problems or other inconsistencies). This is an example of a text where we have a clear addition that would be very difficult to identify without possessing an older stage of the text.

On the other hand, failure to identify this addition would give a distorted picture of when the Sabbath offerings became common. If we possessed only 1 Esdras and, on other grounds, could date it to the fifth century BCE, we would perhaps conclude that the Sabbath offerings had already been significant in the fifth century BCE. A very small addition could thus have a significant impact on our understanding of a historical development. Because of the parallel texts, we now can be fairly certain that the Sabbath offerings are a late addition. In view of its addition in 1 Esdras we may perhaps also assume that these offerings still gained in importance after the textual tradition of 1 Esdras separated from the textual tradition represented by the MT of Ezra-Nehemiah. This underlines the importance of trying to identify even small additions to the text before making far-reaching historical or other conclusions on their basis.

13.3. How an Editorial Change Reversed the Setting between the King and Ezra

First Esdras 8:4 contains a sentence that reverses the setting between Ezra and the Persian king. According to Ezra 7:6, the Persian king Artaxerxes gives Ezra everything he has requested for the trip to Jerusalem because the hand of Yhwh is on Ezra. Ezra pleads with the king and is given what he wants because of Yhwh's approval. The parallel verse 1 Esd 8:4 follows the MT but omits the reference to the hand of Yhwh and has an alternative sentence in its place.

Ezra 7:6

הוא עזרא עלה מבבל והוא־ספר מהיר בתורת משה אשר־נתן יהוה אלהי
ישראל ויתן־לו המלך
כיד־יהוה אלהיו עליו כל בקשתו

This Ezra went from Babylon. He was a scribe skilled in the law of Moses, which ~~Yhwh~~ the God of Israel had given. And the king gave him, ~~because the hand of Yhwh his God was upon him~~, all that he requested.

1 Esd 8:3-4

³ οὗτος Εσδρας ἀνέβη ἐκ Βαβυλῶνος ὡς γραμματεὺς εὐφυὴς ὢν ἐν τῷ Μωυσέως νόμῳ τῷ ἐκδεδομένῳ ὑπὸ τοῦ θεοῦ τοῦ Ισραηλ, ⁴ καὶ ἔδωκεν αὐτῷ ὁ βασιλεὺς <u>δόξαν, εὑρόντος χάριν ἐναντίον αὐτοῦ ἐπὶ</u> πάντα τὰ ἀξιώματα αὐτοῦ.

³ This Ezra went from Babylon as a scribe skilled in the law of Moses, which the God of Israel had given; ⁴ and the king showed [lit., "gave"] him <u>honor, for he found favor before him in</u> all his requests.

In 1 Esdras, the Achaemenid king shows Ezra honor, followed by the king's favor. It is probable that 1 Esdras represents a secondary reading here, because it augments Ezra's role and offers a more fluent text.⁸ The opposite direction of development would imply that Ezra's position in relation to the king was intentionally reduced, but this is improbable. The MT being awkward,⁹ an editor or scribe in the tradition of 1 Esdras removed the syntactically disturbing phrase כיד־יהוה אלהיו עליו ("because the hand of Yhwh his God was upon him"). In this process the sentence was rearranged so that a new object (δόξαν, "honor") was added and Ezra is said to have found favor before the king. The change seems small at first glance, but it effectively has elevated Ezra's position before the king. This change is also well in line with the typical tendency of 1 Esdras to portray the Achaemenid kings as supporting the Jewish cause (see, e.g., how Zerubbabel is elevated in 1 Esd 3:1–4:46). First Esdras 8:3-4 is an example of a case where an awkward older version, represented by the MT, was replaced with a more fluent text. Not only was the text made syntactically clearer, but the content was also altered.

Because the resulting text in 1 Esdras is fluent, it would be very difficult to identify the editorial change if we did not possess the older stage of the text as well. The example thus shows that in some cases a later editorial correction may in fact be contained in a fluent text, in contrast with the conventional assumption in literary or redaction criticism that editorial

---

8. Most commentaries, such as Gunneweg, *Esra*, 118, make no reference to the reading in 1 Esdras, implying that the reading is evidently secondary.

9. The awkwardness of the MT may have been caused by earlier editing. The reference to the hand of Yhwh his God (כיד־יהוה אלהיו עליו) breaks the main sentence and the connection between the verb/subject and object, and it is therefore probably an addition.

changes have to be assumed only when textual roughness and irregularity can be observed in a given text. It should be further noted that in most cases 1 Esdras is expansive in relation to Ezra-Nehemiah, but the present example shows that there are some cases where the expansive tendency of a textual tradition may also include rewriting parts of the older text.

13.4. Leveling Out Inconsistencies and Roughness in 1 Esdras

First Esdras shows a tendency to remove some of the inconsistencies, repetitions, and roughness of the older text. A comparison of Ezra 9:4–5 and 1 Esd 8:69–70 provides illustrative examples.

Ezra 9:4–5

ואלי יאספו כל חרד בדברי אלהי־ישראל על מעל הגולה ואני ישב משומם עד למנחת הערב
ובמנחת הערב קמתי מתעניתי ובקרעי בגדי ומעילי

⁴ And all who feared the words of the God of Israel gathered to me ~~because of the sins of the exiles~~. And I sat mourning until the evening sacrifice. ⁵ ~~At the evening sacrifice~~ I rose from my fast, with my clothes and mantle torn.

1 Esd 8:69–70

⁶⁹ καὶ ἐπισυνήχθησαν πρός με ὅσοι ποτὲ ἐπεκινοῦντο τῷ ῥήματι κυρίου τοῦ Ισραηλ, ἐμοῦ πενθοῦντος ἐπὶ τῇ ἀνομίᾳ, καὶ ἐκαθήμην περίλυπος ἕως τῆς δειλινῆς θυσίας. ⁷⁰ καὶ ἐξεγερθεὶς ἐκ τῆς νηστείας διερρηγμένα ἔχων τὰ ἱμάτια καὶ τὴν ἱερὰν ἐσθῆτα.

⁶⁹ And all who were moved by the word of the Lord of Israel gathered to me, <u>as I mourned because of the sin</u>, and I sat distressed until the evening sacrifice. ⁷⁰ And I rose from my fast, with my clothes and <u>holy</u> mantle torn.

According to Ezra 9:4, the ones who "feared the words of God" gathered to Ezra "because of the sin(s) of the exiles/Gola" (על מעל הגולה). A reference to the sin(s) of the *exiles* is illogical in this passage, because Ezra has just arrived in Jerusalem from Babylon, discovering that the people *who had remained in the land* lived without the Torah and had therefore taken foreign wives. It is probable that the whole verse in Ezra-Nehemiah derives from a later editor who tried to emphasize that only the returnees from the exile form the Jewish community.[10] Similar additions to the older text of Ezra-Nehemiah are found in other parts of the composition as well (e.g., Ezra 6:20-21; 8:35; 10:7; Neh 8:17). Being an idea introduced by later editors with new conceptions, the references to the Gola often disturb or contradict the older text, which apparently does not give any precedence to the community of the returnees.[11]

First Esdras tried to correct some of the inconsistencies caused by the earlier expansions by Gola-oriented editors. In 1 Esd 8:69 the reference to the exiles was omitted and the sentence was also otherwise rendered differently: there is an additional reference to Ezra, and he is said to be saddened because of the sin. First Esdras does not specify whose sin it is, but the context makes it clear that the sin of the people who had remained in the land is meant. The resulting text removes the contradiction with the broader context that the sinners were exiles and not Jews living in the land.[12]

First Esdras 8:70 contains a further illuminating correction. Ezra 9:5 disturbingly repeats a reference to the evening sacrifice. Although the Greek version is evidently less repetitive and fluent, it does not preserve an older text but should instead be seen as an attempt to improve the text by omitting the unnecessary repetition of the evening sacrifice. The repetition was originally caused by the addition of v. 4, which left the text with a double reference to the evening sacrifices.[13] In order to return to the older text, the author of the expansion, rather awkwardly, repeated the sacri-

---

10. See Juha Pakkala, *Ezra the Scribe* (BZAW 347; Berlin: de Gruyter, 2004), 91-92. The author behind this addition thus implies that the people that were in the land were not Jews at all.

11. For further discussion on the Gola additions, see ibid., 263-65.

12. It is very unlikely that 1 Esdras represents the older text here, because the whole verse is an addition and 1 Esdras is familiar with the rest of the verse. Most scholars make no reference to the reading in 1 Esdras. See, e.g., Loring W. Batten, *Ezra and Nehemiah* (ICC; Edinburgh: T&T Clark, 1913), 330-32, 337; Gunneweg, *Esra*, 160, 163; Blenkinsopp, *Ezra-Nehemiah*, 177-79.

13. Note, for example, that v. 5 implies Ezra to have been the only one who mourned, but the editor who added v. 4 wanted to include the most faithful of the community as participating in the mourning. For further argumentation on this verse, see Pakkala, *Ezra the Scribe*, 91-92.

fices.¹⁴ First Esdras 8:69–70 should be seen as an attempt to improve the disturbance caused by earlier editing.¹⁵

Corrections that level out inconsistencies and repetitions are found in other parts of 1 Esdras as well. The reference to the exiles was also omitted in 1 Esd 8:63 (// Ezra 8:35) and 1 Esd 9:3 (// Ezra 10:6). As in Ezra 9:4, the role of the exiles is disturbingly emphasized in Ezra 8:35, while 1 Esdras omits the reference to the Gola altogether.

Ezra 8:35

הבאים מהשבי בני־הגולה הקריבו עלות לאלהי ישראל

Those who returned from the captivity, the sons of the Gola, offered sacrifices to the God of Israel.

1 Esd 8:63

οἱ δὲ παραγενόμενοι ἐκ τῆς αἰχμαλωσίας προσήνεγκαν θυσίας τῷ θεῷ τοῦ Ισραηλ.

Those who had returned from the captivity offered sacrifices to the God of Israel.

It is theoretically possible that 1 Esd 8:63 attests to an earlier form of the text, but in view of 1 Esd 8:69, where the omission is clearly secondary, it is reasonable to assume that the omission is secondary in 1 Esd 8:63 and 9:3 as well.¹⁶ These examples (as well as 1 Esd 8:4, discussed above) show that some editors have leveled out some of the inconsistencies caused by earlier editing. In other words, the editorial development would go in opposite directions, a later editor reversing some of the editing done by an earlier editor. Such editorial interceptions are traditionally not assumed in literary or redaction criticism, and it is evident that they would obstruct

---

14. Ezra 9:4–5 thus contains a typical resumptive repetition (*Wiederaufnahme*), which is often seen in redaction-critical studies as an indication of an addition. After the expansion the editor tried to return to the older text by repeating a part of its text.

15. 1 Esd 8:70 contains a further illuminating addition. According to the MT, Ezra tore his clothes and mantle, but in 1 Esdras Ezra's mantle is a holy one (similarly in Ezra 9:3 // 1 Esd 8:68). This change is in line with the tendency of 1 Esdras to make Ezra the high priest (see below), and therefore he must also be wearing holy garments.

16. Thus also Gunneweg, *Esra*, 157.

attempts to identify editorial changes made to the text. For example, 1 Esd 8:63 would give little indication that something was omitted.

13.5. Changing Ezra's Profession in 1 Esdras

Ezra-Nehemiah variably calls Ezra a scribe and a priest. The roles and functions he takes also vary according to the topic in question (e.g., Ezra 8 emphasizes his priestly aspect, while Neh 8 stresses his role as a scribe). In the background is probably a literary development where the scribe Ezra, as he is portrayed in the oldest text, was later made into a priest in some later additions.[17] The reason for this change is the idea, adopted from Ezra 1–6, that he brought some of the temple vessels to Jerusalem. As the carrier of the holy vessels would have been assumed to be a priest, Ezra had to be made one.

This development went a step further in 1 Esdras. Although 1 Esdras variably also calls Ezra a scribe or a priest, he is additionally called the high priest (ὁ ἀρχιερεύς) in 1 Esd 9:39, 40, and 49. In the parallel passages of the MT and 2 Esdras he is called priest, scribe, or priest and scribe.

Neh 8:1; 2 Esd 18:1	1 Esd 9:39
לעזרא הספר	Ἔσδρᾳ τῷ ἀρχιερεῖ καὶ ἀναγνώστῃ
τῷ Ἔσδρᾳ τῷ γραμματεῖ	
Ezra the scribe	Esdras the high priest and reader
Neh 8:2; 2 Esd 18:2	1 Esd 9:40
עזרא הכהן	Ἔσδρας ὁ ἀρχιερεύς
Ἔσδρας ὁ ἱερεύς	
Ezra the priest	Esdras the high priest
Neh 8:9; 2 Esd 18:9	1 Esd 9:49
עזרא הכהן הספר	Ἔσδρᾳ τῷ ἀρχιερεῖ καὶ ἀναγνώστῃ
Ἔσδρας ὁ ἱερεὺς καὶ γραμματεύς	
Ezra the priest (and) scribe	Esdras the high priest and reader

---

17. For discussion and further literature, see Pakkala, *Ezra the Scribe*, 225–75.

It is evident that 1 Esdras is secondary here, because a reverse development where Ezra was "downgraded" from a high priest to a priest or a scribe is very unlikely.[18] The opposite development, where a Jewish hero gradually gains in importance, is understandable. It was perhaps assumed that a priest who restored the community of Jerusalem and brought back the Torah as well as some of the cultic vessels cannot have been less than a high priest, and his title was changed accordingly in some passages of 1 Esdras.

The example shows that in order to augment the roles of central people portrayed in the stories, the older text could be rewritten. Perhaps the most significant consequence of such changes is their impact on how the reader reads many other passages. After the change has been made, the reader is also bound to see the activity of Ezra in other passages in a different light. For example, the reading of the Torah led by the high priest in 1 Esd 9 is easily seen as an important ceremonial and cultic event closely related to the highest temple services, whereas the MT, where Ezra is "only" a priest and scribe, would give a different impression.

A slight change in 1 Esd 9:41 further developed the text in a similar direction. According to 1 Esd 9, Ezra reads the law in front of the temple, whereas in what is probably the older text here in Neh 8:3 the reading takes place before the Water Gate. The setting was made more priestly and appropriate for a high priest.

Neh 8:3

ויקרא־בו לפני הרחוב אשר לפני שער־המים מן־האור עד־מחצית היום

He read from it in front of the square, which is before the ~~Water~~ Gate, from early morning until midday.

1 Esd 9:41

καὶ ἀνεγίγνωσκεν ἐν τῷ πρὸ <u>τοῦ ἱεροῦ</u> πυλῶνος εὐρυχώρῳ ἀπὸ ὄρθρου ἕως μεσημβρινοῦ.

He read aloud in the square before the gate of <u>the temple</u> from early morning until midday.

---

18. Most commentaries make no reference to these readings in 1 Esdras and follow the MT as the more original. See, e.g., Antonius H. J. Gunneweg, *Nehemia* (KAT 19.2; Gütersloh: Mohn, 1987); Blenkinsopp, *Ezra-Nehemiah*, 283–83.

Both of these examples show that in some cases individual words could be replaced with new ones that had a very different meaning or that would change the setting in the text. They also demonstrate that small changes could considerably influence the intention and the reader's interpretation of the text. It is evident that changes where the older text was completely omitted would be difficult or impossible to identify without the older text being preserved as well.

13.6. Additions in Ezra 10:3 and 1 Esdras 8:90

In some cases the MT may contain a later addition while 1 Esdras preserves an older reading.¹⁹ Such a case is met at the very end of Ezra 10:3, where the MT contains a plus that is missing in 1 Esd 8:90. The passage describes how Ezra dissolved the mixed marriages. In Ezra 10:3 // 1 Esd 8:90 Shecaniah, a leader of the community, gives instructions to Ezra as to how the crisis should be resolved.

Ezra 10:3

ועתה נכרת־ברית לאלהינו להוציא כל־נשים והנולד מהם בעצת אדני והח־
רדים במצות אלהינו <u>וכתורה יעשה</u>

And now let us make a covenant with our God to send away all wives and their children, according to the counsel of my lord and of those who tremble at the commandments of our God. <u>Let it be done according to the law.</u>

1 Esd 8:90

ἐν τούτῳ γενέσθω ἡμῖν ὁρκωμοσία πρὸς τὸν κύριον, ἐκβαλεῖν πάσας τὰς γυναῖκας <u>ἡμῶν τὰς ἐκ τῶν ἀλλογενῶν</u> σὺν τοῖς τέκνοις αὐτῶν, ὡς ἐκρίθη σοι καὶ ὅσοι πειθαρχοῦσιν τῷ νόμῳ τοῦ κυρίου.

---

19. The parallel texts in Ezra 10:3 and 1 Esd 8:90 contain many minor differences, but these need not concern us here. The subject has been expressed with a different term three times in this single verse. First Esdras twice renders אלהינו with τὸν κύριον. The rendering of אלהים with κύριος is not uncommon, but here the first-person plural suffix also finds no correspondence in 1 Esdras. Moreover, a reference to Ezra is expressed with σοι while the Hebrew has אדני.

> In this let us take an oath to the Lord to send away all <u>our</u> wives <u>who are of the foreigners</u>, with their children, according to your counsel and (the counsel) of those who obey the law of the Lord.

According to the MT, the crisis should be resolved according to the Torah,[20] whereas this reference is missing in 1 Esdras. It is probable that the plus is due to a later addition, because its omission in 1 Esdras would be very difficult to explain.[21] Moreover, the version of the MT and of 2 Esdras is also somewhat congested.[22] The text already states that the foreign wives should be expelled "according to the counsel of my lord" (presumably referring to Ezra) and "of those who tremble at the commandment of our God." An additional reference to expelling the wives according to the Torah would be redundant or even compete with the idea that Ezra and the pious should decide how to resolve the issue. Even without the evidence from 1 Esdras one would suspect that something was added to Ezra 10:3. The reference to God's commandments (מצות אלהינו) in the older text may have facilitated the addition and functioned as a midrashic hook for it. By way of association, the addition expands the view from a reference to the followers of God's commandments to acting according to the Torah. The verse is thus an example of how texts could grow by augmenting the perspective.

This verse contains another illustrative addition in 1 Esdras. In order to be more specific about which wives were to be divorced, 1 Esdras adds ἡμῶν τὰς ἐκ τῶν ἀλλογενῶν ("our [wives] who are of the foreigners"), while the reference is missing in Ezra-Nehemiah. Although it is rather clear after v. 2 that only foreign wives could be meant here, 1 Esdras made it explicit and left no space for doubt. Such clarifying additions are often assumed in literary- or redaction-critical investigations, and one is unequivocally demonstrated in 1 Esd 8:90.[23]

---

20. 2 Esd 10:3 follows the MT here and renders τί καὶ ὡς ὁ νόμος γενηθήτω.

21. Surprisingly, many scholars follow the MT. Thus, e.g., Batten, *Ezra and Nehemiah*, 340–41; Gunneweg, *Esra*, 173–75; Blenkinsopp, *Ezra-Nehemiah*, 177–79.

22. For further argumentation of this verse, see Pakkala, *Ezra the Scribe*, 94–96.

23. It is unlikely that the MT is secondary here, for there is no technical reason that could have easily occasioned an accidental omission. Moreover, the plus in 1 Esdras does not contain anything theologically or otherwise offensive that would have caused an intentional omission.

13.7. Results and Methodological Consequences

First Esdras generally represents a younger textual form than Ezra-Nehemiah. Most of the editorial changes in 1 Esdras are additions, which corresponds to the conventional assumption in literary and redaction criticism that the texts developed through expansions. The examples presented in this chapter are typical of the small additions that are found in considerable numbers throughout 1 Esdras. Although 1 Esdras mostly represents a younger text than the MT, there are some cases where the MT contains a secondary reading. This means that each case has to be investigated separately. It also implies that both textual forms continued to evolve after the separation of these textual traditions at a relatively late date, perhaps in the last century BCE or beyond.

Many of the expansions in 1 Esdras could be identified even without a comparison with the earlier form of the text of the MT. Nevertheless, we have also seen examples (such as in Ezra 7:6 // 1 Esd 8:4) where part of the older text was replaced by an addition, so that the resulting text is more fluent than the older version of the text. In these cases it would be very difficult to recognize that something had been altered in the earlier history of the text. Further on, there are some examples where small parts of the older text were omitted without any replacement (Ezra 8:35 // 1 Esd 8:63). The reason for such editorial changes in 1 Esdras seems to have been to remove inconsistencies in the older text. In such cases it would be very difficult to notice that the text had been edited.

14
Evidence for Large Additions in the Book of Esther

The book of Esther, which eventually became part of the canonical collection of the five Megilloth, provides a large amount of evidence for editorial changes because it is preserved in three distinct editions. The MT differs considerably from the two Greek translations, both of which also represent different textual traditions.[1] The older translation, the so-called B-text (also called LXX Esther and Old Greek with siglum o'), is included in most LXX manuscripts, while the younger translation, the so-called A-text (also called the Alpha text or L-text),[2] is usually dated to the first century BCE or to the first century CE.[3]

Both Greek texts contain six large passages that are not included in the MT, and they are commonly acknowledged to be late additions.[4] Since

---

1. The exact relationship between the two Greek translations is debated. According to several scholars, such as Karen H. Jobes, *The Alpha-Text of Esther: Its Character and Relationship to the Masoretic Text* (SBLDS 153; Atlanta: Scholars Press, 1996), they are based on two entirely different Hebrew *Vorlagen*, while others have argued for an inner Greek development. For example, according to Robert Hanhart, ed., *Esther* (vol. 8.3 of *Septuaginta: Vetus Testamentum Graecum*; Göttingen: Vandenhoeck & Ruprecht, 1983), 87–95, the A-text is a revision of the Greek Esther tradition that is largely based on the B-text.

2. L is used because earlier research erroneously assumed that this text is Lucianic.

3. For discussion, see David A. deSilva, *Introducing the Apocrypha: Message, Context, and Significance* (Grand Rapids: Baker Academic, 2002), 114–15; and Kristin De Troyer, *Rewriting the Sacred Text* (Atlanta: Society of Biblical Literature, 2003), 88–89. According to De Troyer, the A-text, which she calls the Agrippa text, was written around 40–41 CE in Rome.

4. Thus most scholars; see deSilva, *Introducing the Apocrypha*, 110–18. However, earlier research (e.g., Charles C. Torrey, "The Older Book of Esther," *HTR* 37.1 [1944]:

most of the other chapters in our book discuss smaller editorial changes, in this chapter our focus will be on the large additions, each of which forms an entirely new passage. Large additions are often assumed in source-critical investigations, but the book of Esther provides unequivocal evidence that later editors factually made such additions. Their large number in Esther provides important information as to what their relationship with the older text is. This is useful information regarding the literary- and redaction-critical method by which similar additions are postulated in texts where we do not possess empirical textual evidence. Before proceeding with the six large additions, a few notes about the nature of the problems pertaining to the book as a witness have to be made.

14.1. The Book of Esther as Evidence of Editing

Although the book of Esther is potentially a very fruitful source for editorial changes, some problems limit its full use. Without question, the book has been heavily edited. Ironically, we may have too much evidence. The problem lies in the fact that the text has been very heavily edited and that it is preserved in three strongly divergent versions. The investigation of many passages has proved to be a very difficult and controversial undertaking. A cursory look at most parallel passages already shows the extent of the differences and thereby the problems. A comparison of one parallel passage, the coronation of Esther, in the MT and B-text of Esth 2:17–20 suffices to illustrate the extent of textual variation in this book.

Esth 2:17–20 B-Text

¹⁷ καὶ ἠράσθη ὁ βασιλεὺς Εσθηρ, καὶ εὗρεν χάριν παρὰ πάσας τὰς παρθένους, καὶ ἐπέθηκεν αὐτῇ τὸ διάδημα τὸ γυναικεῖον. ¹⁸ καὶ ἐποίησεν ὁ βασιλεὺς πότον πᾶσι τοῖς φίλοις αὐτοῦ καὶ ταῖς δυνάμεσιν ἐπὶ ἡμέρας ἑπτὰ καὶ ὕψωσεν τοὺς γάμους Εσθηρ καὶ ἄφεσιν ἐποίησεν τοῖς ὑπὸ τὴν βασιλείαν αὐτοῦ. ¹⁹ ὁ δὲ Μαρδοχαῖος ἐθεράπευεν ἐν τῇ αὐλῇ. ²⁰ ἡ δὲ Εσθηρ οὐχ ὑπέδειξεν τὴν πατρίδα αὐτῆς· οὕτως γὰρ ἐνετείλατο αὐτῇ Μαρδοχαῖος φοβεῖσθαι τὸν θεὸν καὶ ποιεῖν τὰ προστάγματα αὐτοῦ, καθὼς ἦν μετ' αὐτοῦ, καὶ Εσθηρ οὐ μετήλλαξεν τὴν ἀγωγὴν αὐτῆς.

1–40) suggested that some of the additions were included in the original book of Esther.

17 And the king loved Esther, and she found favor beyond all the virgins; and he put the queen's crown on her. 18 And the king gave a banquet to all his friends and great men for seven days, and he highly celebrated Esther's marriage; and he made a release to those who were under his dominion. 19 But Mardochaeus served in the palace. 20 Esther had not revealed her kindred; for thus Mardochaeus had ordered her to fear God and perform his commandments, as when she was with him, and Esther changed not her manner of life.

Some of the differences are small changes of isolated words that are of limited consequence, but many are substantial and change the meaning as well as the intent of the text. For example, v. 20 shows one of the many changes in the Greek texts that increased God's role in the narrative and thereby made the text theologically more acceptable for inclusion in the canonical collection. It should further be added that these differences between the MT and the B-text are only part of the evidence; the A-text of Esth 2:17–20 differs even more from both than these two texts from each other.[5]

The comparison of parallel passages in Esther is further complicated by the nature of the translations. Especially the B-text (or the LXX) is a rather free translation.[6] There are many atypical equivalents of the Hebrew text, and the translator seems to have taken considerable liberties in rendering the Hebrew.[7] As noted by Emanuel Tov: "Esth-LXX goes far beyond freedom, variation, addition and omission of details.… It sometimes adds new ideas and restructures sentences in such a way that it is almost impossible to indicate the word-for-word equivalence between the Hebrew and the translation."[8] Nevertheless, the *Vorlage* of the translator already contained

---

5. For example, Michael V. Fox, *The Redaction of the Books of Esther* (SBLMS 40; Atlanta: Scholars Press, 1991), has shown the complex relationships among the three different versions of the book of Esther. A linear development from one of the versions to the others cannot be assumed. For further discussion of the literary and redaction history of the book of Esther, see also De Troyer, *Rewriting the Sacred Text*, and the contributions in Leonard Greenspoon and Sidnie White Crawford, eds., *The Book of Esther in Modern Research* (JSOTSup 380; London: T&T Clark, 2003).

6. There is a general consensus that the LXX translation is rather free. Thus, e.g., Emanuel Tov, "The LXX Translation of Esther: A Paraphrastic Translation of MT or a Free Translation or a Rewritten Version?" in *Empsychoi Logoi—Religious Innovations in Antiquity: Studies in Honour of Pieter Willem van der Horst* (ed. A. Houtman et al.; Leiden: Brill, 2008), 507–26.

7. For example, some words have been omitted as unnecessary.

8. Tov, "LXX Translation of Esther," 526.

substantial differences with the MT to the extent that Tov has characterized it as a rewritten version.[9] In other words, although some, or perhaps many, of the changes were made in the process of translation into Greek, it is very likely that many were already made before the translation, so that the proto-MT and the *Vorlage* of the Greek translation already differed considerably.

Despite the problems with the translation process, it is evident that the MT cannot automatically be regarded as the more reliable text. In many cases the MT contains an addition in relation to one or both of the Greek versions, and therefore the development of each passage has to be investigated separately, with all three witnesses carrying equal weight. Although one may not be able to solve the development of all passages in Esther, it is perhaps one of the best examples for illustrating how extensively some biblical texts could have been changed by later editors. In that sense, it may function as a possible model for investigating some texts in the Hebrew Bible that are not preserved in three textual traditions.

14.2. Evidence for Large Additions

The Greek versions of Esther contain six major additions, which are usually labeled as additions A–F. These additions are similar to ones often assumed by redaction critics in other parts of the Hebrew Bible, but Esther shows, beyond any doubt, that such additions were indeed made. There is also empirical evidence from other books in the Hebrew Bible that entire passages were added.[10] A chart listing the large additions in the Greek translations of Esther, their location in relation to the MT, and their extent in verses shows how extensively the older composition was expanded by these additions.

---

9. In other words, editorial changes were made prior to the translations into Greek, during the translation process itself, and after the translation process. Ascribing the variants to the translator, many scholars have neglected the LXX of Esther as a witness to variant readings. This common position is rejected by Tov, "LXX Translation of Esther," 515, who notes that "the LXX does reflect variants." He appeals, for example, to the LXX readings that are influenced by Hebrew but that differ from the text preserved in the MT.

10. For example, the scene in the Persian court in 1 Esd 3:1–4:63 or the three major additions to the book of Daniel.

MT	Additions in the Greek Editions	B-Text (Verses)	A-Text (Verses)
	Mordecai's dream (addition A)	18	17
1:1–3:13			
	Haman's edict (addition B)	7	7
3:14–4:17			
	Mordecai's prayer (addition C^1)	11	10
	Esther's prayer (addition C^2)	20	19
5:1–2	Esther meets the king (addition D, which replaced Esth 5:1–2)	16	12
5:3–8:12			
	The king's edict (addition E)	24	23
8:13–10:3			
	Mordecai's dream explained and the epilogue (addition F)	11	9

The Hebrew text consists of 167 verses, while the additions consist of more than 100 verses. This means that the large additions increased the book by roughly 60 percent.[11] The small additions throughout the text inflated the text even more.

Because they were placed at the very beginning and the end of the composition, additions A and F envelop the older narrative. Addition A was placed in front of the older story as Mordecai's dream where he foresees, in symbolic language, the coming events, whereas addition F was placed at the end of the composition to explain the dream. The sections were evidently added by the same editor, because one section would be deficient without the other. Together they provide a framework through which the reader is bound to interpret the older story in a particular way.

---

11. Clearly the verses are of different size, but the comparison of verses still serves to illustrate how extensively the text grew.

Like many of the other additions, additions A and F increase the religious dimension or nature of the story. The same tendency was enhanced by small additions (see, e.g., Esth 2:20 above). It is to be suspected that the same editor who added additions A and F is behind at least some of these small additions in the main corpus of the book. For source and redaction criticism this is significant because this would corroborate the assumption often made in redaction criticism that some books were comprehensively edited from a certain theological perspective (e.g., the Deuteronomistic editing in Jeremiah).

The addition of a new introduction to an older text is an editorial technique also used elsewhere. In her recent study of this technique, Sara J. Milstein has called it revision by introduction.[12] Here a new introduction guides the reader to understand the following narrative from a different perspective. This technique may extensively transform the meaning and intent of a text so that it could be regarded as a new edition.[13] Milstein has collected empirical evidence of the technique from ancient Mesopotamian literature, but it appears to have been in use in the Hebrew Bible as well, addition A being a case in point.[14]

A 1–17	New beginning in B-text/LXX	In the second year when Artaxerxes the Great was king, on the first day of Nisa, Mardochaeus the son of Iairos … saw a dream
1:1	B-text/LXX	It happened <u>after these things</u> in the days of Artaxerxes
1:1–	Original beginning	It happened in the days of Artaxerxes, the same Artaxerxes who ruled over one hundred twenty-seven provinces from India to Ethiopia

---

12. Sara J. Milstein, "Reworking Ancient Texts: Revision through Introduction in Biblical and Mesopotamian Literature" (Ph.D. diss., New York University, 2010). Addition A of Esther would correspond to her subcategory "Reintroduction of the Collection."

13. Cf. ibid., 306.

14. For empirical evidence of the technique of adding a new introduction in the Mesopotamian literature, see ibid., 37–127. She also discusses the technique in Judges and 1 Samuel (pp. 128–293), but here the empirical evidence is missing and her discussion is based on source-critical considerations.

Note that the Greek versions have added the words "after these things" in Esth 1:1. This was done in order to create a bridge between the new beginning in addition A and the original beginning.

MT	B-Text (LXX)
ויהי	Καὶ ἐγένετο
	μετὰ τοὺς λόγους τούτους
בימי אחשורוש	ἐν ταῖς ἡμέραις Ἀρταξέρξου
It happened	It happened
	after these things
in the days of Artaxerxes	in the days of Artaxerxes

In the book of Esther this technique was reinforced by the addition of a conclusion (addition F in the Greek versions) that connects directly to the introduction, and thereby the whole older narrative is framed by the additions. The technique of framing the older text further amplified the impact of the additions. The reader receives a certain interpretative horizon for the book at the beginning and at the end.

Similar framing of the older composition is often assumed to have taken place in other books of the Hebrew Bible, but empirical evidence such as we have in the book of Esther is usually missing. For example, most scholars assume that the older core of Deuteronomy is found in chs. 12–26, whereas the frames in chs. (1–3) 4–11 and 27–34 are regarded as a later development that accumulated in successive stages over centuries.[15] Apparently several successive editors of Deuteronomy attempted to guide the reader to understand the older law from a certain perspective by placing additions as new introductions and conclusions. As in the Greek versions of Esther, the frames of Deuteronomy lead the reader to understand the older core text from a certain perspective. In Deuteronomy this technique appears to have been used by several successive editors.

---

15. See commentaries on Deuteronomy; e.g., Timo Veijola, *Das fünfte Buch Mose: Deuteronomium; Kapitel 1,1–16,17* (ATD 8.1; Göttingen: Vandenhoeck & Ruprecht, 2004).

Similar examples can be pointed out in the book of Judges, where Judg 1 and 19–21 are frequently assumed to be later additions. Framing is also probable in the book of Nehemiah. This is especially evident for the final chapters of the book, Neh 9–13, which were probably accumulated through several successive additions, as commonly acknowledged in source-critical investigations.[16] It is also possible that Neh 1 was added later and that Neh 2 forms the original beginning.[17] The function of Neh 1 would have been to provide background information for the story, and this was, in part, presented as a prayer (compare Neh 1:5–11 with addition C of Esther). The oldest sections would thus be found in the middle of the book, in chs. 2–7. Unlike in Deuteronomy, Judges, or Nehemiah, the Greek editions of Esther provide unequivocal empirical evidence that the oldest text was secondarily framed with additional and later material.[18]

Additions B and E show how the text could be expanded by providing more detail and even documents, purported to be authentic, that are missing in the older text. The MT refers to two edicts that were to be implemented in the kingdom. The first edict, authored by Haman,[19] orders the satraps and governors to destroy all Jews in the kingdom (in Esth 3:12–14), whereas the second edict by the Persian king reverses Haman's edict and allows the Jews to kill their oppressors (Esth 8:9–13). The MT mentions only that such edicts were made and implemented, but the texts of the edicts are not recorded. However, the Greek versions provide the exact text of both edicts, as additions B and E, respectively.

The reference to an edict that is not quoted can be seen as an invitation for later editors who, by including the edict itself, could have developed the text in a direction that corresponded with their own conceptions. Through such additions the editors may also have intended to increase the impression that the text is a piece of authentic historiographic writing and that it therefore provides historically accurate information. The edicts

---

16. See discussion and further literature in Jacob L. Wright, *Rebuilding Identity: The Nehemiah Memoir and Its Earliest Readers* (BZAW 348; Berlin: de Gruyter, 2004), 189–340 (illustrative chart on p. 340).

17. This is suggested by Wright, *Rebuilding Identity*, 25–66. According to him, only Neh 1:1a and 11b are part of the oldest text in Neh 1, whereas much of Neh 2 is original (vv. 1–6, 11, 15*, 16a, 17, and 18b).

18. Here one could also mention the addition of Susanna and the Elders in the book of Daniel. In many Greek manuscripts it is placed before the book of Daniel as its introduction.

19. The edict is given in the king's name, but it is said to be written by Haman.

in the Greek versions of Esther are clearly meant to be read as authentic documents.

The addition of the edicts in the Greek translations is significant for the discussion of similar documents elsewhere in the Hebrew Bible. Many source or redaction critics have suggested such additions in other parts of the Hebrew Bible, while some others have tended to regard documents quoted in the text as old and authentic. For example, there has been considerable discussion about the authenticity of the letters and edicts of the book of Ezra. Some scholars have argued that they are not authentic[20] and/or that they were added later,[21] but others have assumed that they may be the oldest parts of these books.[22] Since there is no manuscript evidence in Ezra-Nehemiah, the case has been disputed, and it remains only a theory that the letters and edicts that are quoted in this book were secondarily created. The book of Esther, however, provides us with indisputable evidence that these kinds of additions to the Hebrew Bible were made during the Second Temple period, and it runs counter to the assumption that such documents would be old merely because of their form as edicts or separate documents. The addition of the two edicts in the Greek versions of Esther suggests that similar additions may have been made in other parts of the Hebrew Bible as well.

The Greek versions include the prayers of Mordecai and Esther (addition C), which are missing in the MT. Both prayers were inserted—probably as a single addition—before Esth 5:1–2, where Esther is said to go to ask the king for a favor and eventually to save the Jews from destruction. The prayers prepare ground for Esther's mission and increase the religious nature of the story more than any other addition in the Greek versions. The prayers are filled with Deuteronomistic terminology (see, e.g., vv.

---

20. Especially Dirk Schwiderski, *Handbuch des nordwestsemitischen Briefformulars: Ein Beitrag zur Echtheitsfrage der aramäischen Briefe des Esrabuches* (BZAW 295; Berlin: de Gruyter, 2000).

21. For example, Artaxerxes's rescript in Ezra 7:11–26 is a later addition that purports to be authentic, but it is very likely a document written by a scribe editor with a heavily Jewish perspective. See Juha Pakkala, *Ezra the Scribe* (BZAW 347; Berlin: de Gruyter, 2004), 40–49, for discussion and further literature.

22. For example, Artaxerxes's rescript is assumed to be original and authentic by Wilhelm Rudolph, *Esra und Nehemia samt 3. Esra* (HAT 20; Tübingen: J.C.B. Mohr, 1949), 73–77. Herbert Donner, *Geschichte des Volkes Israel und seiner Nachbarn in Grundzügen* (ATD Erg. 4.1–2; Göttingen: Vandenhoeck & Ruprecht, 1995), 460, notes that the edict may be the only authentic part of Ezra 7–10.

14–21), and both Esther and Mordecai are presented as pious Jews who acknowledge the sins of the past and seek Yhwh's mercy. After the prayers have been added to the composition, the favorable turn of events later in the account is easily seen as the result of Yhwh's favor and mercy, whereas without the additions the plot puts more emphasis on Esther's own ingenuity and cunning.

Like the edicts, the addition of the prayers is significant for understanding comparable passages in other parts of the Hebrew Bible. Similar prayers are found, for example, in 1 Kgs 8, Ezra 9, Neh 1:5–11, Neh 9, and Dan 9. All of these prayers reflect on the surrounding narrative and its themes, often interpreting the theological meaning of the events of the narrative. Because they appear to be digressions from the main narrative, there has been considerable discussion about their relationship to the rest of the text. Ezra 9, Neh 1:5–11, and Neh 9 in particular have been argued to be later additions.[23] Addition C of Esther seems to confirm that such additions were indeed made to the texts of the Hebrew Bible. Although addition C of Esther as such does not prove that other prayers are later additions, it can and should be used in the discussion about the connection of similar prayers to their contexts in other ancient texts. In concrete terms, if such a prayer was added to Esther, similar additions could also be expected in other parts of the Hebrew Bible where such documented evidence was not preserved.

The large additions imply that the editing of the Greek traditions took place in successive stages. Although the Hebrew or Greek origin of some of the additions in the Greek versions is debated, there is consensus that some were originally written in Greek and some in Hebrew.[24] This implies that the additions were made by different editors, which further suggests that large additions were not an exception, but they could have been made in different contexts at different times by different editors. On the basis of this empirical evidence from the book of Esther, it is fair to assume that

---

23. See, e.g., Pakkala, *Ezra the Scribe*, 89–94 (Ezra 9) and 180–84 (Neh 9). For Neh 1:5–11, see Wright, *Rebuilding Identity*, 10–21. See also discussion on Dan 9 in Hans-Peter Mathys, *Dichter und Beter: Theologen aus spätalttestamentlicher Zeit* (OBO 132; Göttingen: Vandenhoeck & Ruprecht, 1994), 21–36.

24. Additions B and E were probably written in Greek, whereas the other additions were probably written in Hebrew. Nevertheless, some later additions to the large Hebrew additions may have been written in Greek. See, e.g., deSilva, *Introducing the Apocrypha*, 116.

similarly large additions, many of which correspond to entire chapters of modern Bible editions, were made to other books of the Hebrew Bible as well.[25]

14.3. Summary and Methodological Considerations

The book of Esther may provide us with the best empirical evidence for large additions in the Hebrew Bible. They accord with assumptions often made in redaction-critical investigations that entire passages could have been inserted into older compositions. Because of the sheer size of the additions in Esther, the nature of the story changed considerably. The Masoretic book of Esther never refers to God and does not seem have a particularly religious perspective. However, in both of the Greek versions the story receives a clearly religious dimension. This was achieved by the addition of an apocalyptic dream (addition A), its interpretation (addition F), prayers (addition C), and many smaller additions. The edicts were probably added in order to create an impression of authenticity and to guide the text in a particular direction. All in all, Esther is significant in showing how extensively a text could be transformed by the editing. It has changed the nature of the text substantially. This becomes apparent when we compare the complete Greek versions with the (generally) older Hebrew. This is well in line with many source- and redaction-critical approaches that assume significant editing in other books. It also shows how important it is to understand the history of the text.

It is probable that many of the large additions to Esther could be identified as additions even without access to the more original MT. The added religious dimension in most of the additions already contrasts with the older text. The genre and style of the additions would also suggest that they were not written by the same author. For example, the partly apocalyptic style of addition A finds no correspondence in the rest of the composition (with the exception of addition F, which was probably added by the same editors). The prayers also stand out from their contexts because of their religious aspect. As for the edicts, many redaction critics have come to the conclusion that similar additions were made to Ezra-Nehemiah, even

---

25. That some of the large additions were made before the translation also corroborates the idea that already the Hebrew *Vorlagen* of the translators were substantially different from the MT and that the differences were not introduced in the translation process.

though similar textual evidence is not available. It is therefore probable that in Esther, where we know for certain that the edicts were added later, some redaction critics would come to the conclusion that they had been added even if the MT were not available.

15
Evidence for Expansions, Relocations, Omissions, and Rewriting: Joash the King and Jehoiada the Priest in 2 Kings 11–12 and 2 Chronicles 22–24

Because many of the Chronicler's sources are preserved in the books of Samuel and Kings, Chronicles is a productive example for understanding how a source text could be used when a new composition was formed. The creation of an entirely new composition distinguishes the present example from many others in this volume where we compare different textual versions of the same passage (e.g., in Num 13–14) or a passage that was created on the basis of another (e.g., Jer 48 on the basis of Isa 15–16). Although it has a different type of relationship with its source from many other examples of this volume, Chronicles nevertheless shows how some texts related to their sources. This type of relationship to the source text must also be taken into consideration as a possibility when we investigate texts of the Hebrew Bible where a source text was not preserved. In other words, some of the texts investigated in literary and redaction criticism may also be ones created as new compositions on the basis of an entirely different literary work.

Joash's reign is described in 2 Kgs 12:1–22, but the terror reign of Athaliah and her attempt to kill the whole royal family in 2 Kgs 11 functions as a prelude. Second Kings 11 describes how Joash was saved, how Jehoiada the priest staged a coup against Athaliah, and how Jehoiada put Joash in power. Several short examples from these chapters, each with different kinds of editorial changes, illustrate how the Chronicler transmitted and changed the story he found in his source in 2 Kgs 11–12. Although one should not exclude the possibility that 2 Kgs 11–12 was also changed after it had been used by the Chronicler as his source, this does not play a decisive role for the examples presented here.

15.1. A Relocation and an Expansion: Jehosheba Saves Joash from Athaliah

The short parallel accounts of Joash being hidden from Athaliah in 2 Kgs 11:2–3 and 2 Chr 22:11–12 contain several differences.

2 Kgs 11:2–3

ותקח יהושבע בת־המלך יורם אחות אחזיהו את־יואש בן־אחזיה ותגנב
אתו מתוך בני־המלך הממותתים אתו ואת־מינקתו בחדר המטות ויסתרו
אתו מפני עתליהו ולא הוּמָת
ויהי אתה בית יהוה מתחבא שש שנים ועתליה מלכת על־הארץ

² Jehosheba, the daughter of the king ~~Joram, Ahaziah's sister~~, took Joash son of Ahaziah, and stole him away from among the king's children who were about to be killed, (and put) him and his nurse in a bedroom. They thus hid him from Athaliah, <u>so that he would not be killed</u>. ³ He remained with ~~her~~ six years, hidden in the temple of Yhwh, while Athaliah reigned over the land.

2 Chr 22:11–12

ותקח יהושבעת בת־המלך את־יואש בן־אחזיהו ותגנב אתו מתוך בני־
המלך המומתים <u>ותתן</u> אתו ואת־מינקתו בחדר המטות ותסתירהו <u>יהושבעת
בת־המלך יהורם אשת יהוידע הכהן כי היא היתה אחות אחזיהו מפני</u>
עתליהו ולא <u>הֲמִיתָתְהוּ</u>
ויהי אתם בבית האלהים מתחבא שש שנים ועתליה מלכת על־הארץ

¹¹ Jehoshabeath, the daughter of the king, took Joash son of Ahaziah, and stole him away from among the king's children who were about to be killed, <u>and put</u> him and his nurse in a bedroom. <u>Jehoshabeath, who was the daughter of King Jehoram and wife of the priest Jehoiada—for she was a sister of Ahaziah</u>—thus hid him from Athaliah, <u>so that she would not kill him</u>. ¹² He remained with <u>them</u> six years, hidden in the temple of God, while Athaliah reigned over the land.

The most significant difference between the parallel passages is the expansion in 2 Chr 22:11 where the family relationships of Jehosheba (Jehoshabeath)[1] are explained in more detail than in the source text.

---

1. Note that the name is slightly different in the two versions: יהושבע in 2 Kings versus יהושבעת in 2 Chronicles.

At the beginning of 2 Kgs 11:2, Jehosheba is introduced as the sister of Ahaziah. The Chronicler's account has preserved this information, but it has been relocated and incorporated into the expansion in 2 Chr 22:11, which further adds that Jehosheba was the wife of Jehoiada the priest.² This expansion is probably an invention of the Chronicler, who throughout 2 Chr 22–24 portrays Jehoiada as having more influence than what he had according to the source.

Since the expansion was made in a verse where the Chronicler otherwise followed 2 Kgs 11:2 word for word, it is not likely that the expansion derives from a different source as some scholars have suggested.³ Had the author of 2 Chr 22:11 used another source for this passage, one would expect to find here other traces of this source as well. The assumption that there was an isolated piece of information or a separate tradition reporting that Jehosheba was the wife of Jehoiada the priest seems improbable. More important, most of the differences from 2 Kgs 11–12 can be explained on the basis of the Chronicler's theological conceptions.⁴

The change was sparked by the source, where a nonpriestly woman is able to move freely or even live inside the temple area. Second Kings 11:2–3 implies that this was possible during the First Temple period, but it had probably become unthinkable in the Chronicler's own context in the Second Temple period. The Chronicler had to find an explanation and justification for her presence there. Although the whole idea that a woman was able to live in the temple area is bound to have disturbed the

---

2. Edward L. Curtis, *A Critical and Exegetical Commentary on the Books of Chronicles* (ICC; Edinburgh: T&T Clark; New York: Scribner's, 1910), 423, notes that the relocation may have been accidental, but this is unlikely, because the Chronicler also added information in this verse, which implies that the change is intentional.

3. For example, Sara Japhet (*I and II Chronicles* [OTL; Louisville: Westminster John Knox, 1993], 819–24) has suggested that here the Chronicler may have had authentic information not preserved by the author of 2 Kgs 11. Curtis, *Chronicles*, 418–19, and many others similarly assume an additional source. According to Wilhelm Rudolph (*Chronikbücher* [HAT 21; Tübingen: Mohr Siebeck, 1955], 271), the Chronicler deviates from 2 Kgs 11 only when it is theologically disturbing ("Anstößig").

4. For a discussion of the Chronicler's theological conceptions, see Curtis, *Chronicles*, 6–16; Rudolph, *Chronikbücher*, VIII–IX, XIII–XXIV; Hugh G. M. Williamson, *1 and 2 Chronicles* (NCBC; Grand Rapids: Eerdmans; London: Marshall, Morgan & Scott, 1982), 24–33; Japhet, *I and II Chronicles*, 43–49. See also Ehud Ben Zvi, *History, Literature and Theology in the Book of Chronicles* (London: Equinox, 2006), 160–73.

Chronicler,[5] it would have been difficult for him to completely omit the idea that Jehosheba hid Joash in the temple, because many details in the ensuing story are dependent on Joash's hiding place. The temple became the hub of the rebellion according to 2 Kgs 11 // 2 Chr 23, and changing this motif would have meant that entire events concerning the rebellion would had to have been omitted. This would have been too radical, since the Chronicler seems to have been convinced about the general course of events as described in 2 Kgs 11. He found a more economical solution to the problem, as we will see.

That a person was able to move inside the temple would have meant for the Chronicler that this person must have had permission to be there, which then logically meant that she must have been connected to the priests. It is only a short step from here to the idea that Jehosheba was the wife of a priest, and Jehoiada would certainly be the best candidate, because he was the one who taught Joash (2 Kgs 12:3; 2 Chr 24:2). In other words, the addition of the idea that Jehosheba was the wife of Jehoiada the priest can be seen as an interpretation of the source text that is in line with the Chronicler's theological conceptions.

The change of אתה ("with her") in 2 Kgs 11:3 to אתם ("with them") in 2 Chr 22:12 further corroborates the assumption that the Chronicler made Jehosheba the wife of Jehoiada. In the older text, Joash is reported to have been hiding with Jehosheba alone, whereas in the Chronicler's account Joash stays "with them," evidently referring to both Jehosheba and Jehoiada the priest. This would be well in accordance with the idea that Jehoiada taught Joash (2 Kgs 12:3 // 2 Chr 24:2; see below). It would have been logical that Joash had also been taught in his childhood by Jehoiada, during the time that Joash was hiding. In other words, the source text provided the impulse for creating the expansion through imaginative reasoning.

These changes are illustrative of the Chronicler's method in using his source. He found a detail in the source text that did not correspond to his own understanding of who was allowed to enter the temple area. It would have been difficult to omit the problematic reference in this case, and therefore an explanation for this detail had to be found to remove or at least reduce the disturbance. Although the modern reader could inter-

---

5. For example, according to 2 Chr 23:6–7, only the priests and Levites may enter the temple. Verse 7 implies that anyone else should be killed.

pret the addition as a pure invention, it is probable that the Chronicler was convinced about the accuracy of his explanation. For him the source text must have been incorrect or at least unsatisfactory, and therefore it had to be corrected. In other words, a theologically disturbing detail forced a reaction and an editorial correction from the Chronicler. Eventually it was 2 Kgs 12:3 that gave the Chronicler a reason to connect Joash's childhood with Jehoiada (see below).

15.2. A Small Omission with a Large Impact: Jehoiada the Priest Teaches Joash

The Chronicler's account of Joash's reign in 2 Chr 24:1–27 is thoroughly different from that of 2 Kgs 12:1–22, but the beginning of the story was taken almost word for word from 2 Kgs 12. Many details in the source text conflicted with the Chronicler's theological and other conceptions, but especially the basic development of the events as described in 2 Kgs 12 would have been difficult if not impossible for him to accept.

According to 2 Kgs 12, King Joash was a good king because Jehoiada, the priest, had taught him, and consequently Joash took interest in the temple and restored it. Except for the high places, which are a recurrent sin of all good and evil kings of Judah up to King Hezekiah, King Joash is said to have done nothing wrong. According to 2 Kgs 12:19, however, he had to give all the votive gifts (כל־הקדשים) from the temple as well as the gold of the temple and of the palace to King Hazael of Aram. This was done in order to save Jerusalem from an imminent attack by the Arameans. The author of 2 Kgs 12 does not appear to blame the king at all, and the event is described rather neutrally as a necessary action to save Jerusalem from destruction.

For the Chronicler the temple was the center of his theology,[6] and he would have regarded Joash's act of giving the votive offerings and temple treasures to the Arameans as a total catastrophe and a sign of Yhwh's anger and punishment. In view of his conceptions of divine justice and just retribution,[7] there was an evident contradiction between the goodness of King Joash and the robbing of the temple. The course and development of the events as described in 2 Kgs 12 would hardly have been possible for the

---

6. Thus most scholars; see, e.g., Peter B. Dirksen, *1 Chronicles* (Historical Commentary on the Old Testament; Leuven: Peeters, 2005), 19–20.
7. Japhet, *I and II Chronicles*, 44–45.

Chronicler, and this is probably the main reason for most of the changes he made in relation to the source text.

It may have been difficult for the Chronicler to change the general evaluation of Joash as a good king, because he is said to have done many good deeds, such as the repairing of the temple, but at the same time the plundering of the temple had to be given an interpretation. A small omission in the evaluation of the king's reign solved this problem.[8]

2 Kgs 12:1–3

בן־שבע שנים יהואש במלכו
בשנת־שבע ליהוא מלך יהואש וארבעים שנה מלך בירושלם ושם אמו צביה מבאר שבע
ויעש יהואש הישר בעיני יהוה כל־ימיו אשר הורהו יהוידע הכהן

[1] Joash was seven years old when he began to reign, [2] ~~in the seventh year of Jehu Joash began to reign~~, and he reigned forty years in Jerusalem. His mother's name was Zibiah from Beer-sheba. [3] Joash did what was right in the sight of Yhwh all ~~his~~ days, ~~because~~ the priest Jehoiada ~~instructed him~~.

2 Chr 24:1–2

בן־שבע שנים יאש במלכו וארבעים שנה מלך בירושלם ושם אמו צביה מבאר שבע
ויעש יואש הישר בעיני יהוה כל־ימי יהוידע הכהן

[1] Joash was seven years old when he began to reign, and he reigned forty years in Jerusalem. His mother's name was Zibiah from Beer-sheba. [2] Joash did what was right in the sight of Yhwh all the days *of* the priest Jehoiada.

According to 2 Kgs 12:3, Joash was a good king all the days of his life (כל־ימיו) because Jehoiada had taught him. However, the Chronicler omitted a small section of this sentence, thereby changing the whole idea. According to his account, Joash was a good king all the days of Jehoiada (כל־ימי יהוידע), which implies that he was not good all the days of his own life. It is not explicitly stated that Joash was evil, but it is implied that Jehoiada

---

8. The omission of the reference to the year of the king of Israel is a systematic omission in Chronicles and need not concern us here.

kept him from committing evil deeds. That the sentence in 2 Kgs is somewhat ambiguous (whether אשר should be understood as introducing a relative or explicative clause) may have been caused by earlier editing,[9] since the whole sentence beginning with אשר could be a later addition to 2 Kgs 12:3, as some scholars have suggested.[10] Nonetheless, this does not change our case, because the Chronicler was evidently aware of this part of the text: in Chronicles the reference to Jehoiada has been changed so that Joash's piety is limited to a part of his life.

Once Joash's piety was restricted to the time that Jehoiada lived, the door was open for the other changes in the passage that explained the contradiction between the king's goodness and the restoration of the temple on the one hand (2 Kgs 12:2–17) and the catastrophe later in the king's reign on the other (2 Kgs 12:18–19). In the Chronicler's account, Joash's reign is divided by Jehoiada's death into two different periods. The temple is restored during the time that Jehoiada lived, whereas the time after his death is characterized by sin and punishment. Because of this division, the idea of Jehoiada's death had to be added to the Chronicler's account (2 Chr 24:15–16). This was followed by several other insertions. Immediately after Jehoiada has died, Joash listens to the leaders of Judah (v. 17), which then leads to the neglect of the temple and the worship of the Asherim and the idols (v. 18). The prophets sent by Yhwh (vv. 19–20) are ignored, and finally Joash orders Zechariah, the son of Jehoiada, to be stoned to death (vv. 21–22). The words of the dying Zechariah function as the bridge from the sins to the ensuing catastrophe: "May Yhwh see and avenge" (v. 22).

---

9. That the אשר of 2 Kgs 12:3 could be understood as an explicative and not as a relative particle is implied by the suffix in ימי. For it to be understood as a relative clause, one would have to remove the suffix. For example, the Greek translations that understood אשר as a relative pronoun omitted the suffix: καὶ ἐποίησεν Ιωας τὸ εὐθὲς ἐνώπιον κυρίου πάσας τὰς ἡμέρας, ἃς ἐφώτισεν αὐτὸν Ιωδαε ὁ ἱερεύς. However, Paul Joüon and Takamitsu Muraoka, *A Grammar of Biblical Hebrew* (2nd repr. of 2nd ed.; SubBi 27; Rome: Gregorian & Biblical Press, 2009), §158t, 600, understand the word as a relative pronoun that refers to an earlier part of the sentence. More probably, however, we are dealing with an explicative use of the word (cf. ibid., §170e, 638).

10. According to Charles Fox Burney (*Notes on the Hebrew Text of the Books of Kings* [Oxford: Clarendon, 1903], 312) and Christoph Levin ("Die Instandsetzung des Tempels unter Joas ben Ahasja," in *Fortschreibungen: Gesammelte Studien zum Alten Testament* [BZAW 316; Berlin: de Gruyter, 2003], 169–97, esp. 169–71), the sentence is a later addition or a marginal note. Levin further notes (171) that the sentence refers to the reason for the piety and not to its duration.

The attack of the Arameans is described in the following verse. The additional material in vv. 15–22 serves the Chronicler's broader conception that a catastrophe is always a punishment for sins. These verses explain how the king's initial goodness eventually turned into evil. They are necessary to the Chronicler's attempt to transform the story to conform to his theological conceptions.

Consequently, a comparison between 2 Kgs 12:1–3 and 2 Chr 24:1–2 illustrates how theological reasoning could justify an omission of a part of the source text that changed the meaning of the sentence substantially. This small omission then enabled the Chronicler to make other more extensive changes throughout the passage.

15.3. Rewriting: Joash Repairs the Temple

Although most of the general themes of 2 Kgs 12 are preserved in 2 Chr 24, practically all details and the course of events have been rewritten. Some scholars assume that most of the changes in this chapter mainly or exclusively derive from the Chronicler's own pen and not from an unknown source,[11] while others have suggested that the Chronicler used another source besides 2 Kgs 12.[12] Several considerations suggest that the Chronicler used 2 Kgs 12 as the main source. The beginnings of the passages are identical, which implies that the Chronicler certainly knew the beginning of 2 Kgs 12. Although similar parallels are missing in the ensuing text, both passages share vocabulary, and the shared words are often found in the same order in both accounts. The thematic similarities between the passages are even more apparent. All themes of 2 Kgs 12 have a parallel in 2 Chr 24, albeit in a radically altered form. Since the themes are also presented in the same order, the correspondence of themes is probably caused by the Chronicler's attempt to react to the text in 2 Kgs 12. He tried to correct what he saw as incorrect in the source. It should be further noted that the resulting text is an excellent example of the Chronicler's theology,

---

11. Thus, among many others, Curtis, *Chronicles*, 434; Japhet, *I and II Chronicles*, 839–40.

12. Thus, for example, Wilhelm Rudolph (*Chronikbücher*, 273–74) and Steven L. McKenzie (*The Chronicler's Use of the Deuteronomistic History* [HSM 33; Atlanta: Scholars Press, 1985], 110–11) assume that the Chronicler used another source besides 2 Kgs 12.

as noted by Edward Curtis.[13] The cumulative evidence therefore suggests that 2 Chr 24 was written with 2 Kgs 12 in view and that no other source is necessary to explain the differences.

A prime example of rewriting is the repairing of the temple. According to 2 Kgs 12:5–6, the money should be collected from the people in order to repair the breaches (בדק) of the temple. It consists of a tax and voluntary offerings or gifts. One receives the impression from this passage that collecting money for the temple was a onetime event that took place only during Joash's reign. In contrast, the Chronicler's version implies that there was an annual tax or payment for the repairs (מדי שנה בשנה) and that Moses had ordered such a payment (משאת משה).[14] The restoration is also assumed to have been a much bigger issue in the Chronicler's version than in 2 Kgs 12. According to 2 Kgs 12, only the breaches (בדק) were repaired, but when the reference to the breaches was omitted in 2 Chr 24, the limitation was lifted. As a consequence, in the Chronicler's text the whole temple has to be repaired (see vv. 5, 12) or even renewed (לחדש; see v. 12). The Chronicler changed a description of reparation of breaches to an implicit statement that the temple should be renewed every year and that Moses, in fact, ordered the Israelites to contribute financially to the continuous renovation of the temple by paying an annual tax for this purpose. This is well in line with the temple-centered approach of the Chronicler. The comparison of these verses in the two accounts illustrates how extensive the changes were that the Chronicler could, in some cases, make in order to imprint his own theological and compositional conceptions on the text. Of the source text only fractions are preserved in the Chronicler's version.

2 Kgs 12:5–8

ויאמר יהואש אל־הכהנים כל כסף הקדשים אשר־יובא בית־יהוה כסף עובר
איש כסף נפשות ערכו כל־כסף אשר יעלה על לב־איש להביא בית יהוה
יקחו להם הכהנים איש מאת מכרו והם יחזקו את־בדק הבית לכל אשר־
ימצא שם בדק
ויהי בשנת עשרים ושלש שנה למלך יהואש לא־חזקו הכהנים את־בדק
הבית

---

13. Curtis, *Chronicles*, 423.

14. It is not clear which passage in the Pentateuch is meant here, if any. Exod 36:5–29, for example, refers to the gifts that the Israelites gave for the construction of the tabernacle, but they are clearly voluntary gifts, and it is a onetime event.

ויקרא המלך יהואש ליהוידע הכהן ולכהנים ויאמר אלהם מדוע אינכם
מחזקים את־בדק הבית ועתה אל־תקחו־כסף מאת מכריכם כי־לבדק הבית
תתנהו

[5] ~~Jehoash said to the priests, "All the money offered as sacred donations brought into Yhwh's temple, the money for which each person is assessed (tax he is able to pay) and the money from the voluntary offerings brought into Yhwh's temple,~~ [6] ~~let the priests receive from each of the donors; and let them~~ repair the breaches of the temple ~~wherever any need of repairs is discovered."~~ [7] ~~But by the twenty-third year of King Jehoash the priests had made no repairs on the house.~~ [8] So King ~~Joash~~ summoned ~~the priest~~ Jehoiada ~~with the other priests~~ and said to ~~them~~, "Why ~~are you~~ not repairing the house? ~~Now therefore do not accept any more money from your donors but hand it over for the repair of the house."~~

2 Chr 24:4–6

ויהי אחריכן היה עם־לב יואש לחדש את־בית יהוה
ויקבץ את־הכהנים והלוים ויאמר להם צאו לערי יהודה
וקבצו מכל־ישראל כסף לחזק את־בית אלהיכם מדי שנה בשנה ואתם
תמהרו לדבר ולא מהרו הלוים
ויקרא המלך ליהוידע הראש ויאמר לו מדוע לא־דרשת על־הלוים להביא
מיהודה ומירושלם את־משאת משה עבד־יהוה והקהל לישראל לאהל
העדות

[4] <u>Sometime afterward Joash decided to restore Yhwh's temple.</u> [5] <u>He assembled the priests and the Levites and said to them, "Go out to the cities of Judah and gather money from all Israel</u> to repair the temple <u>of your God, the yearly amount; and act quickly in this matter." But the Levites did not act quickly.</u>

[6] So the king summoned Jehoiada <u>the chief</u> (priest) and said to <u>him</u>, "Why <u>have you not required the Levites to bring in from Judah and Jerusalem the tax levied by Moses, the servant of Yhwh, on the congregation of Israel for the tent of the covenant?"</u>

15.4. Evidence for Contradicting the Source by an Omission and an Addition: Joash's Burial

As 2 Kgs 12 describes King Joash in a positive light, he is buried in an honorable way with his fathers in the royal cemetery (v. 22). Because this would have been against the Chronicler's conception that Joash had done many evil deeds after Jehoiada's death, the manner of Joash's burial was changed accordingly. Clearly following his source in the basic reference to Joash's burial, the Chronicler contradicted it by omitting the reference to the fathers and adding a sentence that explicitly notes that King Joash was not buried in the royal tombs (2 Kgs 12:22 // 2 Chr 24:25).

2 Kgs 12:22	2 Chr 24:25
ויקברו אתו	ויקברהו
עם־אבתיו	
בעיר דוד	בעיר דוד
	ולא קברהו בקברות המלכים
and they buried him	and they buried him
~~with his fathers~~	
in the city of David	in the city of David
	but they did not bury him in the royal tombs

Instead of Joash, in the Chronicler's account the priest Jehoiada was buried in the royal tombs (2 Chr 24:16: ויקברהו בעיר־דויד עם־המלכים, "And they buried him in the city of David among the kings"). There is probably an intentional contrast between the good Jehoiada, who, despite being a priest, deserved to be buried with the kings, and the evil Joash, who was held good only as long as Jehoiada lived. This is an illustrative example where the Chronicler could present a diametrically opposing view of an event that he found in his source. It is very unlikely that the Chronicler used a different source here, because the change is in accordance with the other changes he made throughout the passage.[15]

15.5. Conclusions and Methodological Consequences

Although it is probable that many of the changes in 2 Chr 24 are more or less inventions of the Chronicler, he was not entirely free to create the

---

15. For example, Rudolph, *Chronikbücher*, 280, regards it possible that the difference is due to a different source or the invention of the Chronicler. Japhet, *I and II Chronicles*, 853–54, is also hesitant as to whether a source was used or not, but she notes that theological motives are behind the changes.

whole story. Second Kings 12 is the starting point that the Chronicler reacted to, and he also built his own story on the basis of this source. He was bound by the events, which were generally assumed to have taken place, but took the liberty to rewrite the details that were contrary to his own theological conceptions. He evidently could not deny many of the events described in 2 Kgs 12, and he also seems to have been convinced that the general development of the events as described in 2 Kgs 12 was reliable. Perhaps we are dealing with events generally acknowledged by the Chronicler's community to have taken place, and the description of these events could not be completely changed without endangering the credibility of the new text.[16] On the other hand, it seems that the Chronicler was not bound by the source text solely because of external or societal pressure. He clearly also regarded 1–2 Kings as an authoritative and reliable source that he could and in many cases did follow word for word. However, the course of events in 2 Kgs 12 contradicted so much of the Chronicler's own theology that much of its wordage had to be left out. The resulting text describes the reign of Joash as the Chronicler assumed that it must have taken place.

The examples presented in this chapter show that at least in some cases authors who used older sources could make substantial changes to the older text for theological reasons. We have seen an example of an expansion (in 2 Kgs 11:2 and 2 Chr 22:11), similar to what is assumed in conventional literary or redaction criticism. Literary criticism would probably be in a position to identify the addition, because it partly repeats what is already said (cf. "Jehoshabeath, the daughter of the king ... Jehoshabeath, who was the daughter of King Jehoram"). However, parts of the texts (namely, the idea that Jehoshabeath was Ahaziah's sister) were also relocated, and literary criticism commonly does not assume that such processes took place. For literary criticism, the case would thus be complicated, because part of what seems to be an expansion was in fact relocated from another section of the older text. On the other hand, parts of the expansion have no counterpart in the older text. Consequently, it is likely that literary criticism would be able to detect that something was added, but it would not be able to reconstruct the course of editing in full.

---

16. See Ehud Ben Zvi, "Shifting the Gaze: Historiographic Constraints in Chronicles and Their Implications," in *The Land That I Will Show You: Essays on the History and Archaeology of the Ancient Near East in Honor of J. Maxwell Miller* (ed. P. Graham and A. Dearman; JSOTSup 343: Sheffield: Sheffield Academic Press, 2001), 38–60.

We have also seen several small omissions (2 Kgs 12:1-3 // 2 Chr 24:1-2), some of which had considerable impact on the meaning of the text. It goes without saying that literary criticism would not be in a position to reconstruct what was omitted, but it would also be difficult to detect that something was omitted, because the resulting text is rather fluent. Perhaps the most radical change in relation to the source took place in 2 Chr 24:4-6, which is an extensively rewritten version of 2 Kgs 12:5-8. It is evident that the reconstruction of such textual changes would also be very difficult, if not impossible, if we did not possess the source. The same can be said of 2 Chr 24:25, which describes Joash's burial.

The reason for the extensive changes may, at least in part, be due to the way Chronicles relates to its sources. It is a new composition that was created by using different literary works as sources, 1-2 Kings being one of them. Nevertheless, the evidence does provide possible models as to how some texts in the Hebrew Bible related to their sources, and in this respect the evidence should not be ignored by literary or redaction criticism in seeking to understand the earlier history of the texts. In concrete terms, it is possible that the prehistory of some texts where we do not possess the source is similar to that of the prehistory of Chronicles. If a literary-critical investigation seeks to reconstruct the prehistory of such texts, it would go astray unless extensive omissions and rewritings were assumed.

Conclusions:
Empirical Evidence of Editorial Processes

Fifteen passages from the Hebrew Bible have been investigated in this volume. They show that substantial editing took place in the literary history of the Hebrew Bible. The evidence consists of textual witnesses that differ from the MT and of parallel passages within one textual tradition, especially within the MT. This evidence could be characterized as empirical in the sense that the editorial changes can be observed by comparing two or more preserved textual witnesses or parallel texts. The examples thus provide a solid basis for understanding the general nature of editorial processes. It can reasonably be assumed that similar changes also took place in cases where such evidence is not preserved.

The passages were taken from various parts of the Hebrew Bible in order to gain a broad perspective. Although each text is different and needs to be investigated on the basis of its available textual witnesses, the presented analyses can be used as reference material and potential models for investigating other texts. They provide evidence of a variety of techniques used by the editors. Although it has become apparent that the positions and attitudes of the editors toward the older text were not identical and that different processes have been at work, some clear tendencies of the literary history can be detected in the preserved textual material. With regard to this evidence, the existence and the wide range of editorial processes in the history of the Hebrew Bible should no longer be questioned.

1. The Final Text Should Not Be Used for Historical Investigation

The examples unequivocally show that it is imperative to be aware of the complicated editorial processes behind the texts of the Hebrew Bible. This is especially important if these texts are used for historical investigation.

In many cases the text was so substantially changed by later editors that the original meaning was greatly altered. This undermines any attempt to use the final texts for historical purposes. Without understanding how the texts developed and received their latest forms, one would effectively neglect significant and perhaps crucial information. One has to question the viability and validity of any theory that is based on the use of the final texts to reconstruct the culture, history, and religion of ancient Israel and Judaism. In the worst cases, the use of the final texts provides a distorted and misleading picture of the investigated subject.

For example, it is very probable that several editors made changes to Ezra's profession, and some of this editorial activity is preserved in the textual witnesses, as we have seen. Although Ezra was originally regarded as a scribe, later editors increasingly made him a priest as well. The end of this development can be seen in 1 Esdras, where he is regarded as the high priest (ὁ ἀρχιερεὺς in 1 Esd 9:39, 40, 49). The changes in his title and profession were accompanied by changes in the rest of the text, such as the addition of temple vessels that Ezra brings back to Jerusalem. Themes related to the temple and priests were increased. The reader is bound to understand the narrative in a different light after Ezra has been made a priestly character. The reading of the law in Neh 8 will be understood differently depending on whether Ezra the scribe or Ezra the high priest leads the occasion. As Ezra 7–10 and Neh 8 are often used as a significant historical source, a neglect of the fact that substantial editorial changes took place in these texts will inevitably lead to shaky historical reconstructions.[1]

2. The Methods of Literary and Redaction Criticism in the Light of Empirical Evidence

There are several examples in the analyzed passages where the preserved empirical evidence corresponds to conventional theories about the literary growth of the texts (e.g., Num 13:33; 28:16–25; Judg 6:7–10; 2 Kgs 25:8–12; and Jer 52:12).[2] As assumed in literary and redaction criticism,

---

[1]. For example, the Ezra narrative in Ezra 7–10 and in Neh 8 is used rather uncritically as a historical source in Pierre Briant, *From Cyrus to Alexander: A History of the Persian Empire* (Winona Lake, Ind.: Eisenbrauns, 2002), 583–84.

[2]. Num 28:16–25 in relation to the older Lev 23:5–8, the MT of 2 Kgs 25:8–12 in relation to the LXX, the MT of Jer 52:12 in relation to the LXX.

these texts were mainly expanded. Moreover, the expansions in these cases clearly distinguish themselves from the older text, which accords with the assumption in literary criticism that expansions can be identified. They often interrupt the older narrative or its thought sequences and may not completely fit in with the syntax and style of their respective contexts. One can often see a different perspective in the expansion that separates it from its surroundings. The main incentives for expanding an older text would be to explain older passages, provide a different perspective, add something new, or change something that the editor thought was not adequately or correctly discussed. A recurrent motive to insert an additional passage was to update the older text to correspond to changed socio-historical circumstances and to new religious ideas and concepts. Accordingly, incoherent syntax and differing styles, perspectives, tendencies, and topics are regarded by literary critics as significant criteria for distinguishing expansions from older literary layers. In texts where expansions were made, it is in many cases possible to identify the later elements and thus reconstruct, at least in part, the literary development. Thus, an overall methodological skepticism toward the possibilities of reconstructing the literary history of the Hebrew Bible, advocated by some scholars, cannot be held justified. Processes of editing left many traces in the resulting texts, and by investigating these traces it is often possible to reconstruct how texts probably developed. In light of the evidence presented in this volume, we should not ignore these traces in exegesis, and in every case we should try to gain insight into the textual prehistory by using the criteria of literary criticism.

On the other hand, the example passages also demonstrate that in several cases it would be difficult, if not impossible, to reconstruct the editorial changes that have taken place. There is evidence of relocation of parts of the text (e.g., 2 Chr 22:11–12), rewriting (e.g., 2 Chr 24:4–6; Jer 39:8–10; 48:29–33; Ps 108; 1 Esd 8:3–4), and even sheer omissions (Josh 20:1–6 LXX; 1 Sam 10:1; Esth 2:17–20) of parts of the older text. Literary and redaction criticism would have considerable difficulties in determining what has been left out or rewritten. For example, if Jer 39:8–10 were the only preserved passage describing the burning of Jerusalem, it would be next to impossible to reconstruct its older literary stage that is probably preserved in 2 Kgs 25:8–11 and Jer 52:13–16. The same holds true for the rewritten prophecy of Jer 48:29–33 in relation to its probable source text in Isa 15–16.

Literary critics have also been reluctant to assume that parts of the older text were relocated by later editors, but textual evidence suggests that this was not exceptional. Relocations are implied, for example, by the textual evidence from Jeremiah when the LXX and MT are compared. Several verses or even entire passages are now found in different locations in the MT and the LXX.[3] Second Chronicles 36:18–20, in relation to the source text 2 Kgs 25:9–11, illustrates some of the difficulties that one would have if 2 Kgs 25:9–11 had not been preserved. In addition to rewriting many parts of the source, the Chronicler has rearranged the text to accord with his own interests: the destruction of the temple and its paraphernalia is elevated, while the destruction of the rest of Jerusalem has a more marginal role than in the source text 2 Kgs 25:9–11.

Some of the additions are also very well integrated with the older text so that it would be difficult to argue that an addition has taken place by using the conventional criteria of literary criticism. For example, the words שבעת ימים ("seven days") in Num 28:16–25 are now found in the middle of a major expansion, although they derive from the source text in Lev 23:5–8.[4] If Lev 23 had not been preserved, it would be very difficult to come to the conclusion that out of Num 28:19–24 two words were taken from a source and the rest of these verses are an expansion. Furthermore, in some cases merely one or two words have been added later, which would also be difficult to identify as additions on technical grounds, especially if the addition does not conflict with or otherwise stand out from its context. Lists in particular were often updated (e.g., 1 Esd 5:51–52[5] or Num 13:29 SP/LXX), but the critic would have little chance of identifying one member of a list as an addition.

These observations underscore the limits of literary and redaction criticism. The difficulties have to be taken into consideration when reconstructing the literary growth of a text by using the classic criteria of this method. In other words, the evidence points in two opposing directions. Some example texts show that it is possible to gain reliable results by using the literary-critical method. Other example texts, however, indicate that some editorial alterations would be very difficult or impossible to detect, especially many minor changes that nevertheless may affect the meaning

---

3. For example, Josh 8:30–35 MT is placed in the LXX after Josh 9:2; 1 Kgs 20 MT corresponds to 3 Kgdms 21 LXX; and the MT version of Jer 25:13–38 is found in ch. 32 of the Greek version.

4. For details, see ch. 2.

5. The Sabbath offerings in 1 Esd 5:51–52 are missing in the source text in Ezra 3:5 and were thus later added in the textual tradition of 1 Esdras.

substantially. These limitations should be acknowledged in all reconstructions of the literary prehistory.

The difficulties and uncertainties in some texts should not mean that one has to refrain from trying to reconstruct the earlier stages of the literary history of all texts in the Hebrew Bible, as is sometimes implied or suggested (as we have seen in the introduction). It has to be stressed that because of heavy editing the final texts are poor historical sources for any period. Scholars who fail to investigate the earlier stages of the literary history effectively give up understanding large parts of the history and religion of ancient Israel. If we use the texts exclusively as witnesses for the period in which their final form developed, the Persian, Hellenistic, or Roman periods, we would in many cases ignore the complexity of the concepts they contain. This complexity is due to long-standing processes of transmission and editorial activity, and a failure to take this background into consideration would create the wrong idea about what the texts can tell us about the development of concepts. In other words, much of the historical perspective would be lost.

To be sure, one could argue that archaeology and textual discoveries provide very significant information about many facets of ancient society, and their results seem to be much more reliable than the often contradictory theories of literary and redaction criticism. Yet, the Hebrew Bible may provide access to some areas of the ancient Israelite religion, culture, and history that one would not be able to have by other means. Especially important is the development of conceptions, a central area of biblical studies, which is difficult to reconstruct by archaeological and epigraphic evidence. Conceptions are rarely preserved as such in material remains and could thus be studied only indirectly without texts. It also needs to be noted that archaeology and related fields have their own limitations. Like literary criticism, archaeology is based on theories and hypotheses that leave uncertainties as well. Each theory, whether essentially based on archaeological or textual evidence, has to be critically evaluated by scholarly discussion. In other words, since we are in the field of human sciences, we can rarely, if ever, expect to reach fully proven theories. We are dealing with probabilities, and we have to evaluate different theories and hypotheses as to which one offers the most probable explanation to a particular question or area of investigation.

Regarding the question about the origins and development of the Hebrew Bible, we are thus effectively faced with a situation that we have a methodology that cannot provide complete or comprehensive reconstructions of the texts. However, this methodology may be the only possibility to identify, at least in part, later editorial changes and thus to understand that the final texts are the result of long-standing and intricate editorial processes. Consequently, an attempt to understand the prehistory of a given text should be made, if one is not be able to reconstruct it in full. For example, if we had only Num 28 (without the parallel in Lev 23), Judg 6 MT/LXX (without 4QSam[a]), 1 Kgs 6 MT (without the LXX), or Ps 108 (without Pss 57 and 60), we could still develop models of the prehistory of these texts that would cover some of the actual prehistory that can now be seen in the extant parallel texts. At the same time, some of these examples (in particular, Num 28 and Ps 108) show that we should be more cautious in the attempt to reconstruct every detail of the literary history. Since not all changes left discernible traces in the text, reconstructions remain necessarily tentative and, at least in some cases, also incomplete.

Consequently, literary- and redaction-critical analyses should be conducted, and their results should be critically evaluated. Excessively optimistic notions about the methodology should be avoided, and uncertainty about the reconstructions has to be accepted. A theory concerning any aspect of Israel's history should not be built on the literary-critical reconstruction of any single text but should be substantiated by similar observations in many texts. For example, if one can see that a certain theme was added to several different passages in a literary composition, the probability is increased that the theme in general is late, which then should have consequences for our understanding of the past. Here one could mention the observance of the Sabbath, which has been added to many passages in the Hebrew Bible.[6] It therefore stands to reason that the Sabbath became a central idea within the Jewish communities relatively late in the Second Temple period.

Moreover, all literary-critical reconstructions remain unfinished because of their hypothetical nature. The discussion with other scholars has to continue, and the balancing of the arguments will gradually bring us closer to the actual development. Literary-critical reconstructions should also reflect theories rising out of archaeological and other evidence. This

---

6. Such as in the Decalogue—see, e.g., Timo Veijola, *Das fünfte Buch Mose: Deuteronomium; Kapitel 1,1–16,17* (ATD 8.1; Göttingen: Vandenhoeck & Ruprecht, 2004), 160–63, and many others. This development is seen in one of the example texts of this volume, namely in 1 Esd 5:51–52 in relation to Ezra 3:5.

is an open-ended process that gradually increases our understanding through the refinement of the proposed theories.

3. The Relation between Textual and Literary Criticism

The example texts show that the borderline between textual and literary criticism is difficult to draw to the extent that these methodologies have to be implemented hand in hand. Textual criticism is essential for understanding literary criticism. Although textual criticism also deals with mechanical errors as well as translation techniques and revisions of translations, both methodologies share a common field of research, because editorial changes took place not only in the prehistory of the extant texts but also in the textual history as it is preserved in the witnesses. The main difference between the methods is that textual criticism investigates those changes that were preserved in the variant editions, while literary criticism seeks to reconstruct the same processes without such empirical evidence.

To be sure, the scale of the editorial changes seems to have diminished gradually, and the texts began to freeze at a certain point in their history. This was a longer process, the beginning of which is not easy to delimit, and which may have been different for each book. It is probably an unhistorical notion that the texts were at some point deliberately finished by editors, after which the long process of copying began. The evidence implies that scribal editors only gradually turned into scribal copyists and that the continuous processes of editing did not stop suddenly but slowly decreased in scale and frequency.

4. Perspectives for Further Research

In order to improve and refine the traditional methodologies of literary and redaction criticism, it would be helpful to place the scribal techniques that were used by the editors under closer scrutiny. Which kinds of editorial changes were made? A categorization of the changes would certainly be useful for the application of the methodology. How are these changes related to the material aspects of writing and rewriting as they can be observed in material evidence like the scrolls from Qumran? In which cases did editing leave discernible traces in the texts, and in which cases can no such traces be found due to the nature of the editorial technique? Did the editors use some techniques more often than others? How can the editorial freedom be described with regard to the genre of the respective books? For example, were the legal and prose texts of the Pentateuch less prone to changes than the poetical texts of the Psalms? Were some texts more protected from alterations than other texts?[7] Although the results of such an investigation are limited to the range of the extant empirical evidence, they would substantially contribute to a historical understanding of the texts of the Hebrew Bible and advance their investigation.

Another important perspective is of a comparative nature. It is conceivable that similar techniques of editing were, at least in part, used in the cultures of the ancient Near East as well as in the Hellenistic world. Especially the vast Mesopotamian and Egyptian literature could provide significant reference material for understanding the editorial processes of the Hebrew Bible. A well-known example is the Mesopotamian Gilgamesh Epic, which is preserved in several variant editions from different times. Although research has been done in this field,[8] the authors of this volume are convinced that much more can be done in this respect. Further texts should be included for investigation, and a more comprehensive comparison of the editorial processes in different areas of the ancient Near East would certainly be productive.

A further area of exploration is related to the phenomena of canon and canonicity. The crystallization of a canon of "holy scriptures" was not isolated from cultural, sociological, and religious circumstances, but more information about the causal relationships in this respect would certainly be welcome. How is canonicity to be defined, especially in terms of authoritativeness? How is it related to the actual unchangeability of the text? These questions should be developed in comparative studies of different canons of the ancient world.

The most difficult questions are related to the editors themselves. It would be imperative to understand their sociological and religious backgrounds in more detail, and here a comparative study would possibly

---

7. For example, since parts of the Pentateuch or words of the prophets claim to be divine revelations, one could suggest that they have been more protected from changes than the historical books, such as 1–2 Kings, which mainly describe Israel's past. However, this suggestion has never been validated and should be investigated. As the examples in this book have shown, many texts in the Pentateuch and the books of the prophets have been heavily edited as well.

8. Jeffrey H. Tigay, *The Evolution of the Gilgamesh Epic* (Philadelphia: University of Pennsylvania Press, 1982); Sara J. Milstein, "Reworking Ancient Texts: Revision through Introduction in Biblical and Mesopotamian Literature" (Ph.D. diss., New York University, 2010).

provide additional information. Although poorly known, the economic aspects of the vast editorial activity were certainly important. Because of the costs, the production of a new edition of a text could rarely be commissioned by an individual. Institutional support or the support of a broader community is probable in most cases. Here the relationship between the editor and the commissioning authority of the community may also be reflected in the types of changes that were made. For example, was an editor or a group of editors commissioned by someone to update a certain set of texts or to correct them theologically, or did the editor(s) have a more independent role? Here we are faced with the question of how the editors perceived themselves, and whether this perception is somewhere reflected in the edited texts.[9]

Despite growing awareness about the empirical evidence of editing, many questions are still unanswered. Acknowledging that much remains to be done in this field, we hope that this volume will contribute to a better understanding of how the texts of the Hebrew Bible developed.

---

9. Timo Veijola, "Die Deuteronomisten als Vorgänger der Schriftgelehrten: Ein Beitrag zur Entstehung des Judentums," in *Moses Erben: Studien zum Dekalog, zum Deuteronomismus und zum Schriftgelehrtentum* (BWANT 149; Stuttgart: Kohlhammer, 2000), 192–240.

Bibliography

Aejmelaeus, Anneli. "How to Reach the Old Greek in 1 Samuel and What to Do with It." Pages 185–205 in *Congress Volume Helsinki 2010*. Edited by Martti Nissinen. VTSup 148. Leiden: Brill, 2012.

———. "What Can We Know about the Hebrew *Vorlage* of the Septuagint." Pages 71–106 in *On the Trail of the Septuagint Translators: Collected Essays*. Leuven: Peeters, 2007.

Allen, Leslie C. *Psalms 101–150*. WBC 21. Waco, Tex.: Word, 1983.

Amit, Yairah. *The Book of Judges: The Art of Editing*. Biblical Interpretation Series 38. Leiden: Brill, 1999.

Auld, A. Graeme. *I and II Samuel: A Commentary*. OTL. Louisville, Ky.: Westminster John Knox, 2011.

———. *Joshua: Jesus Son of Nauē in Codex Vaticanus*. Septuagint Commentary Series. Leiden: Brill: 2005.

Baentsch, Bruno. *Exodus, Leviticus, Numeri*. HKAT 1.2. Göttingen: Vandenhoeck & Ruprecht, 1903.

Bardtke, Hans. "Jeremia der Fremdvölkerprophet." ZAW 54 (1936): 240–62.

Barthélemy, Dominique, ed. *Critique textuelle de l'Ancien Testament: Rapport final du Comité pour l'analyse textuelle de l'Ancien Testament hébreu*. 4 vols. OBO 50. Fribourg: Éditions Universitaires; Göttingen: Vandenhoeck & Ruprecht, 1982–2005.

———. "L'enchevêtrement de l'histoire textuelle et de l'histoire littéraire dans les relations entre la Septante et le Texte Massorétique: Modifications dans la manière de concevoir les relations existant entre la LXX et le TM, depuis J. Morin jusqu'à E. Tov." Pages 21–40 in *De Septuaginta: Studies in Honour of John William Wevers on His Sixty-Fifth Birthday*. Edited by Albert Pietersma and Claude Cox. Mississauga: Benben, 1984.

Batten, Loring W. *Ezra and Nehemiah*. ICC. Edinburgh: T&T Clark, 1913.

Becker, Uwe. *Exegese des Alten Testaments*. 3d ed. UTB 2664. Tübingen: Mohr Siebeck, 2011.

Benzinger, Immanuel. *Die Bücher der Könige*. KHC 9. Freiburg i. B.: Mohr Siebeck, 1899.

Ben Zvi, Ehud. "The Concept of Prophetic Books and Its Historical Setting." Pages 73–95 in *The Production of Prophecy: Constructing Prophecy and Prophets in Yehud*. Edited by Diana V. Edelman and Ehud Ben Zvi. London: Equinox, 2009.

———. *History, Literature and Theology in the Book of Chronicles*. London: Equinox, 2006.

———. *Hosea*. FOTL 21A.1. Grand Rapids: Eerdmans, 2005.

———. "Shifting the Gaze: Historiographic Constraints in Chronicles and Their Implications." Pages 38–60 in *The Land That I Will Show You: Essays on the History and Archaeology of the Ancient Near East in Honor of J. Maxwell Miller*. Edited by P. Graham and A. Dearman. JSOTSup 343. Sheffield: Sheffield Academic Press, 2001.

Bertholet, Alfred. *Leviticus*. KHC 3. Tübingen: Mohr Siebeck, 1901.

Beuken, Willem A. M. *Jesaja 13–27*. HTKAT. Freiburg im Breisgau: Herder, 2007.

Blenkinsopp, Joseph. *Ezra-Nehemiah*. OTL. Philadelphia: Westminster, 1988.

Blum, Erhard. "Der kompositionelle Knoten am Übergang von Josua zu Richter." Pages 195–97 in *Deuteronomic Literature*. Edited by M. Vervenne and J. Lust. BETL 133. Leuven: University Press, 1997.

Böhler, Dieter. *Die Heilige Stadt in Esdras α und Esra-Nehemia: Zwei Konzeptionen zur Wiederherstellung Israels*. OBO 158. Fribourg: Universitätsverlag; Göttingen: Vandenhoeck & Ruprecht, 1997.

Braude, William G., ed. *The Midrash on Psalms*. 2 vols. Yale Judaica Series 13. New Haven: Yale University, 1959.

Briant, Pierre. *From Cyrus to Alexander: A History of the Persian Empire*. Winona Lake, Ind.: Eisenbrauns, 2002.

Briggs, Charles Augustus, and Emily Grace Briggs. *The Book of Psalms*. 2 vols. ICC. Edinburgh: T&T Clark, 1909.

Bright, John. *Jeremiah*. AB 21. Garden City, N.Y.: Doubleday, 1965.

Brooke, Alan England, Norman McLean, and Henry St John Thackeray, eds. *I and II Kings*. Vol. 2.2 of *The Old Testament in Greek: According to the Text of Codex Vaticanus, Supplemented from Other Uncial Manuscripts, with a Critical Apparatus Containing the Chief Ancient*

Authorities for the Text of the Septuagint. Cambridge: Cambridge University Press, 1930.
Brooke, George J. "The Qumran Scrolls and the Demise of the Distinction between Higher and Lower Criticism." Pages 26–42 in *New Directions in Qumran Studies: Proceedings of the Bristol Colloquium on the Dead Sea Scrolls*. Edited by Jonathan G. Campbell, William John Lyons, and Lloyd K. Pietersen. London: T&T Clark, 2005.
Brueggemann, Walter. *First and Second Samuel*. Interpretation. Louisville, Ky.: John Knox, 1990.
Budd, Philip J. *Numbers*. WBC 5. Waco, Tex.: Word, 1984.
Budde, Karl. *Die Bücher Samuel*. KHC 8. Tübingen: J.C.B. Mohr, 1902.
Burney, Charles Fox. *Notes on the Hebrew Text of the Books of Kings: With an Introduction and Appendix*. Oxford: Clarendon, 1903.
Carmignac, Jean. "L'emploi de la négation אין dans la Bible et à Qumran." *RevQ* 8 (1974): 407–13.
Carr, David M. *The Formation of the Hebrew Bible: A New Reconstruction*. Oxford: Oxford University Press, 2011.
Carroll, Robert P. *Jeremiah: A Commentary*. OTL. Philadelphia: Westminster, 1986.
Clines, David J. A., ed. *The Dictionary of Classical Hebrew*. 8 vols. Sheffield: Sheffield Phoenix, 1993–2011.
Cogan, Mordechai. *1 Kings: A New Translation with Introduction and Commentary*. AB 10. New York: Doubleday, 2001.
Cortese, Enzo. *Josua 13–21: Ein priesterschriftlicher Abschnitt im deuteronomistischen Geschichtswerk*. OBO 94. Fribourg: Universitätsverlag, 1990.
Cross, Frank Moore. "The Ammonite Oppression of the Tribes of Gad and Reuben: Missing Verses from 1 Samuel 11 Found in 4QSamuel[a]." Pages 105–19 in *The Hebrew and Greek Texts of Samuel: 1980 Proceedings IOSCS - Vienna*. Edited by Emanuel Tov. Jerusalem: Academon, 1980.
Cross, Frank Moore, et al. *Qumran Cave 4.XII: 1–2 Samuel*. DJD 17. Oxford: Clarendon, 2005.
Curtis, Edward L. *A Critical and Exegetical Commentary on the Books of Chronicles*. ICC. Edinburgh; T&T Clark; New York: Scribner's, 1910.
Dahmen, Ulrich. *Psalmen- und Psalterrezeption im Frühjudentum: Rekonstruktion, Textbestand, Struktur und Pragmatik der Psalmenrolle 11QPs[a] aus Qumran*. STDJ 49. Leiden: Brill, 2003.

Dahood, Mitchell. *Psalms III: 101–150*. AB 17A. Garden City, N.Y.: Doubleday, 1970.

DeSilva, David A. *Introducing the Apocrypha: Message, Context, and Significance*. Grand Rapids: Baker Academic, 2002.

De Troyer, Kristin. *Rewriting the Sacred Text: What the Old Greek Texts Tell Us about the Literary Growth of the Bible*. Atlanta: Society of Biblical Literature, 2003.

DeVries, Simon J. *1 Kings*. WBC 12. Waco, Tex.: Word, 1985.

de Wette, Wilhelm Martin Leberecht. *Lehrbuch der historisch-kritischen Einleitung in die Bibel Alten und Neuen Testaments*. 7th ed. Berlin: Georg Reimer, 1852.

Dhorme, Paul. *Les Livres de Samuel*. Paris: Librairie Victor Lecoffre, 1910.

Dietrich, Walter. *Prophetie und Geschichte: Eine redaktionsgeschichtliche Untersuchung zum deuteronomistischen Geschichtswerk*. FRLANT 108. Göttingen: Vandenhoeck & Ruprecht, 1972.

———. *1 Sam 1–12*. Vol. 1 of *Samuel*. BKAT 8.1. Neukirchen-Vluyn: Neukirchener Verlag, 2010.

Dillmann, August. *Die Bücher Numeri, Deuteronomium und Josua*. 2d ed. Leipzig: S. Hirzel, 1886.

Dirksen, Peter B. *1 Chronicles*. Historical Commentary on the Old Testament. Leuven: Peeters, 2005.

Donner, Herbert. *Geschichte des Volkes Israel und seiner Nachbarn in Grundzügen*. ATD Erg. 4.1–2. Göttingen: Vandenhoeck & Ruprecht, 1995.

Driver, Samuel Rolles. *Deuteronomy*. ICC. Edinburgh: T&T Clark, 1902.

———. *Notes on the Hebrew Text and the Topography of the Books of Samuel*. Oxford: Clarendon, 1913.

Duhm, Bernhard. *Das Buch Jeremia*. KHC 11. Tübingen: J. C. B. Mohr, 1901.

Ehrlich, Arnold B. *Jesaia, Jeremia*. Vol. 4 of *Randglossen zur hebräischen Bibel: Textkritisches, Sprachliches und Sachliches*. Leipzig: Hinrichs, 1912.

———. *Josua, Richter, I. u. II. Samuelis*. Vol. 3 of *Randglossen zur hebräischen Bibel: Textkritisches, Sprachliches und Sachliches*. 1910. Repr., Hildesheim: Georg Olms, 1968.

Eskenazi, Tamara. *In an Age of Prose: A Literary Approach to Ezra-Nehemiah*. SBLMS 36. Atlanta: Scholars Press, 1988.

Fernández Marcos, Natalio, ed. "The Hebrew and Greek Text of Judges." Pages 1–16 in *The Earliest Text of the Hebrew Bible: The Relationship between the Masoretic Text and the Hebrew Base of the Septuagint*

Reconsidered. Edited by Adrian Schenker. SBLSCS 52. Atlanta: Society of Biblical Literature, 2003.

———. *Judges.* Vol. 7 of *Biblia Hebraica: Quinta editione cum apparatu critico novis curis elaborato.* Stuttgart: Deutsche Bibelgesellschaft, 2011.

Fernández Marcos, Natalio, and José Ramón Busto Saiz, eds. *1–2 Reyes.* Vol. 2 of *El texto antioqueno de la Biblia griega.* TECC 53. Madrid: Instituto de Filología, 1992.

Fischer, Georg. *Jeremia 26–52.* HTKAT. Freiburg im Breisgau: Herder, 2005.

Fishbane, Michael. "Biblical Colophons, Textual Criticism and Legal Analogies." *CBQ* 42 (1980): 438–49.

———. *Biblical Interpretation in Ancient Israel.* Oxford: Clarendon, 1985.

Flint, Peter W. "A Form of Psalm 89 (4Q236 = 4QPs89)." Pages 40–45 in *Pseudepigraphic and Non-Masoretic Psalms and Prayers.* Vol. 4A of *The Dead Sea Scrolls: Hebrew, Aramaic, and Greek Texts with English Translations.* Edited by James H. Charlesworth. Tübingen: Mohr Siebeck; Louisville: Westminster John Knox, 1997.

Fokkelman, Jan P. *King David (II Sam. 9–20 and I Kings 1–2).* Vol. 1 of *Narrative Art and Poetry in the Books of Samuel: A Full Interpretation Based on Stylistic and Structural Analyses.* Assen: Van Gorcum, 1981.

Fox, Michael V. *The Redaction of the Books of Esther.* SBLMS 40. Atlanta: Scholars Press, 1991.

Fried, Lisbeth S. *Was 1 Esdras First?* SBLAIL 7. Atlanta: Society of Biblical Literature, 2011.

Fritz, Volkmar. *Das Buch Josua.* HAT 7. Tübingen: Mohr Siebeck, 1994.

———. *Das erste Buch der Könige.* ZBK 10.1. Zürich: Theologischer Verlag, 1996.

George, Andrew R. *The Babylonian Gilgamesh Epic.* Oxford: Oxford University Press, 2003.

Gerstenberger, Erhard S. *Leviticus.* Translated by Douglas W. Stott. OTL. Louisville: Westminster John Knox, 1996. Translation of *Das dritte Buch Mose: Leviticus.* ATD 6. Göttingen: Vandenhoeck & Ruprecht, 1993.

———. *Psalms, Part 2, and Lamentations.* FOTL 15. Grand Rapids: Eerdmans, 2001.

Gesenius, Wilhelm. *Hebräisches und Aramäisches Handwörterbuch über das Alte Testament.* Edited by Herbert Donner. 6 vols. 18th ed. Heidelberg: Springer, 2010.

Giesebrecht, Friedrich. *Das Buch Jeremia*. HKAT 3.2.1. Göttingen: Vandenhoeck & Ruprecht, 1907.
Goldingay, John. *Psalms 42–89*. Vol. 2 of *Psalms*. Baker Commentary on the Old Testament Wisdom and Psalms. Grand Rapids: Baker Academic, 2007.
Gray, George Buchanan. *A Critical and Exegetical Commentary on Numbers*. ICC. Edinburgh: T&T Clark, 1903.
Gray, John. *I and II Kings*. OTL. Philadelphia: Westminster John Knox, 1963.
Grayson, Albert Kirk. *Assyrian and Babylonian Chronicles*. Winona Lake, Ind.: Eisenbrauns, 2000.
Greenspoon, Leonard, and Sidnie White Crawford, eds. *The Book of Esther in Modern Research*. JSOTSup 380. London: T&T Clark, 2003.
Groß, Walter. *Richter*. Freiburg: Herder, 2009.
Grünwaldt, Klaus. *Das Heiligkeitsgesetz Leviticus 17–26: Ursprüngliche Gestalt, Tradition und Theologie*. BZAW 271. Berlin: de Gruyter, 1999.
Gunneweg, Antonius H. J. *Esra*. KAT 19.1. Gütersloh: Mohn, 1985.
———. *Nehemia*. KAT 19.2. Gütersloh: Mohn, 1987.
Halbe, Jörn. *Das Privilegrecht Jahwes: Ex 34,10–26; Gestalt und Wesen, Herkunft und Wirken in vordeuteronomischer Zeit*. FRLANT 114. Göttingen: Vandenhoeck & Ruprecht, 1975.
Hanhart, Robert, ed. *Esther*. Vol. 8.3 of *Septuaginta: Vetus Testamentum Graecum Auctoritate Academiae Scientiarum Gottingensis*. Göttingen: Vandenhoeck & Ruprecht, 1983.
Harrison, Roland Kenneth. *Numbers: An Exegetical Commentary*. The Wycliffe Exegetical Commentary. Grand Rapids: Baker Book House, 1992.
Hendel, Ronald S. *The Text of Genesis 1–11: Textual Studies and Critical Edition*. New York: Oxford University Press, 1998.
Hertog, Cornelis den. "Jesus: Josue / Das Buch Josua." Pages 605–56 in vol. 1 of *Septuaginta Deutsch: Erläuterungen und Kommentare zum griechischen Alten Testament*. Edited by Martin Karrer and Wolfgang Kraus. Stuttgart: Deutsche Bibelgesellschaft, 2011.
Hertzberg, Hans Wilhelm. *Die Samuelbücher*. ATD 10. Göttingen: Vandenhoeck & Ruprecht, 1956.
Hess, Richard S. "The Dead Sea Scrolls and Higher Criticism of the Hebrew Bible: The Case of 4QJudg[a]." Pages 122–28 in *The Scrolls and the Scriptures: Qumran Fifty Years After*. Edited by Stanley E. Porter and Craig A. Evans. JSPSup 26. Sheffield: Sheffield Academic Press, 1997.

Holladay, William L. *Jeremiah*. 2 vols. Hermeneia. Minneapolis: Fortress, 1986–89.
Holzinger, Heinrich. *Numeri*. KHC 4. Tübingen and Leipzig: J.C.B. Mohr, 1903.
Hossfeld, Frank-Lothar, and Erich Zenger. *Psalmen 101–150*. Freiburg: Herder, 2008.
Housman, Alfred Edward. "The Application of Thought to Textual Criticism." Pages 325–39 in *Collected Poems and Selected Prose*. Edited by Christopher Ricks. Harmondsworth: Penguin, 1988.
———. "The Editing of Juvenal: Preface of MDCCCCV." Pages 395–402 in *Collected Poems and Selected Prose*. Edited by Christopher Ricks. Harmondsworth: Penguin, 1988.
Japhet, Sara. *I and II Chronicles*. OTL. Louisville: Westminster John Knox, 1993.
Jobes, Karen H. *The Alpha-Text of Esther: Its Character and Relationship to the Masoretic Text*. SBLDS 153. Atlanta: Scholars Press, 1996.
Jones, Gwilym H. *1 and 2 Kings*. 2 vols. NCBC. Grand Rapids: Eerdmans, 1984.
Joüon, Paul, and Takamitsu Muraoka. *A Grammar of Biblical Hebrew*. 2d repr. of 2d ed. SubBi 27. Rome: Gregorian & Biblical Press, 2009.
Kaiser, Otto. *Der Prophet Jesaja: Kapitel 13–39*. 3d ed. ATD 18. Göttingen: Vandenhoeck & Ruprecht, 1983.
Kalimi, Isaac. *An Ancient Israelite Historian: Studies in the Chronicler, His Time, Place and Writing*. SSN 46. Leiden: Brill, 2005.
Kallai, Zecharia. "Samuel in Qumrān: Expansion of a Historiographical Pattern (4QSam^a)." *RB* 103 (1996): 581–91.
Kartveit, Magnar. *The Origin of the Samaritans*. VTSup 128. Leiden: Brill, 2009.
Keil, Carl Friedrich. *Die Bücher Samuels*. Biblischer Commentar über das Alte Testament 2.2. Leipzig: Dörfling und Franke, 1864.
Keown, Gerald L., Pamela J. Scalise, and Thomas G. Smothers. *Jeremiah 26–52*. WBC 27. Nashville: Thomas Nelson, 1995.
Klein, Ralph W. *1 Samuel*. WBC 10. Waco, Tex.: Word, 1983.
Knauf, Ernst Axel. *Josua*. ZBK. Zürich: Theologischer Verlag, 2008.
———. "Psalm lx und Psalm cviii." *VT* 50 (2000): 55–65.
Knobel, August, and August Dillmann. *Die Bücher Exodus und Leviticus*. 2d ed. KeHAT. Leipzig: S. Hirzel, 1880.
Knohl, Israel. *The Sanctuary of Silence: The Priestly Torah and the Holiness School*. Minneapolis: Fortress, 1995.

Koehler, Ludwig, and Walter Baumgartner. *Hebräisches und aramäisches Lexikon zum Alten Testament*. 3d ed. Leiden: Brill, 1967–96.

———. *The Hebrew and Aramaic Lexicon of the Old Testament*. Leiden: Brill, 2001.

Kooij, Arie van der. "Textual Criticism." Pages 579–90 in *The Oxford Handbook of Biblical Studies*. Edited by Judith M. Lieu and J. W. Rogerson. Oxford: Oxford University Press, 2008.

———. "Textual Criticism of the Hebrew Bible: Its Aim and Method." Pages 729–39 in *Emanuel: Studies in the Hebrew Bible, Septuagint, and Dead Sea Scrolls in Honor of Emanuel Tov*. Edited by Shalom M. Paul et al. VTSup 94. Leiden: Brill, 2003).

Korpel, Marjo. *The Structure of the Book of Ruth*. Pericope 2. Assen: Van Gorcum, 2001.

Kraus, Wolfgang, and Martin Karrer, eds. *Septuaginta Deutsch: Das griechische Alte Testament in deutscher Übersetzung*. Stuttgart: Deutsche Bibelgesellschaft, 2009.

Kuhl, Curt. "Die '*Wiederaufnahme*'—ein literarkritisches Prinzip?" *ZAW* 64 (1952): 1–11.

Lagrange, Marie-Joseph. "*Les sources du Pentateuque*." *RB* 7 (1898): 10–32.

Lange, Armin. *Die Handschriften biblischer Bücher von Qumran und den anderen Fundorten*. Vol. 1 of *Handbuch der Textfunde vom Toten Meer*. Tübingen: Mohr Siebeck, 2009.

Lemche, Niels Peter. *The Old Testament between Theology and History*. Louisville, Ky.: Westminster John Knox, 2008.

Leuenberger, Martin. *Konzeptionen des Königtums Gottes im Psalter: Untersuchungen zu Komposition und Redaktion der theokratischen Bücher IV–V im Psalter*. ATANT. Zürich: Theologischer Verlag, 2004.

Levin, Christoph. "Die Instandsetzung des Tempels unter Joas ben Ahasja." Pages 169–97 in *Fortschreibungen: Gesammelte Studien zum Alten Testament*. BZAW 316. Berlin: de Gruyter, 2003.

———. *The Old Testament: A Brief Introduction*. Princeton: Princeton University Press, 2005.

Long, Burke O. *1 Kings: With an Introduction to Historical Literature*. FOTL 9. Grand Rapids: Eerdmans, 1984.

Lundbom, Jack R. *Jeremiah 37–52: A New Translation with Introduction and Commentary*. AB 21C. New York: Doubleday, 2004.

Mathys, Hans-Peter. *Dichter und Beter: Theologen aus spätalttestamentlicher Zeit*. OBO 132. Göttingen: Vandenhoeck & Ruprecht, 1994.

McCarter, P. Kyle, Jr. *I Samuel*. AB 8. Garden City, N.Y.: Doubleday, 1980.

McCarthy, Carmel, ed. *Deuteronomy*. Vol. 5 of *Biblia Hebraica: Quinta editione cum apparatu critico novis curis elaborato*. Stuttgart: Deutsche Bibelgesellschaft, 2007.

McKane, William. *Commentary on Jeremiah 1–25*. Vol. 1 of *A Critical and Exegetical Commentary on Jeremiah*. ICC. Edinburgh: T&T Clark, 1986.

———. *Commentary on Jeremiah 26–52*. Vol. 2 of *A Critical and Exegetical Commentary on Jeremiah*. ICC. Edinburgh: T&T Clark, 1996.

McKenzie, Steven L. *The Chronicler's Use of the Deuteronomistic History*. HSM 33. Atlanta: Scholars Press, 1985.

Miller, James Maxwell, and John H. Hayes. *A History of Ancient Israel and Judah*. 2d ed. Louisville, Ky.: Westminster John Knox, 2006.

Miller, James Maxwell, and Gene M. Tucker. *The Book of Joshua*. CBC. Cambridge: Cambridge University Press, 1974.

Milstein, Sara J. "Reworking Ancient Texts: Revision through Introduction in Biblical and Mesopotamian Literature." Ph.D. diss., New York University, 2010.

Montgomery, James A. *A Critical and Exegetical Commentary on the Books of Kings*. Edited by Henry Snyder Gehman. ICC. Edinburgh: T&T Clark, 1967.

Moulton, Warren J. "Über die Überlieferung und den textkritischen Werth des dritten Esrabuchs." *ZAW* 19 (1899): 209–58.

Mulder, Martin J. *1 Kings 1–11*. Vol. 1 of *1 Kings*. Historical Commentary on the Old Testament. Leuven: Peeters, 1998.

Müller, Reinhard. *Königtum und Gottesherrschaft: Untersuchungen zur alttestamentlichen Monarchiekritik*. FAT 2.3. Tübingen: Mohr Siebeck, 2004.

Nelson, Richard D. *Deuteronomy*. OTL. Louisville, Ky.: Westminster John Knox, 2002.

———. *The Double Redaction of the Deuteronomistic History*. JSOTSup 18. Sheffield: JSOT Press, 1981.

———. *Joshua: A Commentary*. OTL. Louisville, Ky.: Westminster John Knox, 1997.

Niese, B., ed. *Flavii Iosephi opera*. 7 vols. Berlin: Weidmann, 1885–95.

Noth, Martin. *Das Buch Josua*. 2d ed. HAT 7. Tübingen: Mohr Siebeck, 1953.

———. *I Könige 1–16*. Vol. 1 of *Könige*. BKAT 9.1. Neukirchen-Vluyn: Neukirchener Verlag, 1968.

———. *Numbers: A Commentary*. OTL. London: SCM, 1968.

———. *Überlieferungsgeschichtliche Studien.* Tübingen: Niemayer, 1957.
O'Connell, Robert H. *The Rhetoric of the Book of Judges.* VTSup 63. Leiden: Brill, 1996.
Pakkala, Juha. *Ezra the Scribe.* BZAW 347. Berlin: de Gruyter, 2004.
———. "Gedaliah's Murder in 2 Kgs 25:25 and Jer 41:1–3." Pages 401–11 in *Scripture in Transition: Essays on Septuagint, Hebrew Bible, and Dead Sea Scrolls in Honour of Raija Sollamo.* Edited by A. Voitila and J. Jokiranta. Brill: Leiden, 2008.
Parry, Donald W. "The Textual Character of the Unique Readings of 4QSam[a] (4Q51)." Pages 163–82 in *Flores Florentino: Dead Sea Scrolls and Other Early Jewish Studies in Honour of Florentino García Martínez.* Edited by Anthony Hilhorst et al. JSJSup 122. Leiden: Brill, 2007.
Pisano, Stephen. *Additions or Omissions in the Books of Samuel: The Significant Pluses and Minuses in the Massoretic, LXX and Qumran Texts.* OBO 57. Fribourg: Éditions Universitaires; Göttingen: Vandenhoeck & Ruprecht, 1984.
Polak, Frank H. "The LXX Account of Solomon's Reign: Revision and Ancient Recension." Pages 139–64 in *X Congress of the International Organization for Septuagint and Cognate Studies Oslo, 1998.* Edited by Bernard A. Taylor. SBLSCS 51. Atlanta: Scholars Press, 2001.
Rahlfs, Alfred, and Robert Hanhart, eds. *Septuaginta: Id est Vetus Testamentum graece iuxta LXX interpretes.* 2d ed. Stuttgart: Deutsche Bibelgesellschaft, 2006.
Richter, Wolfgang. *Die Bearbeitungen des "Retterbuches" in der deuteronomischen Epoche.* BBB 21. Bonn: Peter Hanstein, 1964.
———. *Exegese als Literaturwissenschaft: Entwurf einer alttestamentlichen Literaturtheorie und Methodologie.* Göttingen: Vandenhoeck & Ruprecht, 1971.
Ringgren, Helmer. "Oral and Written Transmission in the O.T." *ST* 3 (1949): 34–59.
Robinson, Joseph. *The First Book of Kings.* Cambridge: Cambridge University Press, 1972.
Rofé, Alexander. "The Acts of Nahash according to 4QSam[a]." *IEJ* 32 (1982): 129–33.
———. "Joshua 20: Historico-Literary Criticism Illustrated." Pages 131–47 in *Empirical Models for Biblical Criticism.* Edited by Jeffrey H. Tigay. Philadelphia: University of Pennsylvania Press, 1985.
———. "Midrashic Traits in 4Q51 (So-Called 4QSam[a])." Pages 75–88 in *Archaeology of the Books of Samuel: The Entangling of the Textual*

and Literary History. Edited by Philippe Hugo and Adrian Schenker. VTSup 132. Leiden: Brill, 2010.

———. "The Nomistic Correction in Biblical Manuscripts and Its Occurrence in 4QSam[a]." *RevQ* 14 (1989-90): 247-54.

———. "Studying the Biblical Text in the Light of Historico-Literary Criticism: The Reproach of the Prophet in Judg 6:7-10 and 4QJudg[a]." Pages 111-23 in *The Dead Sea Scrolls in Context: Integrating the Dead Sea Scrolls in the Study of Ancient Texts, Languages and Cultures.* Edited by Armin Lange, Emanuel Tov, and Matthias Weigold. VTSup 140. Leiden: Brill, 2011.

Rudolph, Wilhelm. *Chronikbücher.* HAT 21. Tübingen: Mohr Siebeck, 1955.

———. *Esra und Nehemia samt 3. Esra.* HAT 20. Tübingen: J.C.B. Mohr, 1949.

———. *Jeremia.* HAT 12. Tübingen: Mohr Siebeck, 1947.

———. *Jeremia.* 3d ed. HAT 12. Tübingen: Mohr Siebeck, 1968.

Ruwe, Andreas. *„Heiligkeitsgesetz" und „Priesterschrift."* FAT 26. Tübingen: Mohr Siebeck, 1999.

Schaper, Joachim. "Der Septuaginta-Psalter: Interpretation, Aktualisierung und liturgische Verwendung der biblischen Psalmen im hellenistischen Judentum." Pages 165-83 in *Der Psalter in Judentum und Christentum.* Edited by Erich Zenger. Herder's Biblical Studies 18. Freiburg: Herder, 1998.

Schenker, Adrian, et al., eds. *General Introduction and Megilloth.* Vol. 18 of *Biblia Hebraica: Quinta editione cum apparatu critico novis curis elaborato.* Stuttgart: Deutsche Bibelgesellschaft, 2004.

Scherer, Andreas. *Überlieferungen von Religion und Krieg: Exegetische und religionsgeschichtliche Untersuchungen zu Richter 3-8 und verwandten Texten.* WMANT 105. Neukirchen-Vluyn: Neukirchener, 2005.

Schmidt, Ludwig. "Leviten- und Asylstädte in Num. xxxv und Jos. xx; xxi 1-42." *VT* 52 (2002): 103-21.

———. *Das vierte Buch Mose: Numeri 10,11-36,13.* ATD 7.2. Göttingen: Vandenhoeck & Ruprecht, 2004.

Schwiderski, Dirk. *Handbuch des nordwestsemitischen Briefformulars: Ein Beitrag zur Echtheitsfrage der aramäischen Briefe des Esrabuches.* BZAW 295. Berlin: de Gruyter, 2000.

Seebass, Horst. *Numeri 10,11-22,1.* Vol. 2 of *Numeri.* BKAT 4.2. Neukirchen-Vluyn: Neukirchener Verlag, 2003.

———. *Numeri 22,2-36,13.* Vol. 3 of *Numeri.* BKAT 4.3. Neukirchen-Vluyn: Neukirchener Verlag, 2007.

Soggin, J. Alberto. *An Introduction to the History of Israel and Judah*. 3d ed. London: SCM, 1999.

———. *Joshua: A Commentary*. OTL. London: SCM, 1972.

———. *Judges*. OTL. London: SCM, 1987.

Steins, Georg. *Die Bücher der Chronik: Einleitung in das Alte Testament*. Edited by Erich Zenger et al. 5th ed. Kohlhammer: Stuttgart, 2004.

Steuernagel, Carl. *Lehrbuch der Einleitung in das Alte Testament*. Tübingen: J. C. B. Mohr, 1912.

Stipp, Hermann-Josef. "Textkritik – Literarkritik – Textentwicklung: Überlegungen zur exegetischen Aspektsystematik." *ETL* 66 (1990): 143–59.

———. "Das Verhältnis von Textkritik und Literarkritik in neueren alttestamentlichen Veröffentlichungen." *BZ* 34 (1990): 16–37.

Stoebe, Hans Joachim. *Das erste Buch Samuelis*. KAT 8.1. Gütersloh: Mohn, 1973.

Sweeney, Marvin A. *I and II Kings: A Commentary*. OTL. Louisville, Ky.: Westminster John Knox, 2007.

Talshir, Zipora. "The Contribution of Diverging Traditions Preserved in the Septuagint to Literary Criticism of the Bible." Pages 21–41 in *VIII Congress of the International Organization for Septuagint and Cognate Studies, Paris 1992*. Edited by Leonard Greenspoon and Olivier Munnich. SBLSCS 41. Atlanta: Scholars Press, 1995.

———. *I Esdras: From Origin to Translation*. SBLSCS 47. Atlanta: Scholars Press, 1999.

Thackeray, Henry St John, and Ralph Marcus. *Jewish Antiquities, Books V–VIII*. Vol. 5 of *Josephus*. LCL. London: Heinemann; Cambridge: Harvard University Press, 1934.

Tigay, Jeffrey H. *Empirical Models for Biblical Criticism*. Philadelphia: University of Pennsylvania Press, 1985.

———. *The Evolution of the Gilgamesh Epic*. Philadelphia: University of Pennsylvania Press, 1982.

Toorn, Karel van der. *Scribal Culture and the Making of the Hebrew Bible*. Cambridge: Harvard University Press, 2007.

Torrey, Charles C. "The Older Book of Esther." *HTR* 37.1 (1944): 1–40.

Tournay, Raymond Jacques. "Psaumes 57, 60 et 108: Analyse et interprétation." *RB* 96 (1989): 5–26.

Tov, Emanuel. "The LXX Translation of Esther: A Paraphrastic Translation of MT or a Free Translation or a Rewritten Version?" Pages 507–26 in *Empsychoi Logoi—Religious Innovations in Antiquity: Studies in*

Honour of Pieter Willem van der Horst. Edited by A. Houtman et al. Leiden: Brill, 2008.

———. "The Relevance of Textual Theories for the Praxis of Textual Criticism." Pages 23–35 in vol. 1 of *A Teacher for All Generations: Essays in Honor of James C. VanderKam*. Edited by E. F. Mason et al. JSJSup 153.1. Leiden: Brill, 2012.

———. *Textual Criticism of the Hebrew Bible*. 2d ed. Minneapolis: Fortress; Assen: Van Gorcum, 2001.

———. *Textual Criticism of the Hebrew Bible*. 3d ed. Minneapolis: Fortress, 2012.

Tsumura, David Toshio. *The First Book of Samuel*. The New International Commentary on the Old Testament. Grand Rapids: Eerdmans, 2007.

Ulrich, Eugene, ed. *The Biblical Qumran Scrolls: Transcriptions and Textual Variants*. Leiden: Brill, 2010.

———. "Deuteronomistically Inspired Scribal Insertions into the Developing Biblical Texts: 4 QJudg[a] and 4QJer[a]." Pages 489–506 in *Houses Full of All Good Things: Essays in Memory of Timo Veijola*. Edited by Juha Pakkala and Martti Nissinen. Publications of the Finnish Exegetical Society 95. Helsinki: The Finnish Exegetical Society, 2008.

———. "A Qualitative Assessment of the Textual Profile of 4QSam[a]." Pages 147–61 in *Flores Florentino: Dead Sea Scrolls and Other Early Jewish Studies in Honour of Florentino García Martínez*. Edited by Anthony Hilhorst et al. JSJSup 122. Leiden: Brill, 2007.

———. *The Qumran Text of Samuel and Josephus*. HSM 19. Chico, Calif.: 1978.

Ulrich, Eugene, et al., eds. *Qumran Cave 4.IX: Deuteronomy to Kings*. DJD 14. Oxford: Clarendon, 1995.

Van Seters, John. *The Edited Bible: The Curious History of the "Editor" in Biblical Criticism*. Winona Lake, Ind.: Eisenbrauns, 2006.

Veijola, Timo. "Die Deuteronomisten als Vorgänger der Schriftgelehrten: Ein Beitrag zur Entstehung des Judentums." Pages 192–240 in *Moses Erben: Studien zum Dekalog, zum Deuteronomismus und zum Schriftgelehrtentum*. BWANT 149. Stuttgart: W. Kohlhammer, 2000.

———. *Die ewige Dynastie: David und die Entstehung seiner Dynastie nach der deuteronomistischen Darstellung*. AASF B.193. Helsinki: Academia Scientiarum Fennica, 1975.

———. *Das fünfte Buch Mose: Deuteronomium; Kapitel 1,1–16,17*. ATD 8.1. Göttingen: Vandenhoeck & Ruprecht, 2004.

———. *Das Königtum in der Beurteilung der deuteronomistischen Historiographie: Eine redaktionsgeschichtliche Untersuchung.* AASF 198. Helsinki: Academia Scientiarum Fennica, 1977.

Waltke, Bruce K., and M. O'Connor. *An Introduction to Biblical Hebrew Syntax.* Winona Lake, Ind.: Eisenbrauns, 1990.

Weber, Beat. "'Fest ist mein Herz, o Gott!' Zu Ps 57,8–9." ZAW 107 (1995): 294–95.

Wellhausen, Julius. *Die Composition des Hexateuchs und der historischen Bücher des Alten Testaments.* 3d ed. Berlin: Georg Reimer, 1899.

———. *Prolegomena to the History of Israel.* Edinburgh: Adam and Charles Black, 1885.

———. *Prolegomena zur Geschichte Israels.* 3d ed. Berlin: Georg Reimer, 1895.

———. *Der Text der Bücher Samuelis.* Göttingen: Vandenhoeck & Ruprecht, 1871.

West, Martin L. *Textual Criticism and Editorial Technique Applicable to Greek and Latin Texts.* Stuttgart: Teubner, 1973.

Wevers, John William, ed. *Numeri.* Vol. 3.1 of *Septuaginta: Vetus Testamentum Graecum Auctoritate Academiae Scientiarum Gottingensis.* Göttingen: Vandenhoeck & Ruprecht, 1982.

Whiston, William, trans. *The Works of Flavius Jospehus.* London: Baynes & Son, 1825.

Wildberger, Hans. *Jesaja 13–27.* Vol. 2 of *Jesaja.* BKAT 10.2. Neukirchen-Vluyn: Neukirchener Verlag, 1978.

Willi, Thomas. *Die Chronik als Auslegung: Untersuchung zur literarischen Gestaltung der historischen Überlieferung Israels.* Göttingen: Vandenhoeck & Ruprecht, 1972.

Williamson, Hugh G. M. *1 and 2 Chronicles.* NCBC. Grand Rapids: Eerdmans; London: Marshall, Morgan & Scott, 1982.

Wright, Jacob L. *Rebuilding Identity: The Nehemiah Memoir and Its Earliest Readers.* BZAW 348. Berlin: de Gruyter, 2004.

Würthwein, Ernst. *Die Bücher der Könige: 1. Kön. 1–16.* ATD 11.1. Göttingen: Vandenhoeck & Ruprecht, 1977.

———. *Die Bücher der Könige: 1. Kön. 17–2. Kön. 25.* ATD 11.2. Göttingen: Vandenhoeck & Ruprecht, 1984.

Ziegler, Joseph, ed. *Jeremias, Baruch, Threni, Epistula Jeremiae.* Vol. 15 of *Septuaginta: Vetus Testamentum Graecum Auctoritate Academiae Scientiarum Gottingensis.* Göttingen: Vandenhoeck & Ruprecht, 2006.

Zyl, A. H. van. *I Samuël.* 2 vols. POut. Nijkerk: G. F. Callenbach, 1988–89.

Index of Sources

Genesis
13:9	72 n. 7
15:18	6
19:15	92 n. 40
20:5	72 n. 7
30:30	84 n. 7
31:15	72 n. 7
34:21	84 n. 7

Exodus
3:8	42
3:17	42
12:6	32
20:9–10	180
20:24	24
21–23	42
23:15	31
23:15(18)	28
23:18	28 n. 2, 31
25:8	107
29:45	107
32:5	24
34	43
34:6–7	34
34:11–26	28 n. 3
34:18	28
34:25	28, 31
36:5–29	213 n. 14

Leviticus
1:2	19 n. 1
2:1	19 n. 1
2:4	19 n. 1
3:7	19 n. 1
7:13	19 n. 1
7:38	19 n. 1
9:22	24
17–26	19
17:1–2	19
17:1–4	20, 24
17:3–4	19
17:4	19, 21, 22, 25
17:5	21
17:8	21
19:5	21
20:3	60
22:18	19 n. 1
22:23	24
22:27	24
23	2, 27, 222, 224
23:5	32
23:6	31, 32
23:7	32
23:5–8	27, 28, 29, 30, 32, 33, 220 n. 2, 222
23:8	31, 32, 33
26	107
26:3	107

Numbers
5:3	107
9:2–11	32
9:5	32
12:16 (SP)	41
13	35, 37
13–14	35, 37, 38, 40, 41, 42, 43, 205
13:1 (SP)	41
13:22	38
13:28	38
13:29 (LXX/SP)	222

Numbers (cont.)

13:29b	42	1:20–23a	41
13:33	3, 35, 36, 37, 38, 40, 41, 42, 44, 220	1:27–32	39, 40, 41
13:33 (SP)	38, 39, 40, 41	1:28	38, 41
13:33 (LXX*)	44	1:39	41
13:33–14:1	38	1:42	41
14	35	1:44	41
14:1	38	1:45a	41
14:1 (SP)	41	4–11	199
14:12	42	5:7	60
14:18	42	5:13–14	180
14:23 (SP)	42, 43	6:10	43
14:23 LXX)	41	6:13	66
14:31 (P)	41	7:1	42
14:40 (SP)	41	9:2	38
14:45 (SP)	41	11:24	6
14:45 (LXX)	41	12–26	199
21:28	156	16:1–8	28 n. 3, 31
24:17	156	19	50, 52, 57 n. 10
28	2, 27, 31, 32 n. 7, 224	19:4–6	51
28–29	27	27–34	199
28:9–15	180 n. 6	28:15	66
28:16	32	34:1	6
28:16–25	27, 28, 29, 30, 31, 32, 33, 220, 222	34:1–3	6
28:17	31, 32		
28:18	32	*Joshua*	
28:19	31	1:4	6
28:19–24	30, 31, 33, 222	8:30–35 (MT)	222 n. 3
28:25	32	9:2	222 n. 3
32	86	19:29	173 n. 23
32:36	173 n. 23	19:35	173 n. 23
35	50, 54, 55, 56, 57 n. 10	20	45, 50, 52, 54, 56, 58
35:9–15	52, 53, 54, 55, 57	20:1	45
35:11–12	50	20:1–6	45, 46, 47, 50, 52, 53, 54, 56
35:12	56, 57	20:1–6 (LXX*)	53, 55, 221
35:12b	54	20:2	45
35:25–28	51, 52, 54, 57	20:2–6	50
35:34	107	20:3	49, 57
		20:3 (LXX*)	53, 56
Deuteronomy		20:3–6	45, 47, 55
1	38, 39, 40, 41, 44	20:3–6 (MT)	58
1–3	199	20:3–6 (LXX*)	54, 55
1:8	43	20:4	47, 48, 49, 53
		20:4b	49
		20:4–5	48, 49, 50, 53, 56, 57 n. 10
		20:4–5 (MT)	54, 56

20:4–6	45, 53	6:10	64, 65
20:5	47, 48, 49, 56	6:10a	60
20:5b	48	6:11	63
20:6	48, 49, 51, 52, 53, 56, 57	6:11–24	60, 61, 63
20:6 (MT)	54, 55, 58	6:13	60, 61
20:6 (LXX*)	53, 55	6:14	60
20:6aα*	49	10–11	86
20:6aβb	49, 56	10:6–9	59
20:6b	54	10:6–16	65
20:7	45	13:1	59
20:7–9	45	19–21	200
20:8	45		
20:9	45, 52, 53	1 Samuel	
24	62	6:18	173 n. 23
24:2	65	7	87
24:2–15	65	8	87
24:8	62	9:1–10:16	69, 87
24:14	66	9:16–17	70, 71, 74, 76
24:14–15	65	9:16	76
24:15–18	62	10	79, 82, 87, 88, 91, 93
24:16–18	60	10–11	87
		10:1	69, 70, 71, 72, 73, 76, 77, 221
Judges		10:1 (LXX)	70, 75
1	200	10:1 (V)	71
2:11–13	59	10:1–8	75
2:11–15	59, 65	10:2–6	73
3:7	59	10:7	73
3:7–8	59, 65	10:9	73
3:12–14	59	10:9b–13	73
4:1–3	59	10:17–25a	79, 87
4:3	86	10:18–19	62
6	59, 62, 63, 65, 224	10:25b–27	79, 88
6:1–6	59, 63	10:27–11:1	69 n. 1, 79, 80
6:6	63	10:27–11:1 (Q)	81, 83, 84, 85
6:6 (LXX^B)	67	11	82, 87, 91, 93
6:6–8	66	11 (MT)	79
6:6–8 (LXX^B)	67	11:1–11	87
6:6b	66, 67	11:5	87
6:7–10	2, 3, 59, 60, 61, 62, 63, 64, 65, 66, 68, 69 n. 1, 220	11:12–14	88
		11:15	87
6:7a	67	12	87
6:7b	67	12:12	80
6:8	65	13 (MT)	76 n. 15
6:8 (LXX^B)	67	13:1	76 n. 15
6:9	62	13:13–14	75

1 Samuel (cont.)
14:47	76 n. 15
15:23	75
15:26	75
22:7	84 n. 9

2 Samuel
1:18	84 n. 9
2:25	84 n. 9
4:2	84 n. 9
7:13	106
13:28	72
23:29	84 n. 9

1 Kings
2:3–4	106
6	101, 107, 224
6:2–10	101, 104
6:9	105 n. 6, 108
6:9a	103
6:9–15	102, 104
6:10–15 (LXX)	103
6:11–13	101, 102, 104, 105, 106, 107, 108
6:11–14	2, 3, 69 n. 1, 101, 103, 105, 107, 108
6:12	106
6:13	107
6:14	104, 105 n. 6, 108
6:15–36	101, 104
8	202
9:6	106
11:34	106
11:38–39	3, 5
19:18	86 n. 21
20 (MT)	222 n. 3
21 (LXX)	222 n. 3

2 Kings
3:19	173 n. 23
10:2	173 n. 23
11	8, 205, 207 n. 3, 208
11–12	205, 207
11:2	207, 216
11:2–3	206, 207
11:3	208
11:4	8, 9
12	122, 209, 212, 213, 214, 216
12:1–3	210, 212, 217
12:1–22	205, 209
12:2–17	211
12:3	208, 209, 210, 211
12:5–6	213
12:5–8	213, 217
12:18–19	211
12:22	214, 215
22:19	209
17:9	173 n. 23
18:8	173 n. 23
23	13, 35
24–25	118
24:12	115
24:15	86 n. 21
25	2, 112, 116, 118 n. 20, 121, 124, 133, 135, 139
25:8	114 n. 12, 115, 116, 117, 118
25:8–11	110, 116, 117, 221
25:8–11 (LXX^B)	111
25:8–12	109, 110, 123, 124, 220
25:8–12 (LXX^B)	112
25:9	112, 113, 118
25:9–11	119, 120, 222
25:10	111, 112, 113, 123
25:10*	123
25:10 (LXX^B)	110, 114
25:11	112
25:12	118 n. 22
25:13–14	121 n. 25
25:13–17	118, 119, 121
25:18	118 n. 22
25:22	132 n. 6, 135
25:22–23	132 n. 6
25:23	132 n. 6, 134, 135 n. 14, 137 n. 21
25:24	133
25:25	127, 128, 129, 130, 131, 132, 133, 135 n. 14, 136, 137, 138, 139, 140, 141 n. 26
25:25 (LXX^B)	129

INDEX OF SOURCES

Isaiah	
15	155
15–16	2, 143, 144, 153, 155, 156, 157, 205, 221
15:2–3	153, 155
15:2–7	144
15:4–6	151
15:5	152, 153
15:5b	144
15:7	153, 155
15:7a	155
16	148, 149, 150
16:6	145, 146, 147
16:6–10	144, 150, 153, 156
16:6–12	144
16:7	146, 147
16:8	148, 149
16:8–9	147, 148, 149
16:9	149
16:10	149
16:11	155
16:11–12	153
16:12	154
24:17–18	156
34:13	173 n. 24

Jeremiah	
1:1	156
1:18	173 n. 23
5:10	148 n. 15
5:17	173 n. 23
16:6	155 n. 28
22:28	155
25:1	133 n. 8
25:4	133 n. 8
25:8–14	113 n. 7
25:17	133 n. 8
25:19	133 n. 8
25:29	133 n. 8
26:23	136 n. 17
27:13	136 n. 17
29:11	146
32:1	115
33:18	155
34:4	136 n. 17
34:7	173 n. 23
34:8–9	133 n. 8
38:2	136 n. 17
39	116, 117, 118, 119, 124
39:4–13	109, 116
39:8	118, 119, 123
39:8–9	116, 117, 123, 124
39:8–10	109, 111, 116, 120, 124, 221
39:9	117, 118 n. 20
39:10	117
39:11	117
39:13	117
40	137 n. 21
40:7	132, 140
40:8	134
40:12	140
41	132, 135, 139
41:1	133, 135
41:1–2	134, 135
41:1–3	127, 128, 129, 130 n. 5, 131, 133, 134, 137, 140, 141
41:2	129 n. 3, 132 n. 6, 135, 136, 137, 138, 139
41:3	129 n. 3, 133, 136, 137, 140
41:4–9	132
41:4–15	134 n. 12
41:5	155 n. 28
41:8–9 (LXX)	133 n. 8
41:10–15	132
41:11–15	137 n. 21
42:17	136 n. 17
42:22	136 n. 17
47:5	155 n. 28
48	2, 143, 144, 150, 152, 153, 155, 156, 157, 205
48 (LXX)	139
48:1 (LXX)	130 n. 5, 136
48:1–2 (LXX)	134, 135
48:1–3 (LXX)	127, 128, 129, 130, 131, 133, 140
48:2 (LXX)	136, 137, 138, 139
48:3 (LXX)	133
48:4 (LXX)	138 n. 22
48:5	144, 152, 153
48:8	149, 155

Jeremiah (cont.)

48:18	149
48:24	150
48:29	144, 145 n. 5, 146
48:29–30	145, 146
48:29–33	144, 150, 151, 153, 156, 157, 221
48:29–38	144, 156, 157
48:30	144, 145 n. 5, 146, 147
48:30–31	147
48:31	146, 147, 155
48:32	147, 148, 149
48:33	147, 149, 150, 155
48:34	151, 152, 153, 156, 157
48:35	154
48:35–38a	153, 156, 157
48:35–38	153, 154
48:36	155
48:36a	155
48:36b	155
48:37–38a	155
48:38a	155
48:38b	155
48:43–44	156
48:45	156
48:45–46	156
49:3	155 n. 28
52	2, 114 n. 10, 116, 118, 121
52:12	114, 115, 116, 117, 220
52:12–15	116, 117
52:12–16	109, 111, 123, 124
52:13	118
52:13–16	221
52:15	110 n. 3
52:16	110 n. 3
52:17–23	118, 119

Ezekiel

45:21–25	30

Psalms

14	159
29	176
31:22	173 n. 22
40:14–18	159
42–83	166, 176 n. 28
53	159
57	159, 160, 162, 163, 166, 171, 172, 175, 176, 177, 224
57:1	174
57:2–12	163
57:4	163
57:6	163
57:7	163
57:8	163, 167, 168, 169
57:8–9	167, 168
57:8–9 (MT)	168
57:8–12	160, 161, 163, 165, 176
57:9	168
57:10	166, 170
57:11	163, 170, 171
57:12	163, 166 n. 10
60	159, 160, 162, 163, 166, 172, 174, 175, 176, 177, 224
60:1–2	174
60:3	164, 171
60:3–5	164
60:3–6	164
60:3–14	164
60:7	164, 171, 176
60:7–14	161, 162, 164, 165, 176
60:8	169 n. 17
60:9	166 n. 10, 169 n. 17
60:9–10	169 n. 17
60:10	172
60:10 (MT)	172
60:11	173
60:12	164, 173, 174
60:12–13	164
60:14	164, 169 n. 17
65:9	172 n. 20
65:14	172 n. 20
70	159
93	176
96	176
97	176
98	176
105	176
107	170
107:1	170

107:8	170	2:20 (B)	195, 198
107:15	170	3:12–14	200
107–150	166	3:14–4:17	197
108	159, 160, 163, 166, 169, 170, 171, 172, 174, 175, 176, 177, 221, 224	5:1–2	197, 201
		5:3–8:12	197
		5:14–21	202
108 (MT)	168	8:9–13	200
108–110	170, 175 n. 27, 177	8:13–10:3	197
108:1–6	165		
108:2	166, 167, 168, 169, 171, 174	Daniel	
108:2 (MT)	168	9	202
108:2 (LXX)	169	11:15	173 n. 23
108:2–3	168		
108:2–6	160, 162, 163, 171	Ezra	
108:4	166, 170	1–6	187
108:5	170, 171	2:1–70	179 n. 3
108:6	166	3:2–3	180
108:7	164, 166 n. 8, 171, 172, 176, 177	3:5	21, 180, 222 n. 5, 224 n. 6
		4:1–6	179 n. 3
108:7–14	161, 162, 164, 165	4:7–24	179 n. 3
108:8	166, 169 n. 17	6:20–21	185
108:8–10	164, 174, 175 n. 27, 176	7–10	201 n. 22, 220
108:9	166 n. 10, 169 n. 17, 175	7:1–5	135 n. 13
108:9–10	169 n. 17	7:6	182, 191
108:10	172	7:11–26	201 n. 21
108:10 (LXX)	173	8	187
108:11	164, 173, 175	8:35	185, 186, 191
108:12	166, 173, 174	9	202
108:12–13	164	9:3	186 n. 15
108:12–14	166, 176	9:4	184, 185, 186
108:14	164, 169 n. 17	9:4–5	184, 186 n. 14
109	174	9:5	185
109:21	170 n. 19	10:3	189, 190
110	174	10:6	186
110:1	170, 174, 175	10:7	185
144:9	166	31:10	146 n. 9
Esther		Nehemiah	
1–17	198	1	200
1:1	199	1:1a	200 n. 17
1:1 (B)	198, 199	1:5–11	200, 202
1:1–3:13	197	1:11b	200 n. 17
2:17–20	194, 221	2	200
2:17–20 (A)	195	2–7	200
2:17–20 (B)	194	2:1–6	200 n. 17

INDEX OF SOURCES

Nehemiah (cont.)			
2:11	200 n. 17	24:21–22	211
2:15*	200 n. 17	24:22	211
2:16a	200 n. 17	24:25	215, 217
2:17	200 n. 17	24:27	86
2:18b	200 n. 17	36:18	121
8	187, 220	36:18–20	119, 120, 222
8:1	187	36:19	121
8:2	187	36:19–20	109, 123, 124
8:3	188	36:20–21	113 n. 7
8:9	187		
8:17	185		
9	202		
9–13	200		

Apocrypha

1 Chronicles		1 Esdras	
16:8–36	176	1:52–53	124
		1:52–54	109
2 Chronicles		2:16–20	179 n. 3
		3:1–4:46	183
		3:1–4:63	179 n. 3, 196 n. 10
		3:1–5:6	179 n. 3
2:3	180 n. 6	5:7–46	179 n. 3
8:5	173 n. 22	5:51	180
8:13	180 n. 6	5:51–52	21 n. 4, 222, 224 n. 6
11:5	173 n. 22	5:66–73	179 n. 3
13:22	86	8:2	190
22–24	205, 207	8:3–4	183, 221
22:11	206, 207, 216	8:4	182, 186, 191
22:11–12	206, 221	8:63	186, 187, 191
22:12	208	8:68	186 n. 15
23	8, 208	8:69	186
23:1–2	8, 9	8:69–70	184, 186
23:6–7	208 n. 5	8:70	185, 186 n. 15
23:7	208 n. 5	8:90	189, 190
24	122, 212, 213, 215	9	188
24:1–2	210, 212, 217	9:3	186
24:1–27	209	9:39	187, 220
24:2	208	9:40	197, 220
24:4–6	214, 217, 221	9:41	188
24:5	213	9:49	187, 220
24:12	213		
24:15–16	211	2 Esdras	
24:15–22	212	10:3	190 n. 20
24:16	215	18:1	187
24:17	211	18:2	187
24:18	211	18:9	187
24:19–20	211		

INDEX OF SOURCES

Qumran Manuscripts

4QJudg^a	62, 63, 64 n. 12, 65, 66
4QLev^d	19
4QPs^a	159
4QSam^a	79, 80, 83, 86 n. 23, 88, 89, 90, 92, 98, 224
10:27–11:1	81, 84, 85
11	93
11:1	92 n. 40
4Q236	159

Septuagint Manuscripts

L	103, 110 n. 4
B	45, 67, 103, 110, 111, 112, 114
N	45
Θ	45
b$_2$	45

Old Latin Manuscripts

Codex Neapolitanensis
  1 Sam 10:1   71 n. 5

Codex Vindobonensis
  1 Sam 10:1   71 n. 5

Josephus

Antiquities
  6.68–71   81 n. 3, 83, 88, 89, 90, 92, 98
  10.8.5   118 n. 21, 124
  13.9.1   175 n. 27
  13.10.2   175 n. 27

Index of Authors

Aejmelaeus, Anneli	4, 74–75, 76	Cogan, Mordechai	4, 103, 107
Allen, Leslie C.	163, 169	Cortese, Enzo	52
Amit, Yairah	64	Crawford, Sidnie	195
Auld, A. Graeme	46, 52	Cross, Frank Moore	79, 80, 83, 84, 85, 86
Baentsch, Bruno	24, 27	Curtis, Edward L.	121–22, 207, 212, 213
Bardtke, Hans	143	Dahmen, Ulrich	159
Barthelemy, Dominique	72, 83, 84, 87, 93, 94, 95, 137	Dahood, Mitchell	162–163
Batten, Loring W.	185, 190	De Troyer, Kristin	193, 195
Baumgartner, Walter	32, 84	deSilva, David A.	193, 202
Becker, Uwe	6, 22	DeVries, Simon J.	4, 107
Ben Zvi, Ehud	3, 12–16, 207, 216	Dhorme, Paul	74
Benzinger, Immanuel	4, 103, 114	Dietrich, Walter	74, 83, 87, 127
Bertholet, Alfred	24	Dillmann, August	22, 24
Beuken, Willem A. M.	143	Dirksen, Peter B.	209
Blenkinsopp, Joseph	181, 188, 190	Donner, Herbert	201
Blum, Erhard	61	Driver, Samuel Rolles	7, 72, 74
Böhler, Dieter	179	Duhm, Bernhard	115, 119, 127, 134, 135, 136, 137
Braude, William G.	169	Ehrlich, Arnold B.	71–72, 134, 136
Briant, Pierre	220	Eskenazi, Tamara	10–11
Briggs, Charles August	167	Fernández Marcos, Natalio	63, 64, 65, 104
Briggs, Emily Grace	167		
Bright, John	143	Fischer, Georg	143
Brooke, Alan England	103	Fishbane, Michael	7, 48, 52
Brooke, George J.	95, 98, 99	Flint, Peter W.	159
Budd, Philip J.	37, 40	Fokkelman, Jan P.	3
Budde, Karl	70, 74–75, 84	Fox, Michael, V.	195
Burney, Charles Fox	4, 103, 106, 107, 211	Fried, Lisbeth S.	179
Busto Saiz, José Ramón	104	Fritz, Volkmar	103
Carmignac, Jean	85	George, Andrew R.	124
Carr, David M.	13, 15	Gerstenberger, Erhard S.	24, 177
Carroll, Robert P.	116, 134, 136, 143, 151	Gesenius, Wilhelm	148
		Giesebrecht, Friedrich	134, 136
Clines, David J. A.	148	Goldingay, John	164, 172

Gray, George Buchanan 27, 31–32, 36, 114
Grayson, Alan K. 116
Greenspoon, Leonard 195
Groß, Walter 61
Grünwaldt, Klaus 24, 27
Gunneweg, Antonius H. J. 181, 183, 185, 186, 188, 190
Halbe, Jörn 28
Hanhart, Robert 46, 103, 193
Harrison, Roland Kenneth 37, 40
Hayes, John H. 114
Hendel, Ronald S. 92
Hertog, Cornelis den 46, 52
Hertzberg, Hans Wilhelm 74
Hess, Richard S. 63–64
Holladay, William L. 143, 144, 149, 150, 151, 153
Holzinger, Heinrich 27
Hossfeld, Frank-Lothar 166, 170, 173, 175
Housman, A. E. 90, 98
Japhet, Sara 207, 209, 215
Jobes, Karen H. 193
Jones, Gwilym H. 113, 114, 127–28
Joüon, Paul 72, 83–84, 85
Kaiser, Otto 143
Kalimi, Isaac 122
Kallai, Zecharia 87
Karrer, Martin 57–58, 63
Kartveit, Magnar 7
Keil, Carl Friedrich 71
Keown, Gerald L. 143
Klein, Ralph W. 74–75
Knauf, Ernst Axel 54, 166, 173, 175
Knohl, Israel 27
Koehler, Ludwig 32, 84
Kooij, Arie van der 97, 99
Korpel, Marjo 11–12
Kraus, Wolfgang 57–57, 63
Kuhl, Curt 22, 67
Lagrange, Marie-Joseph 93
Lange, Armin 20, 64, 65, 88
Lemche, Niels Peter 14–16
Leuenberger, Martin 159

Levin, Christoph 6, 211
Long, Burke O. 107
Lundbom, Jack R. 143, 147, 150, 151, 157
Marcus, Ralph 82
Mathys, Peter 202
McCarter, P. Kyle Jr. 74, 82, 85
McCarthy, Carmel 7
McKane, William 110, 115, 116, 132, 134, 136, 137, 143, 155
McKenzie, Steven L. 212
McLean, Norman 103
Miller, James Maxwell 52, 114
Milstein, Sara J. 198, 226
Montgomery, James A. 103, 105
Moulton, Warren 180
Mulder, Martin J. 4
Müller, Reinhard 62
Muraoka, Takamitsu 72, 83–84, 85
Nelson, Richard D. 7, 52, 61
Niese, Benedikt 81
Noth, Martin 37, 54, 103, 106, 122
O'Connell, Robert H. 64–65
O'Connor, Michael P. 83, 85
Pakkala, Juha 30, 128, 135, 185, 186, 190, 201, 202
Parry, Donald W. 89
Pisano, Stephen 72, 75, 83, 84
Rahlfs, Alfred 46, 103
Richter, Wolfgang 61
Ringgren, Helmer 143
Robinson, Joseph 102
Rofé, Alexander 48, 49, 52, 64, 83, 85–86, 89
Rudoph, Wilhelm 119, 143, 150, 155, 180, 201, 207, 212, 215
Ruwe, Andreas 27
Scalise, Pamela J. 143
Schaper, Joachim 169
Schenker, Adrian 95
Scherer, Andreas 61
Schmidt, Ludwig 37, 49, 53
Schwiderski, Dirk 201
Seebass, Horst 35, 40, 42
Smothers, Thomas G. 143

INDEX OF AUTHORS

Soggin, Alberto	61, 114
Steins, Georg	122
Steuernagel, Carl	27, 122
Stipp, Hermann-Josef	94, 99
Stoebe, Hans Joachim	72
Sweeney, Marvin A.	4–5, 107, 113, 114
Talshir, Zipora	97, 180
Thackeray, Henry St John	82, 103
Tigay, Jeffrey H.	1, 124, 226
Toorn, Karel van der	98
Torrey, Charles, C.	193–194
Tournay, Raymond Jacques	163
Tov, Emanuel	3, 52, 69, 75, 88–92, 96–98, 195
Trebolle Barrera, Julio C.	62
Tsumura, David Toshio	75
Tucker, Gene M.	52
Ulrich, Eugene	62, 63, 66, 67, 83, 88, 89
Van Seters, John	1
Veijola, Timo	61, 62, 106, 181, 199, 224, 227
Waltke, Bruce K.	83, 85
Weber, Beat	167
Wellhausen, Julius	8, 10, 61, 74, 87, 121, 122
West, Martin L.	92, 98
Wette, Wilhelm M. L. de	122
Wevers, John William	36
Whiston, William	118
Wildberger, Hans	143, 145, 147
Willi, Thomas	121
Williamson, Hugh G. M.	207
Wright, Jacob L.	200, 202
Würthwein, Ernst	105, 106, 113–14
Zenger, Erich	166, 170, 173, 175
Ziegler, Joseph	130
Zyl, A. H. van	72

www.ingramcontent.com/pod-product-compliance
Lightning Source LLC
Chambersburg PA
CBHW030340240426
43661CB00052B/1690